THE TRAVELLERS' GOOD HEALTH GUIDE

Ted Lankester is the director of InterHealth, an international travel health centre providing a wide range of services for overseas travellers, and acts as medical adviser to a number of UK aid agencies. Previously a GP, he has travelled widely and spent seven years setting up health programmes in the Himalayas. He is also assistant editor of the journal *Tropical Doctor*.

The Travellers' Good Health Guide

A Guide for Backpackers,
Travellers, Volunteers and Overseas
Workers

Dr Ted Lankester

With a chapter on stress by
Dr Ruth Fowke

This revised and updated edition published in 1999 by
Sheldon Press, SPCK, Holy Trinity Church, Marylebone Road, London NW1 4DU

Text copyright © T. E. Lankester 1999
Original illustrations © Jason Carter

First published in Great Britain in 1993 by InterHealth in association with
Gospel Communication under the title *Healthy Beyond Heathrow*. Second edition
published in Great Britain in 1995 by Hodder & Stoughton under the title
Good Health, Good Travel

British Library Cataloguing-in-Publication Data

A catalogue record for this book is available from the British Library

ISBN 0–85969–827–0

InterHealth is a registered Christian medical charity that specializes in the health
needs of those travelling abroad, including volunteers, aid workers and mission
partners. InterHealth provides a comprehensive range of health care support both for
individuals and their sending agencies, irrespective of their religious affiliation. This
includes medical and psychological selection, health examinations on return,
psychiatric support, counselling and debriefing, the provision of relevant health kits,
equipment, medicines and books, and a comprehensive advisory service.

Typeset by Deltatype Limited, Birkenhead, Merseyside
Printed in Great Britain by
Biddles Ltd, Guildford and King's Lynn

CONTENTS

CONTENTS

ACKNOWLEDGEMENTS

I would like to thank a number of people for their helpful comments on reading through the draft of this manual. They include the late Dr A. J. Broomhall, Mr Stuart Buchanan of CMS, Dr Denis Roche, previously of Interserve, Dr Mark Evason of Crosslinks, Dr Marianne Janosi, previously VSO medical adviser, Dr Mike Jones of Care for Mission, and Mr Steve Price-Thomas of VSO. In addition Mr Frank Tovey OBE and Jackie Fenwick, formerly of InterHealth, have given invaluable advice.

For this new edition I would also like to thank current friends and colleagues at InterHealth for their help, information and encouragement: Dr Ruth Fowke for her chapter on stress, Peter Chapman our director of resources, Annie McCarthy our senior travel nurse and Cathy Travis, manager of our Travel Health Shop.

INFORMATION SOURCES

Information in this book is based on authoritative UK and international sources including the World Health Organisation and the UK Malaria Reference Laboratory.

As far as possible information was correct at the time of publication. However, recommendations on travel medicine frequently change, especially with regard to immunization and antimalarial advice. For this reason the latest edition of this book should always be used or a travel health adviser consulted.

Although every effort has been made to ensure accuracy, neither the author nor the publisher can accept any liability for unforeseen errors or omissions, or for any illness or event resulting from advice or information given in this book.

AUTHOR TO TRAVELLER

A medical friend of mine recently said he preferred working at the top of the cliff, rather than at the bottom. In reply to my puzzled look he explained: 'It's just my way of saying prevention is better than cure.'

The purpose of this book is to help you take sensible precautions and then stop worrying about all the things that may but probably won't happen to you. Many people overseas keep in better health than their friends back home, and the commonest conditions are often the same, including 'accidents', which can happen anywhere. You will probably have bouts of diarrhoea, and you may get malaria, but body-devouring parasites and giant creepy-crawlies are more likely to be met in your dreams than in reality.

So the book is mainly about how to prevent getting ill in the first place, but with plenty of tips about what to do if you're not lucky or successful. Think back to any time you've been abroad and got sick. Could it have been prevented? Being a bit more faithful with the antimalarials and mosquito nets? Declining more of those alluring salads? Working – or playing – that bit less hard and long?

The basic message is this: have your jabs, take your antimalarials, set up rules for sensible eating and personal hygiene, and lead a balanced lifestyle. If it prevents extra trips to the long-drop and increases the odds that your holiday, assignment or adventure are not ruined by bugs, stress or accidents, it will be worth it.

I've tried to write it in as logical an order as possible – Before, During and After:

Section 1 *Before You Go*

Skim through this weeks before leaving, because it's all about getting prepared. It will only take a few minutes but it could save you a lot of 'if only' thoughts when you get to Destination X.

Section 2 *While Abroad*

Read through this before you leave and again when you arrive.

Section 3 *When You Return*

It is better to read this before you head back homewards. When you arrive at the airport, reading a book on keeping healthy abroad is the last thing you'll want to do.

Section 4 *Notes on Common Conditions*

This is mainly for reference, unless you enjoy reading medical encyclopaedias.

And don't forget the Appendices and Further Reading.

Like any book, this health manual will be largely useless if left at home, or lost among the novels and 4 × 4 manuals in the back of beyond. I hope it travels with you and that its pages, made from sustainable forests, soon start looking old and tatty.

This is the third incarnation of the book. The first was called *Healthy Beyond Heathrow*, which people from the south of England liked but which the Scots and Irish were less sure about.

Please let me know if I've left out any mention of your favourite diseases or most hated parasites. With travellers coming and going from a million destinations, and each having vastly different risks, shapes, ages and immune systems it can never be right for everyone. But I would love your comments on how to make any improvements.

This book is dedicated to
my favourite fellow travellers,
Joy, Rachel, Heather and Debbie

SECTION 1
BEFORE YOU GO

CHECKLIST FOR BEFORE YOU LEAVE

There is a great deal to do just before leaving and it's all too easy if you are normally healthy, or very laid back, to leave health matters to the last moment. By planning well ahead, especially for immunizations, you actually save yourself time – and a lot of last-minute hassle.

For all except the shortest journeys to the healthiest places you will need to do the following:

- Complete all necessary *immunizations* (see pages 2–8).
- Obtain any *certificates* that may be required, e.g. yellow fever. Some countries need an HIV certificate or medical form, especially for residence permits.
- Take sufficient *antimalarials* and start them before leaving (see pages 13, 66–74).
- Select and buy appropriate first-aid, medical or needle and syringe kits (see pages 8–13 and Appendices A, B and C).
- Take other *personal supplies*, including medicines, contraceptives etc. (see pages 11–13).
- Know your *blood group*, and keep a written record with you (see pages 93–4).
- Discover any particular *health or security hazards* of the country you are visiting or special precautions that are recommended.
- Visit a *dentist* and have all dental work completed.
- Consider visiting an *optician* for a routine eye check (see page 147).
- Plan ahead for *self-entertainment* and *professional update* if going to a remote area or prolonged assignment (see pages 23, 26, 115–24).
- Find out about any *reciprocal health arrangements* in the country you are going to (see page 27).
- If going to an EU country complete *form E111* and have it stamped.
- Consider having a *medical examination*, especially if you have any known health problems, are over the age of 50 or are going to a

1

developing country for longer than six months (see pages 21–3).

- Take out *health insurance* unless arranged by your company or agency (see pages 26–7).
- Women should be up-to-date with their *cervical smear tests*.
- Consider going on a *first-aid course*, especially if going to a remote area or leading a team or expedition (see page 26).
- Check all *travel documents* and work out a *safe system* for keeping them – and money (see pages 123–4).
- Consider making a *will.*
- *Photocopy important documents*, including the main page of your passport and any outward or return air tickets, and keep the photocopies separately, along with numbers of travellers' cheques.
- Be *well prepared medically* but don't allow worries about health to overshadow or dominate your time abroad.

ARRANGING YOUR IMMUNIZATIONS

A journey to a clinic or surgery with a resultant sore muscle is a small price to pay for protection from several nasty diseases. It is, however, worth noting that less than one disease episode in ten when overseas is preventable by a vaccine. This means that following antimalarial precautions, advice on food and water, and accident prevention is just as important as being jabbed at your local health centre or travel clinic.

What travel jabs will I need?

The menu of jabs gets longer every year. It's possible to get over-immunized – i.e. go for everything just because it's on a comprehensive list – or what is probably worse, be inadequately protected. Unless you are going on a straightforward trip to a low-risk destination, ask your travel health adviser to draw up a list of what is appropriate for you and your journey. This will take into account your age, how healthy you are, and what previous immunizations you have had (try and find a record of these so you only have the jabs you really need).

Your health adviser will also need to know the area of the country you will be living in, any job you may be doing, the length of time you may be staying and the sort of lifestyle you are likely to follow. Settle for just one opinion from an adviser whom you trust – otherwise it's confusion all round.

Here are some guidelines:

1 Immunizations recommended for *all* countries outside Western Europe, North America and Australasia, for which you should be in-date before leaving:

Adults

Hepatitis A
Polio
Tetanus with diphtheria
Typhoid

Children

BCG (for TB)
DPT (diphtheria, pertussis, tetanus)
Hepatitis A (Junior) for children under 16 (or younger depending on risk)
Hib (haemophilus influenzae b)
Polio
MMR (mumps, measles, rubella)
Typhoid (not under eighteen months)

2 Immunizations needed for *some* developing countries depending on your location, occupation and length of time abroad:

All those for adults in 1 plus
Hepatitis B
Japanese encephalitis
Meningitis
Rabies
Tick-borne encephalitis
Yellow fever (you must also obtain a certificate)

3 Immunizations only rarely needed:

Anthrax
Cholera (an effective live oral vaccine exists but is not licensed in the UK)
Influenza
Measles for adults
Mumps
Plague
Pneumococcus
Rubella (for women of child-bearing age with no immunity)

In addition Anti D immunoglobulin may be needed by some rhesus-negative women who become pregnant or who plan to give birth while overseas (see page 127).

How should I set about having immunizations?

Here are some guidelines:

Discover which immunizations you will need

If you are travelling independently, ask your GP or practice nurse for advice or visit a travel clinic (see Appendix D).

If going with a company or sending agency, you will normally be provided with a list of recommended immunizations for your trip. If you are not, ask for one.

Work out a time schedule

Do this with the doctor or nurse likely to be giving you the majority of your immunizations. If you have been given a recommended list take this along. Let the clinic work out a schedule with you, rather than spend too much time working out your own. Usually immunizations can be completed in two or three visits to the health centre or travel clinic.

Allow plenty of time to fit them all in

If going to a developing country, try to allow three months unless you have travelled in the past three years. This way you will be able to complete courses without having to take vaccine with you. If you don't have this much time your schedule can usually be telescoped.

Understand the spacing rules

If you are one of those travellers who like to keep track of what is being done to you, read on!

- You can have two or more non-live* vaccines together.
- You can have one live and one or more non-live vaccines together.
- You can have two live vaccines together, but if they are not given on the same day they should be at least three weeks apart (because of effectiveness, not safety).
- If using gammaglobulin to protect against hepatitis A, you should ideally have this at least three weeks after (or three months before) any live vaccine except yellow fever. This is again because of effectiveness, not safety. If you are in a hurry this rule can be set aside, with minimal effect.
- Leave gammaglobulin to the week before you go because it loses its effectiveness quicker than others.

Note: *Live vaccines are oral polio, BCG, yellow fever, mumps, measles, rubella and oral typhoid.

Taking booster doses with you

Sometimes it is not possible to complete a course of immunizations before you leave.

Although most vaccines will keep for a short time unrefrigerated, it is better to carry them in a chilled vacuum flask containing a sealed ice pack and then put them in a fridge on arrival. *Vaccines should not be frozen and therefore should not be put in the aircraft hold.* Yellow fever should not be taken with you.

Some GPs or travel clinics will provide supplies for overseas. When abroad the vaccines should be given by a doctor or nurse using a sterile syringe and needle. They must be kept reliably cold between 2° and 8 °C unless otherwise specified.

Where should I go for my travel jabs?

You will need to weigh up the three considerations of availability, convenience and cost. In the UK you will have two main choices:

1 Your NHS health centre or GP surgery

There are great differences between GP surgeries both in terms of what jabs they have available and the amount they charge. Find out what is available and how much different vaccinations will cost. Only a few surgeries are licensed to give yellow fever immunization. Some surgeries may be able to order less common vaccines for you or give you a private prescription to collect one from a chemist.

A debate is going on at the present time about whether any immunizations should be freely available on the NHS. Many people feel that NHS resources should be used for other health priorities and that those able to afford foreign travel should pay for immunizations. At the time of writing the following are usually available free on the NHS:

- Hepatitis A (either the vaccine or gammaglobulin).
- Hepatitis B for accredited health workers.
- Polio.
- Tetanus or tetanus with diphtheria.
- Typhoid.

Plus the immunizations for children listed above.

2 A travel clinic

There are three types of travel clinic: those run by hospitals with travel health or tropical health departments; networks of private travel health centres, of which the best known are British Airways Travel Clinics; and

ARRANGING YOUR IMMUNIZATIONS

Table 1 Immunization summary chart for commonly used vaccines

Name	Original course	Boosters due	Takes effect after	Side effects	Lowest age
Diphtheria +tetanus	3 at monthly intervals	Every 10 years	At once after 3rd dose or booster	Serious reactions rare	10 years
Hepatitis A vaccine	One	After 6 to 12 months then every 10 years	2 weeks	Nil serious	Adult from 16 years Junior from 1 year
Hepatitis A Gamma-globulin	One	After 4 months	At once	Serious reactions rare	Any age
Hepatitis B	3 at months 0, 1 and 6*	3 years	At once after 3rd dose or booster	Serious reactions rare	Birth
Japanese encephalitis	3 at days 0, 7–14, 28	Every 3 years	14 days after 3rd dose or booster	Occ. more serious, sometimes a few days after 2nd or 3rd dose	1 year
Meningitis 'Mengivac' 'AC Vax'	One	Every 3 years	15 days	Serious reactions rare	18 months (Mengivac) 2 months (AC Vax)
Polio	3 at monthly intervals	Every 10 years	At once after 3rd dose or booster	Serious reactions rare	Birth
Rabies	3 at days 0, 7–14, 28	Every 3 years	At once after 3rd dose or booster	Serious reactions rare	1 year
Tick-borne encephalitis	Two, 4–12 weeks apart	After 1 year, then every 3 years	At once after 3rd dose or booster	Serious reactions rare	Obtain advice
Typhoid	One	Every 3 years	14 days after 1st, at once after booster	Occ. pain fever first 48 hours	2 years
Tuberculosis (BCG)	One	Not needed	About 2 months	Local nodule should appear	Birth
Yellow fever	One	Every 10 years	10 days after 1st, at once after booster	Occ. fever 5–10 days after injection	9 months

* Accelerated course available (see page 211).
For further details on each of these vaccines, see Appendix F. There are minor variations in details on some vaccines and schedules, depending on instructions from varying sources and manufacturers.

medical charities, of which InterHealth is an example. Most of these clinics are convenient to use and keep all immunizations in stock. Prices vary considerably. Some medical charities offer reduced rates for those working abroad with charitable organizations.

Differing advice!

It can be bewildering (and annoying) when different doctors seem to give different advice. It helps to understand some of the reasons: correct advice changes frequently both because of new vaccines and differing country-by-country recommendations (experts do not always agree); advice from UK sources is not always the same as that from European or North American colleagues: For many immunizations risk and benefit have to be weighed against each other.

It is usually simplest to follow the advice of one person. If going with a company or agency, follow their medical adviser's recommendations; otherwise follow advice from a travel clinic or your GP or practice nurse.

Pregnancy and breastfeeding

Live vaccines (see list on page 4) should be avoided *in pregnancy*. Non-live vaccines should only be given if going to very high-risk areas, except for gammaglobulin and tetanus, which are known to be fully safe.

Vaccinations can be given *when breastfeeding*.

Special note for parents

Children going abroad need even more jabs than their friends staying in the UK. By following a few simple rules, the trauma for them (and for you) can be reduced.

- Be relaxed when going with them to the doctor.
- Tell them, preferably on the way to the clinic and almost in passing, that they will be having a jab. Mention it may hurt a little, but not very much.
- Don't build up to the event, and don't pile on sympathy.
- Have a sweet or treat ready to encourage the last-minute falterer or to use as a bribe or reward.
- Follow the doctor's or nurse's instruction, and hold your child firmly.
- Try not to let your child see the nurse preparing the injection.
- Use paracetamol suspension (Calpol) over the next few hours and during the first night if your child seems fretful.

Special note for experienced travellers

As a seasoned traveller or long-term expatriate you may assume that your hard-won immunity removes the need for immunizations. Your risks are no less than for the first-time traveller. Follow standard immunization advice like everyone else.

KITS, MEDICINES, ANTIMALARIALS AND OTHER HEALTH SUPPLIES

As you will soon discover, this is a growth industry. There are dozens of kits, medicines and items of equipment you could take, and a bewildering mix and match of needles, first-aid items and medicines. Before coming to any decision, ask yourself these questions:

- *Location*: will you be based for the majority of your trip in a country with good, medium or poor health facilities? Will you be near a large city or in remoter areas? What is the remotest area you are likely to visit, for example on holiday, and how far will it be from good health care?
- *Your basic health*: do you have any medical conditions likely to put you at greater risk when travelling? How old are you and what is your level of physical fitness?
- *Your lifestyle*: where will you come on the spectrum between living in air-conditioned limos and lounges, or roughing it in the outback?
- *Length of time abroad*: are you on a short-term visit, a longer-term assignment, or not sure when you will come back?
- *Occupation*: does this put you at special risk, e.g. as an aid worker, missionary or volunteer, anthropologist or journalist; a water engineer, vet or health care worker; a dedicated adventure traveller?
- *Your personality*: do you feel uncomfortable unless prepared for almost any situation, or do you tend to go with the flow?
- *The practicals*: space, luggage allowance. How much health kit would you put in your case or rucksack when travelling out from your overseas home or hotel?

Thinking these through will help you decide what's worth taking.

Needles and syringes

The World Health Organisation estimates that every year ten million people worldwide catch hepatitis B or C from unclean syringes. Tens of thousands also become infected with HIV. About one injection in three is potentially contaminated.

Having packed a needle and syringe kit you must remember to have it with you when you need it. Rather more difficult is to insist that the doctor or nurse uses it. This may require courage and tact but if you fail to ask, you may worry about it afterwards.

Customs officials rarely seem to object when they come across medical supplies in your personal luggage. However, you should always have a signed doctor's note with you – preferably in your travel documents – which states that these supplies are for your personal, medical use only. Those travelling to a few countries, e.g. Malaysia, Singapore, should avoid taking needles and syringes because of the risk of being misidentified as a drug addict.

General recommendation for needle and syringe kits:

> If going to a developing country for all but the shortest, lowest-risk trips, take clean needles and syringes, ideally as part of a first-aid kit.

First-aid kits

These come in a wide range of contents, combinations and cost. Here are some guidelines:

- *Basic first-aid supplies* such as plasters, scissors and bandages. It is always sensible to have these, regardless of where you travel. For simple trips you can merely add to any supplies you have at home by buying the extras you need. For longer trips it may be easier to buy a simple kit.
- *More advanced supplies* for higher-risk travel. You will need more than the basics if you are going abroad for a longer time or taking up an assignment. Also if you are travelling extensively on dangerous roads or planning adventure pursuits. Your kit will need to include equipment for suturing, putting up intravenous drips and a wider range of first-aid items for more serious injuries. It will probably be better to buy a ready-made kit. You can save money if travelling in a group or team by sharing one or more kits between you.
- *Transfusion substitutes* for extensive travel in high-risk areas. You should consider taking a kit that in addition to the above also includes

blood substitute if travelling extensively on dangerous roads or by light aircraft in countries where HIV is common.

AIDS protection kit

Blood transfusions are a serious HIV and hepatitis B risk in a growing number of countries. In much of sub-Saharan Africa, south Asia and Latin America, blood is often obtained through private suppliers who may buy blood from those living on the streets, many of whom will be HIV positive. Screening is often inadequate, or non-existent.

You should therefore avoid a 'blind' blood transfusion in a developing country except in a life-threatening emergency. The purpose of the HIV protection kit is to enable two or three bottles of intravenous fluid to be administered, either to avoid the need for blood altogether or to buy time until safe blood is available (see page 91). Until recently, fluids known as plasma expanders were the preferred choice (e.g. Haemacell or Gelofusine), but recent evidence suggests that simple intravenous fluids such as Hartmann's solution are a better choice, used early before veins have collapsed from too much blood loss. Normally we can survive blood loss of about 20% before needing replacement.

The AIDS kit can only be used by someone familiar with putting up an intravenous line, such as a medical travelling companion or a trained onlooker at any accident. This does mean there is a possibility that the kit cannot be used at the time you need it. Any colleagues travelling with you should know that a kit is available. Many experts still consider it is better to have one with you in case it can be used, than not to have one at all. The worst scenario is to be in an accident, need your kit, have a trained nurse on site but to have left your kit in the cupboard at home.

General recommendations for first-aid kits:

- For short low-risk trips buy a simple first-aid kit or make up your own.
- If going to live abroad, taking up an assignment or planning adventure travel, obtain a more comprehensive kit including an intravenous giving set, a needle and suture kit and a wider range of dressings.
- If planning to travel extensively by road or light aircraft where HIV is prevalent, consider in addition taking 2 litres of intravenous fluid, preferably as part of an HIV protection kit.

Medicine kits and personal medical supplies

First, personal medical supplies. Take with you ample supplies of any permanent medication you need. GPs *may* be willing to prescribe enough for a few weeks on the NHS, but after that you will need to ask your GP or another doctor for a private prescription. If you are going abroad for more than a year consider having further supplies sent out or, better still, brought out to you.

Remember that all medicines have both a trade name (usually in bold print), which varies from place to place, and a generic name (usually in small print), which is the worldwide scientific name. You should get used to recognizing and using the generic name.

Where possible it is better to take medicines as blister packs or in bottles well packed with cotton wool to prevent transit damage, especially when backpacking. Make sure the tops of ointment tubes are firmly done up, especially at high altitude. Having arrived at your destination keep your supplies in a cool place, out of direct sunlight and away from the reach of rats, ants – and children.

If you use *contact lenses* take plenty of cleansing fluid as well as a pair of glasses. If you are a *diabetic* take all the supplies you may need with you (see page 139).

Women should take a supply of *tampons* unless enquiries confirm that reliable and acceptable supplies are available where you are going.

A note on expiry dates. Many medicines have a use-by date two to four years from the date of manufacture. This means some items in your medical kit are likely to pass their expiry date if your assignment is long-term. However, many medicines, if well stored and neither crumbling, damp nor discoloured, will remain both safe and effective for some time after their expiry date, though this cannot be entirely guaranteed.

Second, medicine kits. Although many countries sell a huge range of medicines, good quality essential supplies may be harder to obtain. In some countries fake products are sold. For simple destinations and short trips just put together a collection of the medicines you are most likely to need – for example, pain killers, antihistamines, travel sickness pills and antiseptic cream.

Most medicine kits contain only non-prescription supplies, but some more comprehensive kits are available in which prescription-only medicines, such as antibiotics, are included. You will need to follow guidelines carefully when buying these and only obtain them from ethical suppliers that follow established protocols. Also carry a doctor's letter and list of contents in case either foreign customs or, on return, British customs raise any questions. A good form of wording for a doctor's letter is as follows:

'These medicines are only for the personal, private use of . . . (name of traveller).' This should be signed by the doctor and have the practice stamp, including the doctor's name and qualifications.

General recommendations for personal medicines and medicine kits:

Take an ample supply of any medicines you usually use until you discover whether these are obtainable in the area in which you will be living or travelling. Consider taking a medicine kit if you will be travelling in remote areas, living in a country where good quality supplies are not easily available or living at a distance from good health facilities. Medicine kits are especially useful for families or those travelling in groups, teams or expeditions, when contents can be shared.

Dental kit

Emergency dental kits are worth taking if you are living for any length of time in remote areas where dentists are few and far between, or where there is a high level of HIV infection (see page 192).

Antimalarials (see also pages 58–85)

If you are travelling to a malarious part of the world *it is essential to take antimalarials.* Usually it is easier and cheaper to take these from the UK, rather than buy them abroad, unless you have personal knowledge of a reliable overseas supply. You should include *both* malaria prophylactics (pills to prevent malaria) *and*, if living or travelling in areas remote from good medical care, an emergency supply of standby tablets for treatment. See pages 68–72 for the names of tablets recommended for different areas.

Some antimalarials (e.g. chloroquine and proguanil (Paludrine)) are available from chemists without a prescription. All others have to be prescribed by your GP (there is usually a charge) or obtained from travel clinics – see Appendix D, page 203.

If you are going to an area where malaria is common or where chloroquine-resistant malaria is known to occur, you may still get malaria even if you take your tablets regularly. You should therefore take these further supplies with you:

- A *mosquito net*, pre-soaked in the safe mosquito-killer, permethrin. Try to find out if a net is available at your destination. Take extra permethrin to resoak your net if you are going for longer than six months.
- *Insect repellent*: take plenty of this, ideally a brand containing DEET (see page 64).
- *Coils* or, better, *vaporizing mats* help keep mosquitoes at bay (see page 66).

13

Contraceptives

Because supplies usually have to be taken with you it is worth planning what contraception to use well before leaving. If you are using the pill for the first time try to take two or three cycles before you go abroad to make sure it suits you.

If there is any chance you may need condoms, take a supply with you. If buying condoms in the UK use only the kite-marked brands. It is usually better not to rely on local supplies. Keep condoms in a cool place, away from the light and check the expiry date.

If you are planning to live abroad it is worth considering other forms of contraception, such as an injectable contraceptive or an IUCD. Talk this over with your family planning clinic or GP, several months before you leave.

Suggestions for those taking the pill when travelling

- *Ample supplies.* Take plenty with you unless you know the pill of your choice is available overseas. There are many brand names for each pill, so keep a packet cover with you with both the brand name and exact formulation written on it. Split your supply between different parts of your baggage in case of theft.

  Your GP may be willing to prescribe enough for up to three months, your family planning clinic possibly for longer. Otherwise you can obtain a private prescription from your GP or from some travel clinics. Make sure all your supplies expire after the latest date you might need them.

- *Time zones.* When crossing these make sure you take a pill at least every twenty-four hours, preferably at the same time, until you gradually adjust to your new timetable. During this adjustment the time between pills can be less than twenty-four hours but should ideally not be longer, though some advisers extend this to 27 hours.

- *Diarrhoea*, stomach upsets and courses of antibiotics (in particular ampicillin and tetracycline) can reduce absorption of the pill. In such situations take the pill as usual, avoid having sex or in addition use a barrier method such as male or female condoms during these risk periods and for seven days after. This is known as the seven-day rule. Also check the instructions in your packet, which will explain exactly what to do if you forget a pill or are late taking it, both easy to do when you are travelling.

- *Vomiting.* If this occurs within three hours of taking a pill, take another. If vomiting then continues, use additional protection as above and follow the seven-day rule.

- *Avoiding periods* when travelling. You can do this for one or two cycles by taking the pill continuously. If you plan to do this, remember to take extra packs with you. It may be possible for you to use this method even if you do not take the pill for contraception – discuss with your doctor well before leaving.

- *Types of pill.* A fixed combination oestrogen-progestogen pill is probably the most appropriate. This is usually known as the combined contraceptive pill. The progestogen-only pill is less appropriate for travel and gives less good protection, especially when crossing time zones or with stomach upsets. Biphasic and triphasic pills with dose formulations that vary with the time of the month are less flexible for travelling.
- *Hepatitis.* If you go down with this it is best to avoid the pill for six months.
- *Hot climates.* Pills should remain effective provided your pack is within the expiry date, it remains intact and you keep it in as cool a place as possible.
- *Emergency contraception.* If there is a serious chance you may have become pregnant against your wishes, you can take oral contraceptive pills within the first 72 hours, the sooner the better. There are three ways of doing this:
  - The Yuzpe method is still the best known: take two doses of a preparation, 12 hours apart, each containing ethinyoestradiol 100 micrograms and levonorgestrel 0.5 mg. This is equivalent to taking 2 Ovran contraceptive pills, and a further two after 12 hours.
  - The second method, slightly more effective, is to take two pills, twelve hours apart, each containing 0.75 mg of levonorgestrel. This preparation, except in combination, is not available in the UK at the time of writing.
  - A third alternative is simply to take two combined contraceptive pills of whichever brand you use, followed by 2 more 12 hours later. This is *not* an ideal solution.

It is important to realize that all the above are unlicensed for this use and that occasional side effects, sometimes serious, can occur. Note most especially that none of these regimes guarantee pregnancy will be prevented.

Other health supplies

Most regular travellers keep a list in their head or in their top drawer. If you don't, start making one now:

- *A hat.* This is an essential item if you will be regularly out in the sun as part of your job or when on holiday!
- *Sun cream.* Buy cream with a sun protection factor of at least 15 if you

do not burn easily or factor 24 or more if you do, or if you are travelling with children. Also take a sun-protecting lip-salve.

- *Water filters.* If you will be living abroad in an area where boiling is not an easy option (e.g. fuel supplies are unreliable), consider buying a domestic water filter unless good brands are available locally. If you will be travelling extensively decide whether to buy a portable water filter for the road (see page 41).
- *Water sterilizing tablets.* Iodine (the most effective) or chlorine tablets are always worth taking with you.
- *Appropriate clothing* to stop you from getting too hot, cold or wet and that will not offend the local population.
- *A torch* to avoid hazards in the dark such as snakes or for village latrines.
- *A medic-alert bracelet or pendant* if you have any severe allergies or serious conditions that others need to know about (see page 206).

Appendix B gives suggested contents for a range of kits. Appendix A gives a list of suggested medicines.

TRAVELLERS WITH SPECIAL HEALTH RISKS

More and more people are travelling today who even a few years ago might have been advised by their doctor, friends or relatives against exchanging suburbia for the Sahara.

If you are concerned about a health problem and whether it might affect your overseas travel, seek medical advice before dreaming of an exotic holiday or planning any mission or assignment. If you will be employed by an agency or company, their medical adviser or anyone to whom they contract out occupational health services will need to be assured you are fit enough to travel.

Two questions need to be answered. First and most important, do you, or any agency you are going with or for, feel that the risks of travelling are acceptable? Second, can health clearance be given in a way sufficient to enable you to take out travel health insurance?

There are three main sources of medical advice you can tap into. First, your GP, especially if they know you well, should be your first port of call, and can offer a range of advice: whether you should go at all; whether your itinerary and plans are suitable; any precautions you should take; any follow-up you may need overseas; and details of medication including dosage and how to obtain supplies abroad. Second, if you are attending a hospital clinic or have recently done so, the consultant is worth talking to, especially if the problem is quite serious or complicated. Third, there are travel medicine specialists who have experience of how overseas travel affects various health problems.

The information given below does not replace the specific advice you should obtain from one of the sources mentioned above.

Back and joint problems

Minor *aches and pains* often improve in warm climates; *arthritis* is unpredictable. *Backache* can be worsened or caused by the rigours of travel. If you have had recent severe backache, sciatica or numbness in the foot or leg, make sure you seek medical advice before you travel (see page 153).

Diabetes

See pages 138–9.

Epilepsy

Although most people with controlled epilepsy or absences travel with little extra danger, it is worth being aware of a few potential problems. A severe bout of malaria with fever might increase the risk of having a further fit. Chloroquine and mefloquine should not be used as antimalarials in those with a past or present history of epilepsy as they may trigger an attack. Doxycycline is often the antimalarial of choice, but certain anticonvulsants reduce its effectiveness, meaning you may have to increase the doxycycline dosage (see page 72).

If your epilepsy is poorly or partially controlled you should get expert advice from your GP or specialist, and preferably travel with a friend or companion.

Headaches

Both *migraine* and *tension headache* often become worse overseas, especially when under stress, when dehydrated or with frequent changes in altitude such as when travelling or trekking in mountains. If you have significant headaches it is worth consulting your doctor to discuss how best you can manage these. Take with you a supply of your favourite painkillers and work out an appropriate lifestyle (see also pages 95–100).

Heart problems

It is generally unwise to visit a developing country or to take up residence abroad within three to six months of having a confirmed *heart attack*.

If you have suffered from *any serious heart disease* or remain under treatment, make sure that your future location and occupation are unlikely to cause undue strain. Try to organize your actual travel to be as stress-free as possible. Have someone with you who can carry your luggage, or arrange in advance with the airline to use a wheelchair.

Precautions overseas include living within reasonable access of adequate health care and avoiding unduly stressful, hot or humid conditions. An air conditioner is a good investment. It is hard to generalize about altitude as ability to tolerate this is so variable. Discuss any exposure to altitudes over 2,000 metres (about 6,500 feet) with your doctor.

Some *blood pressure tablets* may lead to increased giddiness in hot climates, and in addition tablets called betablockers can cause shortness of breath at higher altitudes. If your blood pressure has been raised in the past, have it checked at least once every three months or as your doctor advises.

Carry copies of ECGs (EKGs) with you, especially your most recent and that taken at the time of any heart attack. This can be most valuable should you have any chest pain and need a further ECG while overseas.

Travellers taking *anticoagulants* must ensure that facilities for checking prothrombin time or an equivalent are present at the point of destination, and that adequate doses are taken to cover flights (when the risk of leg thrombosis increases). Make sure that no travel medication you are given affects the dose. Being on anticoagulants makes bleeding more likely and therefore increases the possibility of a blood transfusion, especially in an accident or during surgery. Intramuscular injections and immunizations may also be more painful as slight bleeding may occur into the injection site.

Those with *pacemakers* should tell security officials and discuss with the airline in advance. Although devices in international airports in western countries are set so as not to cause problems, this is not always the case in developing countries.

Those with heart or lung problems should seriously consider having jabs against flu and pneumococcus, especially if travelling during winter in either the northern or southern hemisphere.

Kidney and bladder problems

Kidney stones are common in those who live in the tropics. If you have previously suffered the agony of passing one, ask your GP if an abdominal X-ray, IVU or ultrasound can be arranged before you go, to make sure no others are lurking. Keep your fluid intake up, by drinking far more than usual, ideally enough to keep your urine pale. *Bladder infections (cystitis)*, especially in women, can be brought on by long or bumpy car journeys, especially in the heat; also by sexual activity. Treat cystitis with antibiotics and plenty of fluids (see page 194). Men who have symptoms of *prostate trouble* should have this checked by a doctor before any long-term assignment overseas, and those over the age of 50, with or without symptoms, should have a Prostate Specific Antigen (PSA) blood test.

Overweight

Being markedly overweight makes overseas travel more difficult. In a hot climate, tiredness, difficulty keeping up with others, slowness acclimatizing and a greater tendency to skin infections can all take their toll. You will also be at greater risk of heat exhaustion (see page 104). Start losing weight before you go rather than assume it will happen automatically as you head off for the tropics. Many people actually put on weight overseas.

Pregnancy

See pages 124–30.

Previous splenectomy

If you have had your spleen removed you are slightly more likely to pick up infections while travelling, and they may progress more rapidly. Falciparum malaria is a special risk: take every antimalarial precaution possible and try to avoid areas where this type of malaria is known to be common (see page 59). You should have all the normal travel jabs plus immunization against pneumococcus, haemophilus influenzae b (Hib) and meningitis. When abroad you should also take prophylactic antibiotics such as amoxycillin 250 mg daily or erythromycin 250 mg daily (adult doses). In addition take sufficient extra with you to treat any infection with the maximum dose (amoxycillin 500 mg three times daily or erythromycin 500 mg four times daily for seven to ten days). Consult your doctor before going and seek medical advice if you become ill overseas.

Psychological problems

As a general rule those embarking on an overseas assignment or adventure travel should be mentally healthy. The stresses and strains of working in a developing country are considerable, and psychological problems are one of the commonest reasons for emergency repatriation or for cutting short an assignment.

If you feel worried about going abroad because of previous emotional problems or mental illness, see your doctor. Some organizations sending people to frontline or long-term placements will ask applicants to see a psychiatrist or a clinical psychologist before they are accepted.

Depression often (but by no means always) recurs under prolonged, difficult conditions. If you are prone to *anxiety*, counselling or advice on stress management can be helpful. Those who have had *psychotic* illnesses or a recent history of *alcohol abuse* should generally avoid overseas assignments. If you *smoke*, try hard to give up before travelling because it increases your risk of becoming ill. Volunteers who have suffered from *anorexia* or *bulimia* in the past (or are present sufferers) are encouraged to discuss this openly with their sending agency and at any medical.

Respiratory problems

Asthma is unpredictable abroad, many travellers improving (especially in rural areas), some suffering more severe problems. The pollution of many tropical cities, e.g. Cairo, Karachi, Mexico City, Delhi, Calcutta and Kathmandu, may cause it to worsen or start for the first time.

Because asthma is so unpredictable and the range of overseas situations so broad, it is worth getting specific first-hand information from someone who has been living in the area you are planning to visit. If your asthma is severe, it may be worth making a short trial visit to test out a location for yourself.

Take a supply of the medication you would need for the *worst* attack you have recently suffered. This will probably include an inhaler (e.g. Ventolin as the new CFC-free Ventolin Evohaler, and/or Becotide), and may include steroid tablets and antibiotics. Dry powder systems such as Rotahaler and Spinhaler can get clogged in humid climates, and sealed dry powder systems such as Turbohaler and Diskhaler are probably better. A few people may want to take a nebulizer (which requires reliable electricity, compatible plugs, battery drive etc.), but an excellent alternative is the Nebuhaler, used for example with the drug terbutaline (Bricanyl), or the Volumatic.

Work out an action plan with your normal medical adviser so that you know exactly how to use the medicines you take with you, and when you should seek medical advice. If you are a more severe asthmatic it is worth taking a peakflow meter with you for keeping an accurate record of your readings. High altitude does not usually affect asthma, but if you happen to have an attack of asthma or chest infection at altitude it could be more serious because of decreased oxygen.

If you have severe *allergies*, e.g. to bee and wasp stings or to nuts, take adrenalin injections with you. Two preloaded Epipen self-injectors are ideal but need to be prescribed. There is a junior form for children.

Sinusitis is also unpredictable, usually becoming worse in dusty or polluted areas, though often improving elsewhere (unless you visit Britain in winter).

Coughs and colds usually continue as usual, especially in families. *Hay fever* commonly improves.

Skin conditions

Psoriasis improves in the sun but can worsen under stress. Chloroquine occasionally makes it worse. *Eczema* may flare up in hot or humid climates or with swimming, and is more likely to become infected. However, it often improves with the sun. Widespread, infected eczema is a dangerous condition in the tropics. Ensure your eczema is well controlled before travelling and take a copious supply of all the creams you are likely to need, plus a broad-spectrum antibiotic such as amoxycillin (see page 198). *Fungal infections*, especially of the toes (athlete's foot) and of the groin commonly get worse. Take appropriate cream or powder with you (see also pages 184–7).

Stomach disorders

Peptic ulcers commonly recur overseas, especially under stress, but are easily treated with modern drugs. If you have a history of peptic ulcer and are going on a lengthy overseas trip, ask your GP for a Helicobacter blood or breath test. This germ is a cause of many ulcers and can be eradicated with a week's course of triple drug therapy. A history of past or present *ulcerative colitis* will need very careful assessment and may worsen when overseas, especially after attacks of diarrhoea. *Crohn's disease* also needs caution. *Irritable bowel syndrome* may worsen, e.g. after repeated bouts of diarrhoea, but would not normally stop you travelling. Those with well-controlled *coeliac disease* usually survive travel quite well, providing they do research on the local food and availability of gluten-free products before travelling and take extra care to avoid diarrhoea.

A history of *bleeding from the rectum*, usually put down to piles, should be carefully checked by a doctor before you go overseas. Any *hernia* should be repaired before leaving.

MEDICALS AND TRAVEL HEALTH ADVICE

Most travel clinics and many GP surgeries try to give time for travel health advice and to answer questions at the time you have your immunizations.

Travel to exotic destinations is not only becoming more common, it is also in many areas becoming less safe. There are various reasons for this, including a greater risk of road accidents, more widespread malaria, increased alcohol abuse, the worry and reality of HIV infection and greater risks to personal security.

Immunizations only prevent about one disease episode in ten, so make sure when you get your travel jabs that you also find out about how to keep healthy abroad – defeating malaria, avoiding accidents, reducing risks of HIV infection and dealing with the almost inevitable nuisance of diarrhoea. Because so many clinics are busy you may have to make a point of asking about these things.

You should certainly arrange a travel health consultation if you are going to a developing country – unless your trip is short and low-risk. For any longer trip, assignment or stay overseas it is essential to be well informed, talk to a travel health nurse face-to-face and take away information you can read at your leisure.

In addition to a travel health consultation with a nurse, many people benefit from having a medical before going abroad. Obviously this is not usually needed for the average holiday or short-term trip, but it can be useful if you come into one of the following categories:

- You are travelling off the beaten path, adventure travelling or joining an expedition for three months or longer.
- You are going on an overseas assignment for six months or longer, or on a shorter high-risk mission.
- You are planning to live overseas.
- You have a pre-existing medical condition you are concerned about or that may affect your travel.
- You are aged 50 or over.
- You are planning any especially arduous activities such as mountain-eering or scuba diving.
- You are going with an aid or mission agency, company or organization that requests a medical.

GPs will be able to arrange a medical if you book well in advance. You are not entitled to one on the NHS, and GPs can charge £60 or more if they wish. Some specialist travel clinics will also carry out medicals (see page 203). If you are going as an employee, missionary or aid worker, you will usually be told where to have your medical. If it is not a requirement it may still be in your interest to have one.

You may be going with one of the increasing number of organizations that ask applicants to be seen by a psychiatrist or clinical psychologist. Sometimes psychometric testing is also included. Don't be taken aback by this. The main purpose is not to exclude people from going abroad but to help ensure that your own placement is consistent with your gifts and temperament.

When you do have a medical or have to complete a questionnaire, it is worth being complete (and honest). Holding back information isn't doing yourself a favour. Questions asked are mainly to protect your health in situations where health care may be poor quality, and to make sure you are placed in a safe and appropriate location.

If you do not know your blood group, or those of other family members, this is a good time to find out. Your GP may be willing to arrange it, but there is usually a charge. Alternatively, you can give blood, though it may occasionally take several weeks before your donor card with a note of your blood group is sent to you.

Certain conditions preclude you from giving blood in the UK, including: hepatitis within the past year, being a hepatitis B or C carrier, pregnancy, any past history of malaria or a sexually transmitted disease, any skin piercing or surgical operation within the past year, any past homosexual encounter, history of self-injection with drugs, high blood pressure or diabetes/epilepsy requiring medication.

Phone the National Blood Transfusion Service on 0345–711711 for further details of how and where to give blood.

PREPARING FOR AN OVERSEAS ASSIGNMENT

If you are planning to spend any length of time in a new country, it is worth learning as much as possible about its customs and lifestyle. Apart from being interesting in itself this has two main benefits: it helps to reduce your own culture shock on arrival, and it also makes it less likely that you will cause offence to the local people by dressing or behaving in a way that is out of keeping with local traditions. This can be especially important in Islamic cultures.

Here are a few suggestions:

- *Be prepared for culture shock.*
  Of course you may not experience this, especially if you love travel, have a laid-back temperament, are lucky enough to have a stimulating assignment and close friends, or manage to retain a large measure of control over your life and lifestyle.

  However, you probably will come to recognize the four typical phases shown in Figure 1, and just being prepared for them can be helpful. You then realize it's probably normal to be feeling the way you are, rather than wonder what on earth is happening to you.

  The four phases are often described as:

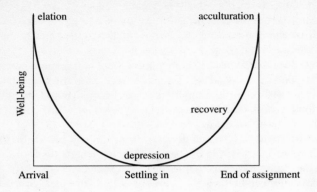

Figure 1 The U-curve pattern of adjustment to a new culture (Modified from *Social Work* (1993), 38 (6), pp. 694–704; after *International Social Science Bulletin* (1955), 7, pp. 45–51.

- **Elation** You are excited by all the new sounds, smells, sights and experiences.
- **Depression** The excitement and newness wears off. It gets replaced by irritation at the hassles and inefficiency and annoyance with your companions. You feel homesick, missing the people, parties and good times – and all your home comforts. You wonder whether you can possibly last out the rest of your assignment – so do your friends and relatives, who get worried about what you write home.
- **Recovery or integration** You start to value the good experiences and cope with the bad. You are grieving less about the people and places back home. Of course, despite integrating these aspects of your life, you still have bad days.
- **Acculturation** You get used to the culture and people and come to accept them, warts and all. You may start enjoying life to such an extent that the idea of leaving fills you with horror. And the more good friends you make and the greater the experiences you have, the better it all feels. Of course, if you've had a really stressful time, some bad experiences or problems with your assignment, you may not feel this way at all (if that is the case be sure to get a proper debriefing when you get home).
- *Meeting people.* There may be people from the country you will be visiting who are studying or living in the UK. It can be mutually enriching to get to know them and discover something of their beliefs and lifestyle.

It is also valuable to talk to any expatriate who has actually lived in or visited the area you are going to. By asking specific questions you will be able to prepare yourself both mentally and practically. It will give you a chance to find out what items are locally available and what clothes and personal belongings you should take with you.

- *Reading*. Time allowing, it is worth reading history books, travel books, novels and any literature covering your own profession or field of interest. Selective reading of a travel guide, e.g. the Rough Guide or Lonely Planet series, helps to give ideas for leisure activities.
- *Watching films*, videos, TV programmes or cultural events (art exhibits, dances, drama) of the country you are visiting.

    The wider your background knowledge the greater will be your appreciation and understanding of what you see – and the more you'll probably be able to contribute, which is satisfying for everyone.

- *Learning some language*. A little of the host language can go a long way, stimulate interest and help give you a head start when you wander through the bazaar or join the language school.

    You will probably be able to find someone here who speaks the language you need to learn. Alternatively, select the most appropriate language guide or consider using a Linguaphone or BBC course.

- *Adjusting expectations* to a sensible level, especially in terms of your job or assignment. This is especially important for goal-orientated professionals, who will need to learn that people are often more important than projects, and good local relationships of greater value than a list of achievements in newsletters home.

    In terms of time management, it helps to realize before you go that the process of living (e.g. shopping, cooking, communicating, travelling) may often take many times longer than at home, effectively reducing your 'productive' working life by half. You may need to spend a day each year, or even a day each month, sitting in an office to obtain a permit, visa, or permission for something absurdly trivial. Being prepared for delays, inefficiency, corruption and red tape enables you to use time spent waiting productively (e.g. for language-swotting, knitting, reading), rather than prolong the process by outbursts of expatriate anger.

- *Discovering ways* to minimize cultural differences. Clothes and gadgets should be selected and worn with care. The uncovered arms or legs of women may be quite acceptable in some countries, but enough to cause stones to fly in others. Photographic and electronic wizardry may draw gasps of admiration from the local inhabitants, but at the expense of you being seen as a provider of foreign merchandise rather than as a straightforward friend.

- *Avoiding gaffes*. Customs, habits and clothes that we take for granted may cause offence or amusement in other cultures. Do some homework first so as to avoid social clangers that can put your local acceptance rating back to zero. Classic examples include eating or giving gifts with the left hand, baring your flesh in public (e.g. Islamic cultures) and failing to remove your shoes when entering a local home. Passing wind may cause amusement or extreme offence – travellers with Giardia please note (see page 53).

- *Preparing for leisure.* Before going abroad decide to build into your lifestyle adequate leisure and time off. In practice this can be difficult if you live in a remote area, travel is dangerous or you are confined within the four walls of a hospital, training centre or compound. A few well-chosen books, games, raw materials for a creative hobby (e.g. oil paints) and a pair of binoculars can pay huge dividends.

- *Decide to keep a diary or record.* Quite apart from being fun to read to yourself in twelve months' time, or to grandchildren in future years, it helps you to see your life in perspective. Sometimes writing down a difficult, annoying or frightening episode can deprive it of its sting. It also stimulates you to continue being a student of the country where you are living.

- *Orientation course.* Most sending agencies or large companies run training courses, briefing weekends or even residential terms for preparation. If one hasn't been arranged try to join one. By helping you to think through situations before they arise, they enable you to handle the human, emotional, physical and spiritual conditions you are likely to meet.

- Finally consider doing a Teaching English as a Foreign Language (TEFL) or Teaching English as a Second Language (TESL) course, a week on vehicle maintenance and, especially if you are going as a team leader, a first-aid course run by the local branch of the British Red Cross or St John/St Andrew's Ambulance.

HEALTH INSURANCE FOR TRAVEL ABROAD

If you are travelling *independently* it is essential to take out an insurance policy. This should cover the following:

- Medical and emergency expenses abroad, including medivac when needed.
- 24-hour emergency assistance in case of accident or severe illness.
- Availability of fully screened and tested blood within 24 hours.

- Medical emergency expenses in your home country if medically repatriated.
- Personal accident to cover death and disability.
- Insurance to cover loss of money and damage to or theft of baggage and personal possessions.
- Personal liability to cover injury to third parties, including legal costs.
- Cancellation and curtailment of trip due to ill health of traveller, family member or business associate.
- Optional availability of cover for adventure sports, and travel in war zones, or to cover the older traveller.

If you are working overseas *with a sending agency or company*, health insurance will probably be arranged for you, but make sure. Ask your organization about its policy and consider taking out additional insurance if it doesn't cover the list above. For any visit to the USA you must have full health insurance (up to £5 million) to cover against potentially enormous medical fees.

Make yourself aware of any 'reciprocal health care' you may be entitled to in your host country. *Health Advice For Travellers* (page 220) gives this information.

Within the European Union, and in some other countries, reciprocal health arrangements are available for British citizens. In order to make use of this you will need to produce your passport, NHS medical card and form E111. The latter is found in the booklet *Health Advice for Travellers*, available from any post office. The E111 has to be completed and stamped before it is valid (at a post office for a holiday in Europe, at the DSS Newcastle Office if going on to live abroad afterwards – see details on form E111). Health cover in Europe is less comprehensive than under the NHS in the UK, and some items will be excluded. Keep all receipts and proofs of purchase of medicines or treatment.

Outside the European Union, some countries offer certain free or subsidized health facilities. Further details can be found in *Health Advice for Travellers*. In practice there are virtually no reciprocal arrangements with most developing countries. When travelling, make sure you have a readily available means of paying any hospital bills.

Special schemes for charitable workers

Some insurance companies are now providing special insurance packages for those working with charitable organizations. One scheme that is both comprehensive and economic is run by Banner Financial Services (see Appendix D for details).

THE FLIGHT

Flying is extremely safe, and for many people enjoyable. Usually any pre-flight nerves quickly settle as the plane takes off, and thoughts of distant places (or an impending hot bath at home) take over.

Travel sickness

As well as reaching for the travel pills, also try simpler methods. Pre-book seats near the middle of the plane and in the most central blocks of seats. This way there is less pitching and rolling. The same applies in boats. Closing the eyes may help, especially if you also lie flat on your back – admittedly not a popular option on most flights unless your neighbours are especially tolerant or charming.

In some countries a hyoscine patch is available to apply behind the ear. This has recently been withdrawn in the UK. Some people swear by Sea-Bands. These are cuffs that you wear on the wrist and that probably work by wishful thinking rather than 'acupressure', making them especially useful with children.

As most of us have discovered, taking sickness pills after you start feeling sick means you've probably lost the battle. However, you will be better motivated to start earlier next time round.

For children (or adults) the drive to the airport is as likely to cause nausea as the flight itself. Give your favourite sickness pill in plenty of time, and take spares for any subsequent journeys overseas and the return flight. Hyoscine (Kwells) is a favourite brand, especially for children, and promethazine (Avomine), dimenhydrinate (Dramamine) and cinnarizine (Stugeron) – not for children under five – each have their followers. They are available over the counter.

Remember to take sickness pills at least two hours before their effects are needed, though one hour is sufficient for Kwells. All cause a degree of drowsiness, often manifested in children by either greater or lesser charm than usual at check-in.

Cabin pressure

For most planes this is maintained at the pressure normally found at an altitude of 6,000 to 7,000 feet above sea level. This explains why body gases expand, especially in stomachs and ears, and why the amount of oxygen slightly decreases, the latter important only to those with severe heart or lung problems. Incidentally, if you do feel short of breath or wheezy you can ask the cabin attendant for oxygen.

You can ease distension of the stomach by wearing loose clothing, avoiding excessive carbonated drinks, eating slowly and avoiding large

meals. Ear problems can usually be prevented by sucking a sweet during take-off and landing, or by regular jaw-opening or swallowing. Those with sensitive ears, including children with recent ear infections or catarrh, should have a combination of an antihistamine and pseudoephedrine known in the UK as Sudafed Plus (tablets or syrup) one hour before take off and, on longer flights, again before landing (do not use in children under two). Again this preparation is available over the counter.

In-flight drinks and food

Cabin air is extremely dry and dehydration occurs on all long flights. Alcohol, tea and coffee unfortunately make dehydration worse (they cause you to lose more urine than the fluid you take in) and you are best to stick to frequent soft, uncarbonated drinks and fruit juices.

It is a cause of regret to many, not least the returning aid worker and volunteer, that alcohol, fizzy drinks and large, rich meals are the very things travel doctors say are best avoided on board the aircraft.

From the point of view of hygiene, aircraft food prepared or loaded in developing countries should carry the same health warnings as meals eaten out in the country of origin. Keep to the rules on page 35, taking special care to avoid salad, including lettuce and tomatoes.

Clots in the legs

There is an increased risk of getting blood clots in the legs on long-haul flights. They occasionally travel up to the lungs, giving a pulmonary embolism days or weeks after arriving. 'Economy-class syndrome', as it is now called, is due to sitting still for long periods of time, being wedged into tight seats, going to sleep in peculiar positions and becoming dehydrated. You can prevent it by frequently flexing your leg muscles, stretching your legs, walking about every one or two hours and having plenty of soft drinks or water throughout the flight. Many of these measures will also help your feet to swell less. Taking half an aspirin before the flight reduces the danger of blood clots by making the blood cells less sticky on the inside of the blood vessels.

If you have previously had a deep vein thrombosis or have varicose veins it is probably worth wearing elastic stockings during the flight. Also discuss with your doctor having a subcutaneous injection of low molecular weight heparin or taking low-dose warfarin tablets.

Jet lag

All long flights, especially where sleep is lost, cause tiredness, as true for north-south flights as for transmeridian flights (east-west/west-east). After crossing time zones there is in addition a disturbance of the normal body rhythms, including sleep patterns. This is largely responsible for the downside of intercontinental flying, jet lag, which for most people tends to be worse going from west to east.

Certain seasoned travellers affirm they have learnt the secret of dealing with this, but for most of us it has to be endured and perhaps helped to a degree by a few commonsense precautions. These include trying to ensure at least one good night's sleep before a long journey, trying to sleep on the plane (especially on an eastward flight), avoiding caffeine and allowing yourself time to adjust on arrival (organizers of travel itineraries please note).

For a flight across five or more time zones, i.e. losing or gaining five hours or more, it is worth planning twenty-four hours in your new destination before any important activity or meeting. Also, if your schedule allows, try to arrive as near as possible to your normal bedtime.

Most people have heard of melatonin, claimed in the USA to work miracles for a variety of complaints and available there in health-food shops. In the UK it is not yet licensed, but many people are convinced it reduces jet lag, a view supported by scientific evidence.

Melatonin helps to induce sleep and reset your body clock. But take care driving after taking a dose as it can make you feel sleepy.

Tips for beating jet lag

- *Sleeping tablets.* Zolpidem 10 mg is short acting. You can take it on any flight of five hours or longer and/or at bedtime after eastward flights for three or four nights.
- *Melatonin tablets.* Take 3-5mg at bedtime (new time zone) for three to four days after arrival.
- *Light.* Expose yourself to light in the morning for eastward flights, and at the end of the day for westward flights.

Two final points. First, before you go: only bid into expensive lag-busting diets, massage regimes or computer programmes if you are very desperate or very rich. Second, on arrival: if you are feeling doped and gormless, try one or two sachets of Oral Rehydration Solution (see page 50). They can be very reviving, especially if you dried out on the flight.

Insomnia

Only the lucky few are able to sleep on a long flight, and then to appear annoyingly fresh and enthusiastic on the day of arrival at the other side of the world.

For some people lack of sleep during flight and/or for a few nights after arrival can be a serious nuisance. This is especially true for those with important engagements or whose transworld responsibilities involve frequent crossing and recrossing of time zones.

In such cases there is a place for the use of sleeping pills. The three golden rules are: use in the lowest dose that works; use for as few nights as possible; and choose a short-acting preparation with minimal after-effects. Current favourites are temazepam 10 mg (Normison), zolpidem 10 mg (Stilnoct) or zopiclone 7.5 mg (Zimovane). In the UK they all have to be prescribed by a doctor (see Appendix A). Alternatively, just buy diphenhydramine (Nytol) over the counter.

Those unfit to fly

If in doubt about flying you should discuss this with your own doctor or the medical officer of the airline. If you have any serious condition be sure to notify the airline well in advance.

Medical conditions that make flying unsuitable or unsafe

Except in special circumstances international airlines will usually debar anyone with the following problems in the categories stated:

- *Heart problems*

Myocardial infarction (heart attack) within ten days if uncomplicated, within ten days of persistent recovery if initial complications; uncontrolled heart failure, unstable angina or uncontrolled arrhythmia; open-heart surgery within ten days; angioplasty within 14 days if stent used

- *Blood and bleeding disorders*

Severe bleeding or clotting disorder within ten days; untreated deep venous thrombosis; unstable anticoagulation; anaemia with an Hb of 7.5 g/dl or less; history of sickling crisis within seven days

- *Respiratory problems*

Pneumothorax (collapsed lung) not fully inflated; major chest surgery within two weeks; unresolved pneumonia; marked shortness of breath at rest

- *Stomach and bowel problems*

Bleeding from the gastro-intestinal tract within ten days

- *Neurological problems*

Uncomplicated stroke within ten days; grand mal fit within 24 hours; brain surgery within ten days

- *Ear, nose and throat problems*

Acute sinus or ear infection; middle ear surgery within ten days; removal of tonsils within one week

- *Eye problems*

Eye surgery or penetrating eye wound within seven days

- *Mental health problems*

Any acute problem unless escorted by competent trained escort and special permission granted

- *Pregnancy and childbirth*

After 36 weeks if no complications; after 30 weeks if multiple pregnancy or any serious complication of pregnancy or history of premature delivery; babies should be 48 hours old, ideally seven days

- *Infectious illness*

Any major infection in the infectious stage including TB, unless confirmed sputum negative

- *Decompression illness*

Any cases with symptoms within ten days; any scuba diving activity within 24 hours

- *Fractures*

Within 24 or 48 hours depending on site of fracture and type of plaster

Have children, will travel

Check with the airline what arrangements they have for children. You can probably pre-book a sky-cot near a bulkhead for children up to 12 or even 18 months. Most airlines let children under the age of two years or 18 months fly free, but if you want them to have a seat in which to use your own safety carrier or capsule you will usually have to pay, unless the flight is fairly empty.

Many children feel sick going to the airport, so give your preferred antisickness pill (see page 28) at the correct time before leaving. Planes are exciting to start with, but especially for younger children can become frustrating after a time. Take with you a supply of small, appropriate toys, books, puzzles and treats, which can be produced at magic intervals to treat, bribe, or prevent boredom.

Children get very thirsty on planes – make sure they get plenty to drink as unrecognized thirst can make them bad-tempered. You can be sensitive to the needs of others on the plane without hedging your own children in with too many prohibitions.

Medical supplies in transit

Remember that anything placed in the aircraft hold is liable to freeze deeply. This means that any immunizations and insulin should be taken in your hand luggage, preferably in a vacuum flask containing a sealed ice pack. Tubes of ointment can ooze owing to pressure effects, so screw up all containers tightly. Put ball-point pens in plastic bags.

In-flight emergencies

Although we read stories of in-flight heart attacks and cabin staff delivering babies, such events are rare. As far as you are concerned they are rarer still if you avoid travelling against doctor's advice or if you come in or near the categories shown on page 32.

Some air companies are tightening up on in-flight health equipment and back-up. Specialist advice is available in the best carriers via electronic link-up to medical experts on the ground. However, it is always pot-luck whether any doctor is on board, let alone any who are expert at dealing with in-flight emergencies.

Fear of flying

Although this is very common, it may become so severe that it overshadows your trip or makes you want to cancel the flight.

If the fear is specific to a particular route or particular airline, then make arrangements that avoid these as far as possible. Sometimes discussing your fears with a friend or member of the family can help you to see it in perspective. For elderly travellers or those unfamiliar with flying it helps to arrive at the airport in plenty of time, so avoiding last-minute panic and hassle; or even do a trial run from home to check-in.

It is worth remembering that a crash or hijack is extremely rare and that even if there were three times more air accidents than at present, flying would still be considered safe. If it's any comfort you are more likely to be killed in a car crash going to the airport than be involved in a plane crash; the airflight is likely to be the safest part of your whole overseas trip.

If the problem still seems to be getting on top of you then British Airways puts on a special seminar and flight from either Heathrow or Manchester. For details of this service, for which there is a charge of between £150 and £200, phone 0161–832 7972. You do not need to be booked on a BA flight.

SECTION 2
WHILE ABROAD

PRECAUTIONS WITH FOOD

First the bad news: only a lucky few who visit or live in a developing country avoid getting stomach upsets or diarrhoea. Not surprisingly, fact and myth are often hopelessly mixed together on the vital topic of how to avoid Delhi Belly or Pharaoh's Revenge.

Now the good news: most bouts of diarrhoea clear up on their own after a few days.

In trying to avoid the runs it is helpful to steer a *middle path* between two extremes, typified on the one hand by the seasoned globetrotter with an apparently cast-iron stomach seizing any opportunity to savour the most exotic and ethnic fare; and on the other hand by the obsessional doomster who produces plastic mugs, disposable cutlery and paper napkins at the first sniff of indigenous food.

Of course by carefully preparing your own food at home you can eat virtually whatever you wish – and usually survive. Dangers mainly arise when eating out. Remember: restaurants are only as safe as the cleanliness of their kitchens and personal hygiene of their food handlers; in this respect budget travellers and five-star diplomats are more equal than they appear. One useful tip: check out with local expatriates which restaurants to visit and which to avoid. They will often have learnt by bitter experience.

Foods – safe and unsafe

You probably won't come to grief if you stick with the following rules:

- **Okay:** *Food, recently cooked and served still hot.* Any food that has just been fried or cooked at or above the normal boiling point of water for fifteen minutes or more is perfectly safe. Fortunately, much food comes into this category.

- **Okay:** *Fruit, either sterilized (see page 37) or carefully peeled (see below).*
- **Okay:** *Food (and drink) from sealed packs or cans.*
- **Avoid:** *Shellfish, lobsters, crabs or prawns.* In coastal areas known to be contaminated or where cholera is present these should be avoided altogether. Otherwise they can be eaten *if you are sure* they have been boiled for at least ten minutes (not easy to ascertain). *Avoid raw fish and remember that sushi always carries a health warning.*
- **Avoid:** *Salads* unless carefully home-prepared.
- **Avoid:** *Uncooked vegetables or fruit* unless known to have been treated (see below).
- **Avoid:** *Ice, ice cream, milk, cheese and yoghurt* unless from a safe, preferably pasteurized source.
- **Avoid:** *Food once hot but served cold*, or on which flies may have settled.
- **Avoid:** *Food that has been reheated*, unless it is known to have been thoroughly recooked. This is especially important for rice.
- **Avoid:** *Eggs, unless cooked until the yolk goes solid.*
- **Avoid:** *Meat if any part of it remains pink.* Pork and beef may give you tapeworm, and chicken, Salmonella.
- **Avoid:** *Fancy, cold foods* that have involved much handling in their preparation.
- **Avoid:** *Table sauces*, as they are often diluted with unsafe water.

In summary: 'Cook it, peel it, clean it or leave it'.

Preparing food at home

Vegetables should be *cleaned* of gross dirt, *peeled* where appropriate and then either *cooked* thoroughly, or *sterilized* (see page 37).

Consider *planting* your own vegetable garden, where you can grow leafy vegetables such as lettuce and spinach.

Fruit should be *cleaned* of gross dirt, then *sterilized*, then *peeled*. Peeling an unwashed piece of fruit is an excellent way of transferring germs progressively inwards. Mango-eaters will understand this. Bananas are of course an exception.

Milk should be *boiled* for five minutes, then *cooled* immediately and kept *covered* and cool. A glass disc (or something equivalent that does the job) placed in the milk prevents it from boiling over and is worth buying before you go abroad or improvising while there.

Sterilization. You can sterilize fruit and vegetables by adding tincture of iodine or water sterilization tablets at three times the dose normally used for decontaminating water (see page 42). Then *soak* for at least twenty minutes, drain, or even better rinse over with boiled water to remove the iodine and the taste of chlorine (you can buy special neutralizing tablets that help mask the taste). Potassium permanganate is ineffective.

Washing hands. Before eating or preparing food *wash your hands* thoroughly with soap. If you are interrupted, have to change nappies, go to the toilet or touch any domestic animal or pet, wash your hands again. Young children's hands should be washed before meals and their nails *kept clean and short*.

Separating cooked from raw food. Don't allow fresh or cooked food to come into contact with raw or contaminated food. This commonly occurs on surfaces, chopping boards and with knives. Beware of raw meat juice dripping in the fridge onto the shelf below. Keep all kitchen surfaces meticulously clean. Never use the same cloth on the floor and on clean surfaces.

Storing cooked food. Leftover food should either be stored near or below 10 °C or kept hot – near or above 60 °C. This is essential if you store food for more than four or five hours. Food for infants is better not stored at all. One word of warning: only place warm food in the refrigerator in small quantities – the centre may not cool and bacteria may explode in numbers.

Reheating food. All parts of the food must reach at least 70 °C, in other words, be thoroughly recooked to kill any organism that may have multiplied during storage.

Failed fridges. If the power supply fails disconnect the power supply, keep the door closed, cover the fridge with a soaked blanket and keep the blanket moist. Throw away any food that has returned to room temperature.

Food storage. Protect your food from flies by netting or covers. A netted cupboard also protects from rodents. To keep ants away, the legs of such cupboards can be placed in cups containing oil or salty water (the salt stops mosquitoes breeding).

Drainage. Plates and cutlery should be *drained* in racks after washing, and if possible be protected from flies.

Cooks, houseboys and ayahs. Anyone you employ for cooking at home, in an institution or on an expedition should have *regular* (*e.g. six-monthly*) *stool tests* as cooks are commonly carriers of Amoeba, Giardia or even typhoid. They should be encouraged to follow the same handwashing habits as you insist on for other family members. *Anyone with diarrhoea or a stomach upset should not be on cooking duty.*

Local hospitality – beware

At home, and to a large extent when eating in restaurants, you have control over what you eat. This is certainly not the case when invited to a meal by friends, the tribal chief, an important political leader or the local bishop. Unless you think fast you may have downed a whole range of suspect food (and drink) before you know it. As a guest your twin aim is to avoid offending both your host and your own digestion. Seasoned travellers can add their own suggestions to the advice given below:

- *Identify safe foods* and concentrate on those.
- *Identify and avoid foods* you consider suspect (including those you can't identify).
- *If in serious trouble*, play with and pretend to eat your food without actually doing so, or eat the smallest amounts possible.
- Explain *you are fasting* for religious or other reasons. Many cultures will readily understand this.
- Play the eccentric who is quaintly apologetic for his strange food habits and weak digestion.
- Consider *saying 'grace'* before meals. It was originally intended for gratitude – and protection.
- *If really in a corner* play the health card. Apologize that although you have always longed to eat raw camel's tail, your doctor has absolutely forbidden it.

A balanced diet

It is nearly always possible to eat a balanced diet overseas, meaning you will not need to take extra vitamins.

There are a few exceptions to this: long-term travellers or volunteers who run low on money and skimp on proper food; those with chronic bowel problems or tropical sprue, especially in South Asia, who will need antibiotics and folic acid (see page 39); pregnant women and those considering pregnancy who will need extra folic acid – 5 mg daily if taking the anti-malarial proguanil (Paludrine), and a lower daily dose otherwise.

The *golden rule of nutrition* is to maintain adequate balanced intakes of the three main nutritional groups:

- *Carbohydrates* or energy foods (the staple food crops mentioned below).
- *Protein* or body-building foods from two or more sources such as meat, fish, eggs, lentils and grains. If you are going to be involved in any strenuous pursuits, especially mountaineering, eat plenty of protein, preferably meat.
- *Vitamins* – protective foods – especially vitamin A (green, leafy vegetables and yellow vegetables and fruit), B (whole grains and meat), and C (citrus fruit and other fresh fruit and vegetables). Vitamin D is largely made in the skin, when exposed to sunlight. Folic acid is present in fresh vegetables and liver, and is important for women who are either pregnant or planning pregnancy.

In addition *minerals*, especially iron, are also needed. Iron-rich foods include green leafy vegetables, eggs, fish and meat including liver. Calcium is especially needed by children, pregnant women and breastfeeding mothers. It is found mainly in milk and dairy products.

Each part of the world has a staple crop – either rice, wheat, maize, millet/sorghum or roots and tubers, e.g. cassava, potatoes, sweet potatoes and yams.

As well as eating enough of these staples each day, which will be your main supply of energy (calories), you will need to add a protein source and locally available foods containing the three main vitamins. Only in exceptional circumstances will you need to take vitamin tablets if you eat correctly.

A reasonable rule of thumb is that a plateful of food containing three or more distinct colours (e.g. white/yellow for the staple food, green for vegetables containing vitamins A and C, and brown for meat containing protein, vitamin B and iron) is likely to be well balanced. Make sure, however, that vegetables are well (but not over-) cooked and not eaten in the form of hastily prepared salads.

Vegetarians

It is possible, but in practice not always easy to be healthily vegetarian overseas. You must, however, ensure you are eating sufficient protein from several different sources. In practice vegetarians tend to lose weight more easily, especially in the Indian subcontinent or after repeated stomach upsets. In these situations they are more likely to become anaemic and deficient in folic acid, and should consider taking iron and folate supplements.

A sensible aim for all travellers is to maintain normal, i.e. correct body weight overseas. If overweight before departure try for an appropriate reduction before leaving and during the first few months abroad. In many developing-world cultures a *minor* degree of obesity is a sign that you are a person of substance or success, and small reserves may be useful if you fall sick or find yourself in an appetite-depleting zone such as West Africa or monsoon Asia.

SAFE DRINKING

Although drinking mineral water in the UK may be more a cult than a necessity, obtaining sufficient clean water in the tropics is a major health issue. In the heat and humidity we need a huge supply of fluids, and a safe supply has to be set up.

Contaminated water causes many diseases. These include hepatitis, diarrhoeas and dysentery, typhoid, cholera, and giardiasis. All these are caused by taking in organisms through the mouth, from sources contaminated by faeces. Some diseases, in particular bilharzia (schistosomiasis), are spread through the skin and are caught by swimming, splashing or washing in contaminated water.

Ways of making water safe

Step 1: Identify a source

Find the nearest, cleanest source, such as a spring, a deep well or a rainwater tank (except where roofs are painted with lead or made of thatch). If using tapped water identify where it comes from and make sure pipes and joints are sound. Hot tap water left to cool is a useful source in a hotel. Treat claims that all drinking water is boiled with extreme caution. Beware of shallow tube wells, which are often contaminated. An ideal water supply is cool, clear and odourless.

Step 2: If cloudy, let it stand

Then decant it, or filter it through a cloth, fine gauze or Millbank Bag.

Step 3: Sterilize it

There are three possible ways of ridding water of germs:

1   *Boiling*
This is the most reliable method and kills all organisms including viruses and amoebic cysts. Unless your water is known to be from a safe source *or* there is a serious lack of fuel, boiling is the method of choice.

Experts disagree about the exact length of time needed. A good rule of thumb is to boil (a rolling boil) for five minutes plus one minute extra for every 1,000 metres (3,000 feet) you are above sea level. Boiling for ten minutes kills all known organisms, but also wastes fuel. There is never any need to boil longer than this.

After boiling let the water cool and stand for a few hours to improve the taste, or shake it in a sterilized non-plastic container to mix it with air.

When making hot drinks at home such as tea and coffee, remember to let the water boil for five minutes. This means avoiding electric kettles that switch themselves off on boiling.

Use boiled water for cleaning your teeth, keeping a separate supply in the bathroom. In an emergency just use toothpaste and saliva.

2   Filtering
Water is filtered for one of two reasons:

- To remove suspended material prior to boiling (see step 2 above).
- As a convenient alternative to boiling, and when there is a shortage of fuel or time.

Water should *not* be filtered after it has been boiled, despite some fondly-held traditions. It risks recontamination, and is the equivalent of 'washing whiter with Persil' and then finishing the job off with ordinary soap.

The best filters, used correctly and cleaned regularly, are almost as reliable as boiling, though some viruses may not be excluded.

Water passes through a filter either by gravity or through an attached pump or direct from a tap through a special attachment.

There are two recommended materials used for filtration:

- *Ceramic* filters, using porcelain 'candles'. The pore size should be as small as possible, ideally 0.5µ, and the filter impregnated with silver, which kills most micro-organisms. Katadyne is a well-known brand. Ceramic filters are suitable for home use.
- *Iodine resin* filters. Contact with iodine kills micro-organisms and releases a low level of iodine for continuing disinfection. These are ideal when on the road but should not be used long term (see page 43 for suggested models).

All filters need to be carefully maintained according to the manufacturer's instructions. Ceramic candles should be regularly cleaned, handled with care and checked for any breaks or cracks, which will render them useless. They should be boiled once a week or according to instructions unless impregnated with silver.

3 *Disinfecting*

This is slightly less reliable than boiling and the best filtering.

Chlorine-based disinfectants can be used. These kill most organisms but not amoebic cysts and some rarer organisms. Puritabs and Steritabs are well-known brands. Household bleach can also be used: add two drops of a 5–6% solution of available chlorine to one litre, or add eight drops of a 1% solution. (One drop is about 0.05 ml.) The water should smell and taste faintly of chlorine.

Iodine is rather more effective, killing most organisms and having some action on amoebic cysts. Buy Potable Aqua tablets and dissolve one in a litre of water, or as per manufacturer's instructions. An alternative is to add five drops of 2% tincture of iodine (2% is the normal concentration) to one litre of water (neutralizing tablets will help remove the unpleasant taste). Current advice is not to use iodine for longer than six weeks, and to use it only occasionally when pregnant, in those under six years of age, or if suffering from thyroid problems. If you do use iodine sterilization, including iodine-resin filters regularly for more than three months, have a thyroid blood test arranged at your next medical check.

You can double all the above doses of chlorine or iodine in the short term if the water is cloudy.

After adding the tablets or solution to the water, allow to stand for twenty to thirty minutes at normal room temperatures, or for one to two hours if very cold.

Step 4: Storing water

Boiled water should ideally be stored in the container in which it was boiled. Alternatively it can be poured into a previously sterilized narrow-necked earthenware jar and placed on a clean, dry surface. The jar will need careful and regular cleaning and should be kept covered. No one should be allowed to dip into it.

Many expatriates keep two large kettles, using each in turn first to boil, then to store. In this way there is a constant supply of cool, boiled water.

Water is best removed from its storage container through a tap or spout. Dippers are unsafe as they frequently get left on the floor and contaminate the whole supply. A good rule is 'Tap or tip, don't dip'.

Safe fluids – on the road

When on the road or in difficult conditions, boiling or filtering is not always possible. Many cases of diarrhoea are caused by thirsty travellers drinking what's offered and hoping for the best.

Here are some suggestions:

- Keep to *hot* drinks. Tea and coffee are usually safe, the milk usually being added to the brew and boiled up together. Try to avoid any cup that is obviously cracked or has just been swilled out with dirty water. In some countries, it is cultural to swill out cups and rice bowls with boiling tea and pour them out.
- Keep to *carbonated* soft drinks from bottles with metal tops from reputable firms. Such drinks are usually clean and their slight acidity kills some organisms. Avoid bottles with loose or suspect tops, and soda or mineral water bottles whose contents may have been replenished from a tap.

   Bottles of mineral water are now available in many countries. Although some of them are undoubtedly clean and genuine, others definitely are not. It takes an experienced eye to tell them apart. *Only use those with unbroken seals*, and preferably bottles where both main label and bottle-top have identical names. If in doubt ask an experienced expatriate about brands known to be reliable – or unreliable.

   Make sure all soft-drink bottles are opened in your presence. If drinking straight from the bottle, clean the rim with care as it may have been resting in contaminated water to keep cool.
- Carry a *vacuum* flask or other container with a clean drink of your choice. ✻
- Always have some *water sterilizing tablets* with you. They should be dry and reasonably fresh (yellowing tablets are losing their potency). ✻
- If using a *plastic water bottle* for travelling or trekking, allow boiled water to cool first before pouring it into the bottle, otherwise the taste will be nauseating.
- Carry a small, portable *water filter* such as a Travel Well, Personal Water Purifier, or the cheaper and lighter Pentapure Travel Cup. ✻ Check the specifications from one of the suppliers in Appendix C to make sure it exactly fits your needs. Because they contain iodine you should follow the same precautions on restricted use mentioned under iodine tablets above.
- *Avoid ice.* Freezing does not kill organisms and ice often comes from an impure source.
- *Avoid milk* unless just boiled.
- *Avoid* excessive *alcohol.* It disinhibits, dehydrates and does not sterilize, making it a low entry on the tropical drinks hit parade.

Swimming

Avoid swimming in contaminated *lakes*, *seas*, *rivers* or *ponds*. Not only are you likely to take in disease-carrying organisms, but you can catch skin infections. In many areas of Africa, east Asia and parts of South

America, bilharzia is a risk (see pages 154–7). Crocodiles and sharks are not reported to have lost their appetites.

Avoid swimming on *beaches* near to cities if there is a known cholera outbreak, or where the sea is obviously polluted.

Swimming pools that smell of chlorine are generally considered safe.

When babies and very young children swim or have a bath they often take in water. Make the bath as hot as possible then let it cool to the right temperature for bathing.

HYGIENE AT HOME

You can prevent most illnesses in the tropics by setting up an appropriate lifestyle, avoiding malaria and taking care with food and water.

Clean personal and domestic habits also have an important part to play.

In hot countries it is essential to *wash* frequently, not only because of the heat and dust but also because of the great number of germs that find your body surface a cosy environment. When the weather is hot, try to wash twice daily, at least once with soap, preferably using a shower. This will help prevent boils and skin infections. Water supply allowing, leave the shower to run briefly before getting under it, as this reduces the risk of getting legionnaires' disease from contaminated water tanks. Also try to avoid getting the water into your mouth. To reduce the likelihood of getting worms, keep your fingernails clean and short and wear shoes when outside the house – this helps avoid hookworm.

You should change your *clothes* regularly and keep them well laundered. This especially goes for underwear and socks.

Ideally you should dry clothes on a line, not on the ground, even though this may be commonly done by the local people. In areas where the Tumbu-fly is found (see page 114), you should either dry all clothes in the house or, better still, hot-iron any clothes that may come into contact with the skin, including underwear and non-disposable nappies.

It is worth being very careful with *domestic* hygiene. Scraps of food left around quickly decompose or attract insects and animals. Take care that the house is swept regularly and the *kitchen* is kept really clean. Make sure that any rag used for the floor is both separate and obviously different from any cloth used for wiping tables (and explain this carefully to anyone who works for you).

Toilets, whatever their type, easily attract flies and you will need to have them regularly cleaned, especially where children are using them. If you are building a latrine it should be twenty metres or more from any water source or river, and on a lower level. It should have a tight-fitting lid and ideally be based on a 'VIP' pit-latrine, or water-seal model.

Keep the *surrounds* of the house or camp clean, free from standing water (to reduce risk of malaria and dengue fever) and free from thick or high vegetation (to reduce the risk of snakes entering). Make sure you have a good *drainage system* for household water, keeping soakaways clean and de-slimed. Any *rainwater tank* needs to be well maintained, have a tight-fitting lid to prevent mosquitoes from breeding, and be allowed to wash through at the start of the rainy season. Keep your *windows*, doors and screening in a good state of repair to reduce the number of insects (especially mosquitoes) entering the house.

House temperature can be kept lower by making sure all outer walls are pale or white, and that you use a non-heat-absorbing roofing material. If this is not possible paint the roof white. Other measures that will keep the house cool are over-hanging eaves, and insulating the roof by placing a layer of bamboo, grasses or thatch on top. Tall rooms with openings near the top and with large lower windows set opposite each other help air-flow.

You can keep *flies* to the minimum by good household hygiene, screening, swatting and the use of insecticides and fly-traps. Pyrethroid insecticides are effective against *cockroaches*. *Ants* should be killed with an appropriate antkiller before they get established, otherwise it will be ants and marmalade for breakfast. Food should always be carefully stored, covered or screened so that no insect or animal can touch it.

Household rubbish needs to be appropriately disposed of. In rural areas you can separate it into material suitable for burning, composting and burial. Any rubbish dump, either household or communal, needs to be deep, a good distance from the house and kept covered with earth so that animals and children don't scatter the contents. Rubbish awaiting disposal should be stored in a strong container, kept raised off the ground and have its lid secured for protection against raiding animals.

Household pets can easily introduce diseases into the house. Take special care with dogs, which will need to be restricted in where they roam, be kept clean, be carefully housetrained and have deworming medicine every six months. From the age of three months dogs and cats should be kept up-to-date with their rabies injections. Three-yearly boosters of a live attenuated vaccine are normally used, which if not available where you live can be brought out from the UK. Dogs should

not be 'kissed', and after petting them or playing with them you should wash your hands (and those of your children).

Finally if you employ a *house servant* who is not used to working with expatriates explain basic rules of hygiene. This, along with a medical check and regular stool test, will help to keep the whole household more healthy. Encourage anyone you employ who has a persistent cough to have a sputum test or chest X-ray to exclude TB, especially if they work with you, regularly visit your house or have regular contact with your children.

DEALING WITH DIARRHOEA

'Travel broadens the mind but loosens the bowel'

For most travellers in developing countries diarrhoea is not a matter of If but When. This section, which is therefore quite detailed, aims to help you deal with the almost inevitable, and to recognize and treat the more serious. It covers the following:

- Who is most at risk?
- What are the main types of diarrhoea?
- Action plan for acute diarrhoea (up to seven days)
- Action plan for persistent diarrhoea (over seven days)
- Amoebic infection
- Giardiasis

- Antibiotics to prevent traveller's diarrhoea
- Diarrhoea in the local population
- Cholera
- Typhoid fever

Prevention of diarrhoea through water and food hygiene is dealt with separately (see pages 35–8).

Who is most at risk?

This depends on the area you are travelling to, your lifestyle and precautions, resistance and good luck.

Area being visited

We can broadly divide the world into three bowel zones:

- High risk: South and South-East Asia (including China), Africa and South America.
- Medium risk: Russia and the former Soviet states, the Caribbean, Southern and Eastern Europe, the Near and Middle East, Japan and the Pacific islands.
- Low-risk: North America, Australia, New Zealand and Western Europe.

Within these countries you are generally more likely to get diarrhoea in hot and humid conditions and during the rainy season or monsoon.

Lifestyle and precautions

The more careful you are, the less likely you are to get diarrhoea. But the kitchens of five-star hotels may be no healthier than street vendors, especially if you buy something sizzling hot from the side of the road. Many downtown or seaside restaurants must be treated with care. The key to bowel-calm lies more in the precautions you take than the lifestyle you lead.

Resistance

Some of us have more than others. We all know of those who seem to have cast-iron stomachs and others who fall to the first meal out in terra exotica. Medical sleuths in Nepal have recently discovered that expatriates living there for two years or more develop substantial resistance. Foreign travel within the previous six months may also give some short-lived protection. If you have a pre-existing condition, such as Crohn's disease or colitis, diarrhoea can hit you harder. Irritable bowel syndrome can make your gripes worse. The use of some antacids may lower resistance. The very young and very old are at greater risk.

What are the main types of diarrhoea?

Although more than one hundred organisms are known to cause diarrhoea, experienced travellers find it helpful to divide the runs into one of three main types:

1 *Acute watery diarrhoea* lasting a few days, with little or no fever, is the commonest form. Four out of five cases are caused by either E. coli, Campylobacter, Shigella or Salmonella. Viruses, especially Rotavirus, account for most of the remainder, especially in children. Malaria can sometimes cause diarrhoea (see figure on page 53).

Cholera, rare in expatriates, can cause extremely severe, almost continuous watery diarrhoea (see below).

2 *Acute diarrhoea with blood* (usually known as *dysentery*). There are two common types:

- In *bacillary* dysentery (caused by Shigella) there is profuse bloody diarrhoea, usually with mucus (often twelve or more stools in twenty-four hours), with severe straining, griping and a feeling of doom. Fever is present.
- With acute *amoebic* dysentery the symptoms are usually less severe, with little or no fever and rarely more than six to twelve stools in twenty-four hours.

Other organisms can cause blood in the stools, including Campylobacter (similar though usually less severe than bacillary dysentery), typhoid (see below), rare forms of E. coli and schistosomiasis (see page 154).

3 *Chronic diarrhoea* (lasting seven days or more). Any of the above can persist. However, chronic diarrhoea is often caused by amoeba or Giardia, as well as more exotic germs such as Cryptosporidium, Cyclospora and Blastocystis. In many cases no cause is found (see below and figure on page 53).

48

Action plan for acute diarrhoea

Here are five broad categories. Treat according to which most obviously applies to you.

1   Mild symptoms
You have symptoms that do not interfere with normal activities; you feel generally well. Treatment: keep up fluid intake and eat a light diet if you feel like it. (Children should still be fed.)

2   Moderate symptoms
Your symptoms threaten normal activities or travel; you feel reasonably well, and have no fever or dysentery.

Treatment: as in 1 above plus the following:

- loperamide 2 mg tablets (Imodium) two together then one every four hours until symptoms improve;
- ciprofloxacin 250 mg tablets two together as a single dose (ciprofloxacin is most useful for short trips and should be used more sparingly for attacks of diarrhoea when you are resident overseas).

3   More severe symptoms
You are unable to carry out normal activities, feel unwell, may have a fever but have no dysentery.

Treatment: as 2 above except continue ciprofloxacin 250 mg tablets two daily for three days.

4   Dysentery
You have blood in your stool and/or fever and feel unwell, possibly seriously so. Treatment: as 3 above, making absolutely sure you keep up fluids. Try to see a doctor and get a stool test. The stool must be fresh, preferably still warm, and examined without delay in a good quality lab or doctor's clinic.

5   Treating according to stool test
Ciprofloxacin 500 mg daily for three days will usually be an effective treatment for Shigella, Salmonella and E. coli. The best treatment for Campylobacter is erythromycin 250–500 mg every six hours for five to seven days.

Please note that ciprofloxacin must be used with plenty of fluids, and is not suitable for those under 16 years of age, in pregnancy or breastfeeding. It can occasionally affect driving ability and may cause slight temporary confusion in the elderly. For these and other side effects of antibiotics, see Appendix A and consult the Patient Information Leaflet with your supply.

Treatment for children

Keeping up fluids is by far the most important treatment (see below). Drugs are less important and should not normally be used as a home remedy in children under four.

For children four and over with more severe symptoms you can use the following:

- loperamide (Imodium) as a blocking agent in doses four times a day for a twenty-four hour period as follows: age 4–8, 1 mg; age 9–12, 2 mg. Loperamide comes both as tablets and as a liquid suspension.
- antibiotics as follows: either cotrimoxazole or erythromycin or furazolidone (not available in UK) as per doctor's or manufacturer's dosages.

  Treatment with these antibiotics in most parts of the world will be rather less effective than the ciprofloxacin used for adults. This is because of widespread drug resistance to those antibiotics that are safe in children.

Treatment for pregnant women

Pregnant women should generally use rehydration only and avoid drugs unless seriously ill. Of the drugs mentioned above, only erythromycin is safe.

Keeping up fluids in diarrhoea

You can use any appropriate non-alcoholic or non-milk based fluid, such as soft drinks (e.g. Sprite, 7-Up or Coke, shaken until flat), weak tea or light soup. A simple method is to buy packets of Oral Rehydration Salts (ORS) and mix them with water as per instructions. Common brands are Dioralyte, Rehydrat or other sachets recommended by the World Health Organisation (WHO).

It is also possible to make your own mixture. The methods and amounts recommended vary considerably. In a leaflet for travellers produced in June 1991 the WHO recommends mixing six level teaspoons of sugar with one level teaspoon of salt in one litre of safe, preferably boiled drinking water. Children under two are spooned one quarter to one half cup after each stool, those from two to ten sip half to one cup per stool, older children and adults as much as they require, usually at least one cup per stool. Breastfed children should continue to receive breastmilk.

If signs of dehydration occur, e.g. dry lips and tongue, inelastic skin, absent or highly concentrated urine, double the amount until these symptoms disappear. If vomiting also occurs sips should be taken more slowly, until the nausea improves.

Remember that after severe diarrhoea you can feel extremely weak and faint, especially on standing. As you take rehydration solution these symptoms will improve, sometimes dramatically. Continue to drink until your urine is no longer dark.

When to see a doctor

You should seek further help under the following situations:

- your symptoms do not largely subside within 48 hours;
- you are seriously ill;
- you have uncontrollable vomiting and/or marked abdominal pain;
- you (or your children) are severely dehydrated.

Don't forget that diarrhoea may mean you have malaria. If in doubt get a blood smear.

Action plan for persistent diarrhoea

Diarrhoea lasting seven days or more (see page 48) tends to cause much concern and discussion among travellers. Before treating it or imagining a giant amoeba eating away at your intestines, it is worth trying to identify the cause. The two ways are:

- A stool test. Take a fresh stool in a labelled, waterproof container to a reliable laboratory and await the result. If the first is negative arrange two further tests.

    Often germs will not be identified, and if they are, treatments you are given may not always be appropriate. Correct doses for germs showing up on stool tests in persistent diarrhoea include the following:

    – Amoeba and Giardia – see separate section below.
    – Blastocystis hominis: adults, metronidazole 400 mg tablets, two tablets three times daily for seven days; children's doses as for amoeba. Blastocystis does not always cause symptoms.
    – Cryptosporidium: no treatment reliably effective.
    – Cyclospora: adults, cotrimoxazole 480 mg tablets, two tablets twice daily for seven days. This is frequent in Nepal and other areas of the tropics, especially in the rainy season. Children's doses as for acute diarrhoea – see page 50.
    – Schistosomiasis (S. haemotobium): adults, praziquantel 600 mg tablets, two tablets twice daily for one or three days, see page 156. Dosages for children 40 mg/kg daily in two divided doses for one or three days.

- Strongyloides: adults, albendazole 400 mg daily for three days. Children two or over, same dose.
- Inspired guesswork. If a stool test is negative, impossible to arrange or thought to be unreliable you will need to try to match cause to symptoms according to the descriptions below:

Amoebiasis (chronic amoebic disentery)

This is common in most developing countries. *Symptoms* include mucus and sometimes blood in the stool, but these are often overlooked. Loose bowels may alternate with constipation; lower abdominal pain is common. There may be some weight loss. Chronic sufferers often become ill-tempered and introverted.

Occasionally amoebas travel upstream to the liver causing amoebic hepatitis or an abscess. Suspect this if you develop a fever (often, but not always high or 'swinging') or pain in the upper right part of the abdomen or under the right rib cage. This must be treated urgently.

Treatment of amoebiasis is as follows: tinidazole 500 mg (Fasigyn), four tablets together after food on three successive evenings, *or* metronidazole 400 mg (Flagyl), two tablets three times a day for five days. If you suspect liver involvement, see a doctor urgently and take metronidazole 400 mg, two tablets three times a day for ten days.

Dosages for children are as follows. Tinidazole: 50–60 mg/kg daily for three days. Metronidazole: one to three years of age, 200 mg every eight hours; three to seven years of age, 200 mg every six hours; seven to ten years of age, 400 mg every eight hours. All for five days. There are slight variations to this on some packet instructions, in which case follow product leaflet. Metronidazole is available in the UK as a syrup for children under the brand name Flagyl.

These drugs can make you feel ill, often causing headache, nausea and a conviction that the treatment is worse than the cure. Alcohol should be strictly avoided as it worsens the side effects. Avoid in pregnancy. These drugs can make breastmilk taste bitter, especially in high dosages, but are probably harmless to the baby.

After finishing your course of Fasigyn or Flagyl, you should ideally take diloxanide 500 mg (Furamide), one tablet three times a day for ten days (this kills the amoebic cysts). Children's dose is 20 mg/kg daily in three divided doses, for five days.

It is unwise to take *repeated* courses of amoeba treatment unless there is evidence on a fresh stool test of active motile forms (trophozoites), or you have very typical symptoms. Amoebic cysts on stool tests more often than not belong to a form of amoeba that does not cause symptoms. Only treat for amoeba if you do have typical symptoms, not just because cysts were found in the stool.

Amoebas are sometimes overlooked; they are often also unfairly blamed for a variety of afflictions. An obsession with amoeba is as common as an infection, and there comes a time when a self-imposed ban on 'The Amoebes', both in conversation and in letters home, is the most appropriate action.

Giardiasis

This is also common in many areas of the tropics, in Eastern Europe and the former Soviet states. *Symptoms* include offensive wind and diarrhoea, loss of appetite, nausea and heartburn. It sometimes leads to milk (lactose) intolerance (see Figure 2).

Treatment is as follows: *either* tinidazole 500 mg tablets (Fasigyn), four together after food, repeat same dose in two weeks, *or* metronidazole 400 mg tablets (Flagyl), five tablets together (2 gm) daily after food, for three days, or one tablet, three times daily for five days.

Avoid alcohol while on treatment, and again be warned of the side effects.

Giardiasis is common in young children. They may have few symptoms but still cause infection by passing cysts. Treatment in children is as follows. Tinidazole 50–75 mg/kg as single dose, and repeated after two weeks. Metronidazole: one to three years of age, 500

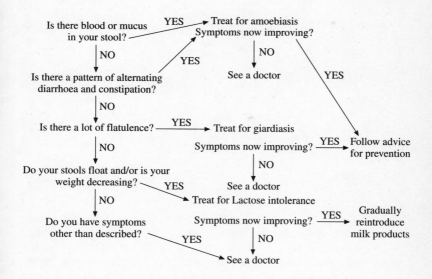

Figure 2 Flow chart for persistent or recurrent diarrhoea (seven days or longer)

mg daily; three to seven years, 600–800 mg daily; seven to ten years, one gram daily. All for three days.

Lactose intolerance

Giardiasis and some other bowel infections can lead on to *lactose (milk) intolerance*, which is one cause of persistent diarrhoea and flatulence. One way of telling whether you have this is to drink one to two pints of boiled milk and see if your symptoms of diarrhoea and flatulence obviously worsen over the following few hours. If they do, consider avoiding all dairy products for a period of three months, then gradually reintroduce them.

Malabsorption

Sometimes repeated bowel infections, including Giardia, Cryptosporidium or Cyclospora, cause the lining of the small intestine to be less efficient in absorbing food. This is known as *tropical malabsorption* or *tropical sprue*. Typical symptoms are floating frothy stools, loss of weight, thinning muscles and decreasing energy. The condition is especially seen in those living, or budget travelling, in South Asia. If you suspect you have it, you must see a doctor.

A variety of other germs can cause persistent diarrhoea, including some that first cause acute symptoms and then remain as unwelcome visitors. They cannot be identified by guesswork and most will eventually disappear on their own. If you have had repeated or persistent bouts of diarrhoea you should have a stool test on your return home, and see a doctor with experience in travel medicine as persisting bowel problems are quite a medical challenge. Many of these will eventually be diagnosed as irritable bowel syndrome (IBS), better thought of as post-infectious or post-tropical IBS if your symptoms only started after your travels. If you have these symptoms arrange for a special stool test for Blastocystis as this can mimic IBS.

Occasionally non-tropical bowel problems first start in the tropics or after returning home, meaning *you should always report any persisting symptoms*.

Antibiotics to prevent diarrhoea

These, though quite effective, are not generally recommended for routine use for the following seasons:

1 Their widespread use may lead to drug resistance.
2 They may cause side effects (occasionally including diarrhoea).
3 There are fewer medicines in reserve if you do need treatment.

4   Modern drugs usually cure diarrhoea if you do develop it.

There are, however, two situations in which it is worth considering preventive antibiotics:

1   Your trip is especially important and even a minor bout of diarrhoea might cause you to miss a crucial journey or cancel seeing the President.
2   Your health is indifferent, you have bowel problems that could be worsened by diarrhoea, you consider yourself to be frail or elderly.

In these cases the best drugs to prevent diarrhoea are either ciprofloxacin 500 mg daily, norfloxacin 400 mg daily, ofloxacin 300 mg daily, starting each twenty-four hours before leaving, continuing for forty-eight hours after returning, and restricting the total length of treatment to no longer than fourteen days.

Slightly less effective alternatives are trimethoprim 200 mg daily or doxycycline 100 mg daily, each of which can be taken for longer. None of these should be used in pregnancy.

Diarrhoea in the local population

If living in a developing country, it is likely that diarrhoea will be one of the commonest causes of severe illness and death among children where you live. You should become familiar with the nationally recommended or local method of making oral rehydration solution (see pages 50) so that you can use and demonstrate this when you are consulted by your neighbours. It is better not to hand out routine antibiotics.

Cholera

Extent: Cholera has become much more widespread in the 1990s and numbers are likely to remain high. There continue to be outbreaks in many countries of South and Central America, tropical Africa and Asia. A virulent strain, 0139 or Bengal cholera, is present in South Asia.

Cause: cholera is a disease of poverty and is most common in areas of social and economic deprivation or civil war. It is spread by faecal contamination of water supplies and food, in particular fish and shellfish, raw fruit and vegetables. The germ that causes it is known as Vibrio cholerae.

Risk and prevention: Cholera is very rare in travellers. You can prevent it by taking care with personal hygiene and by following strict rules on drinking water and food preparation (see pages 35–46). If travelling with a family or leading a group, make sure everyone knows and obeys basic rules of hygiene.

The standard cholera vaccine previously used is no longer recommended. If you hear that customs officials are asking for cholera certificates, obtain an official stamp from an immunization clinic on a certifcate stating that you are exempt for medical reasons. An effective live oral vaccine (Orochol, Mutacol) exists, giving protection for at least six months. It is not currently licensed in the UK.

Symptoms: Most cases of cholera cause nothing more than mild diarrhoea. However, typical life-threatening episodes have to be recognized and treated urgently as they can cause death from dehydration within just a few hours. They usually start suddenly, with massive painless watery diarrhoea, often resembling rice water. There is commonly vomiting. Dehydration occurs rapidly.

Treatment: This depends on immediate rehydration with oral rehydration solution or a suitable equivalent (see page 50). Vomiting is best treated by drinking: start with small amounts at a time and increase as rapidly as possible. Slow sipping often eases the nausea.

If you strongly suspect cholera take either ciprofloxacin 250 mg tablets, four together, or doxycycline 100 mg tablets, three together. If you are going to an area where cholera often occurs or there is a current outbreak, take these tablets with you. GPs will usually be willing to give you a prescription, probably a private one, if you explain why you want them.

Even in an epidemic area you are in fact very unlikely to get cholera if you take sensible precautions. You may, however, get other forms of diarrhoea that you should manage according to the guidelines given. The main treatment of all forms of acute diarrhoea, including cholera, is oral rehydration solution.

If your symptoms or those of your colleague suggest cholera you should follow this procedure:

• Start oral rehydration solution at once and continue until the diarrhoea has improved and a good output of urine is produced.

- Take medication as recommended above.
- See a doctor or reliable health worker as soon as possible.

Typhoid fever (Enteric fever)

Typhoid fever is not uncommon in travellers, especially long-termers and those travelling in Asia. It is probably overdiagnosed, especially in Africa. Quite often a blood test known as the Widal test is used to diagnose typhoid, but this is not very specific and may be raised anyway especially if you have had a typhoid immunization.

Symptoms: diarrhoea may occur with typhoid, especially after the first week, but constipation and cough are often present early. A typical attack of typhoid causes a severe and worsening illness, head and body ache, a temperature that rises higher each day, with the pulse staying relatively slow, often at about eighty beats per minute. After one or two weeks diarrhoea usually develops, often with blood, offensive breath and abdominal pain.

If you have been immunized against typhoid, you can still get the illness but symptoms may be less severe and harder to tell apart from other conditions. Typhoid may occasionally be the cause of persistent or intermittent diarrhoea, low-grade fever or worsening health.

The best treatment for those aged 16 and over is ciprofloxacin 500–750 mg twice daily for ten to fourteen days. An alternative is chloramphenicol 500 mg four times daily for two weeks, but this is not always effective, especially in Asia. These drugs are not appropriate in pregnancy, when you should use ampicillin 500 mg four times daily for 14 days. If you suspect typhoid see a doctor.

Even after typhoid is apparently cured it is still possible to be a carrier. Anyone preparing or cooking food who may have had typhoid should first have a negative stool test.

Please also see Appendix F, pages 217–18.

Constipation

For many travellers constipation is as much a problem as diarrhoea – often they seem to alternate with annoying frequency – sometimes through overdoing the Imodium or because of underlying amoebic infection.

Methods of coping with constipation are obvious, though not always effective. Drinking enough to keep the urine dilute, especially during travel, is the most important. Keep eating a high-fibre diet with plenty of vegetables and fruit (hygienically prepared). When travelling try not to suppress a bowel motion unless you really can't face the toilets, or there are none available as internal traffic jams will only make the problem worse. Finally, make sure you pack your favourite laxative to use either to treat the problem or help prevent it in the first place. Senokot is a good choice, see page 199, Appendix A.

DEFEATING MALARIA

When did you start your tricks, Monsieur? . . . But I know your game now, streaky sorcerer.

From 'The Mosquito' by D. H. Lawrence

Please read this section carefully before you go to a malarious area.

The World Health Organisation estimates that one person in 20 is infected with malaria at any one time, and that 350 million new cases occur each year. During 1998 there was an increase in the number of travellers returning to the UK with malaria.

In many developing countries malaria is the most important and most serious disease you are likely to face. It is therefore worth being extremely careful about *preventing* it, and being well informed about how to recognize and *treat* it. Ways of doing this are described below, and you will need to take various supplies with you. These must include both antimalarial tablets as well as other items to prevent you from being bitten. Make sure you are well informed, well prepared and well stocked before leaving home. (See also page 13.)

Where is malaria found?

At the present time malaria is found in over 100 countries and 2.4 billion people are at risk (see Figure 3). Malaria is thought to kill over one million children per year in Africa alone.

Within individual countries malaria may be common in some areas, absent in others. It is rarely found above about 2,000 metres (about 6,500 feet), though recently in parts of East Africa it has been climbing higher. Some cities within malarious areas may be virtually free, while nearby forested areas or irrigated fields may be badly affected. In some countries, e.g. parts of lowland tropical Africa, malaria is found throughout the year, while in other areas, e.g. some highland areas of Africa and in monsoon Asia, it tends to be more seasonal.

In many areas malaria is becoming both more common and more

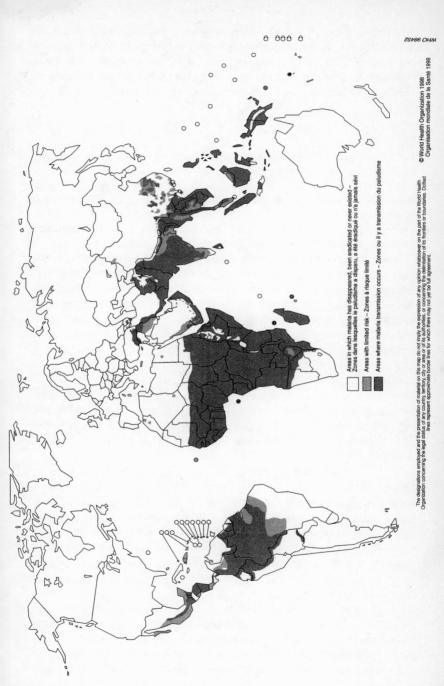

The designations employed and the presentation of material on this map do not imply the expression of any opinion whatsoever on the part of the World Health Organization concerning the legal status of any country, territory, city or area or of its authorities, or concerning the delimitation of its frontiers or boundaries. Dotted lines represent approximate border lines for which there may not yet be full agreement.

© World Health Organization 1998
Organisation mondiale de la Santé 1998

Areas in which malaria has disappeared, been eradicated or never existed –
Zones dans lesquelles le paludisme a disparu, a été éradiqué ou n'a jamais sévi

Areas with limited risk – Zones à risque limité

Areas where malaria transmission occurs – Zones ou il y a transmission du paludisme

Figure 3 Areas where malaria is found (WHO 1998)

WHO 98452

difficult to treat. There are several reasons for this. Mosquitoes are becoming resistant to insecticides, and Plasmodium, which causes malaria, is becoming resistant to drugs, especially chloroquine. Worsening economic conditions, war, the opening up of frontier regions and human migration also encourage the spread of malaria.

What are your risks as a traveller or expatriate?

Each year over 30,000 European and American travellers get malaria. Some become seriously ill; a few (usually unnecessarily) die. In the UK about 2,000 imported cases occur most years, the great majority from sub-Saharan Africa, South and South-East Asia and a few from Latin America and the Pacific Islands. Many more cases go undiagnosed or unrecognized. Countless cases of malaria occur among travellers and expatriates while overseas, many of them treated inadequately.

Your risk depends not only on which *country* you are visiting, but also on your *occupation* and *lifestyle*. Above all it depends on *how well you protect yourself. By taking a few simple precautions and following them rigorously, you are much less likely to get malaria. If you start treatment as soon as suspicious symptoms develop you are very unlikely to become seriously ill.*

What causes malaria?

Malaria is caused by a single-celled organism called Plasmodium. This is carried by the female Anopheles mosquito (see Figure 4), and is injected into the blood stream through a bite. After an incubation period of at least seven days, and sometimes very much longer, the disease develops.

There are two main forms of malaria. *Malignant* malaria caused by Plasmodium falciparum is the more serious and in many areas, including Africa, the commoner. *Benign* malaria caused by P. vivax, ovale or malariae tends to be more a nuisance than a danger, is rarely fatal, usually responds to chloroquine, but still needs to be diagnosed and treated promptly. It can only reliably be told from falciparum malaria by a blood smear.

What are the symptoms of malaria?

These are extremely variable. Although 'classic' symptoms are quite rare in travellers, these are the three phases. First a sudden onset (the *cold phase*), when shivering and shaking start suddenly and last up to one hour. This is followed by a *hot dry phase* lasting two to six hours,

Figure 4 **Anopheles mosquito (female 4–6 mm long)**

when the temperature may rise up to 40 °C (104 °F): there is headache, pains in the joints and often vomiting and diarrhoea. Finally comes the *hot wet phase* lasting two to four hours, when the patient sweats profusely and then feels better.

Left untreated these phases tend to recur every two days (tertian fever – P. falciparum, vivax or ovale) or much more rarely every three days (quartan fever – P. malariae).

However, most attacks of malaria do not follow these phases, especially if you are taking antimalarials. Malignant malaria in particular may cause a variety of symptoms, including continuous or more often irregular fever. Malaria in children under three months may not cause fever at all.

This means that malaria can mimic a whole range of illnesses. Experienced hands learn to recognize them. Mild fever, headache, a bout of vomiting and diarrhoea or simply feeling off-colour may indicate an attack. A severe cold, an operation and a time of stress or exhaustion may cause a relapse and bring out symptoms. The strain of bringing a family, or just yourself, back to the UK may trigger an attack. In fact travel itself often precipitates malaria, making holidays and the days and weeks following international flights high-risk periods.

Malignant malaria, if not treated early, can progress rapidly and cause serious illness within hours. Cerebral malaria (always caused by P. falciparum) affects the brain and may cause fits and fluctuating levels of consciousness before leading to coma and death. Danger signs, usually obvious, include drowsiness, confusion, absent urine, shortness of breath, jaundice and persistent fever. Repeated attacks of malaria may lead to exhaustion and contribute towards depression. The spleen may enlarge and anaemia can become severe.

How can you avoid malaria?

There are two main ways – *avoiding mosquito bites* and *taking prophylactics.*

Prevention tactic number one: avoiding bites

Here are some ways of reducing the risk:

 1 Sleep under a mosquito net (bed-net)

Use these in areas where malaria is known to occur, even if there don't seem to be many mosquitoes. Just a single bite is enough to cause infection, especially in parts of Africa because so many mosquitoes are carriers. Check there are no holes in the net.

They also keep out bed-bugs and creepy-crawlies – and the fear of them. Of course mosquito nets also help to protect against several other insect-borne diseases. There is such a variety of mosquito nets on the market that some basic understanding is necessary to help you choose the most appropriate one.

* Shapes
  - **Rectangular or box nets** are suspended at four corners and are the standard nets used in many homes, guest houses and hotels. They come in double, single and cot size.
  - **Bell nets** are suspended on a hoop above the bed and hang from a single hook in the ceiling. These nets are now commonly made in one size that can be used for cots, single or double beds. They are convenient and agreeable to use, both at home and when travelling.
  - **Pyramidal nets** hang from a single point and **wedge nets** from two points, making both easy to carry around and suspend when you are travelling and camping.
* Strength, mesh size and material
  Nets come in various strengths or Denier, the higher the stronger. 40 Denier would not be very robust, 70–100 would be tough and durable. Mesh size in the UK is still usually measured in number of holes per square inch. 150 would be large-holed giving plenty of air-flow, 250 would be small-holed giving less air-flow but an increased rate of protection, especially if the effect of permethrin is wearing off. None of these nets guarantee protection against sandflies.

Most nets are made with synthetic fibres and are more durable than cotton nets. Cotton nets, though widely available overseas, are harder to obtain in the UK. Being cooler they can have finer mesh size (which helps to keep out sandflies), and can still be soaked in permethrin.

Whichever net you choose, make sure it is presoaked in permethrin or deltamethrin, or a newer substance, lambdacyhalothrin (trade name, Icon). Permethrin is an insecticide that kills mosquitoes (and other biting insects). Nets soaked in it are far more effective than standard nets and can safely be left to hang loose (ideally right down to the floor), without being tucked in. They also act as mosquito killers, so reducing the number of flying insects in the house. Remember, however, to resoak them at least every six months and whenever they are washed. Instructions on how to do this come with the permethrin solution. Icon lasts for at least one year, but its use is otherwise similar.

Before you take up an overseas posting, find out if an appropriate net is provided or available locally and if not, take an impregnated one with you, along with sufficient permethrin for resoaking if you are going for more than six months.

2   Cover your skin

Mosquitoes commonly bite at sunset then continue late into the night – skilfully co-ordinating their day's work with your evening's pleasure and arriving as unwelcome intruders at the very time you want to relax outside. They also favour dawn, so affecting the early risers.

Mosquitoes will go for any part of the body, but tend to specialize in wrist and face, **ankles** and **feet** (catching you unawares under the table). Climate allowing, wear long cotton sleeves and long trousers if you go out in the evening, preferably of light-coloured material. Remember that a determined mosquito can bite through socks or two pairs of tights, which means that cover alone is not always enough. We have recently heard that mosquitoes from Southern Sudan have broken the jeans barrier.

3   Use an insect repellent

In order to be effective this must contain either the active ingredient DEET (diethyl-toluamide), dimethyl phthalate, or 'natural' lemon eucalyptus oil. Citronella-based products are probably less effective. Repellents can be applied in various ways: direct to skin, as a cream, gel, stick, roll-on or spray. They last up to about four hours and are reasonably effective, but may leave an unpleasant sticky feeling to the skin. Autan and Jungle formula are well-known brands containing DEET. Mosiguard Naturel is eucalyptus based.

You should certainly use a DEET concentration of 20% or more, and there is evidence suggesting that the higher the concentration of DEET the more effective it is. You would only need to use concentrations higher than 50% in severe conditions. Concentrations of 35% or thereabouts are commonly used.

For young children use concentrations of DEET of about 10%. Do not use at all in children under 12 months. Do not apply to the lips or eyelids. DEET tends to destroy plastic, nail varnish and synthetic fabrics. In the rare case of an allergic reaction, e.g. itching, swelling, blistering, stop using it immediately – and take an antihistamine. Ideally, test DEET on a small patch of skin first for a few hours before applying it more widely, to ensure you are not allergic to it.

Lemon eucalyptus oil hardly ever causes reactions and does not destroy fabrics.

4   Soak or spray your clothes

You have two choices:

- *Using concentrated (90–100%) DEET* you can soak cotton garments in a solution of 30 ml of DEET added to 250 ml of water.

  Ankle- and wrist-bands can also be pre-soaked in DEET. Clothes and bands should be kept in a sealed container when not being used as this increases their useful life to about 120 hours before needing a resoak. Bands are more useful on the ankles than the wrists as mosquitoes are attracted to feet.

  Use DEET-soaked clothing with caution in children, and do not use with babies.

You can also spray concentrated DEET (e.g. Expedition 100 insect repellent) both onto skin in adults and older children and onto cotton clothing or cotton/woollen socks. Follow instructions carefully.

- *Permethrin.* You can soak clothes in permethrin using the solution according to manufacturer's instructions. Permethrin does not harm synthetic materials. For technical reasons it is not licensed for use on clothing (as opposed to mosquito nets) in the UK, though it is in the USA and France.

Remember that DEET repels mosquitoes but does not necessarily kill them; permethrin kills but does not necessarily repel them.

Here are some suggestions for areas where there is a severe mosquito or insect nuisance:

- When outside in the evening wear appropriate clothing, thoroughly apply a DEET-based insect repellent and wear wrist-bands and ankle-bands or pre-soaked socks.
- Inside the house use permethrin-impregnated bed nets (and curtains).
- When walking outside in highly affected areas, including trekking in tick- and leech-infested country, use DEET insect repellent on the skin and permethrin-soaked clothing.

Those who are likely to be outside after sunset in malarious areas are strongly recommended to apply insect repellent thoroughly to all exposed areas of the skin.

5 Screen your room

In areas with many mosquitoes you can fix fine metal screening to your windows and doors, and make sure they are kept closed from about two hours before sunset to well after sunrise. Check for any holes or gaps in the screening. The netting should have six or seven threads per centimetre width. Where dengue is common (see page 159), keep your windows and doors closed throughout the day – especially for two hours after sunrise and two hours before sunset when the Aedes mosquito is on the warpath.

6 Use an aerosol or flit gun

These, also known as knock-down sprays, contain a pyrethroid insecticide and can be used in the house every evening. Spray sleeping areas, being careful to include dark corners, hidden areas behind cupboards, under beds and most important of all the bath or shower room. These sprays do not necessarily kill mosquitoes that arrive after you have finished spraying, i.e. they have little 'residual' effect.

7 Other night-time precautions

Mosquito coils can be burned. They are effective and their vapour is safe. Under a fan or in a breeze they may run out before dawn. They are available cheaply in many tropical countries, but beware of fake products.

Vaporizing mats. A tablet of pyrethroid insecticide is placed on a mains-operated heating plate. These are available in many countries but depend on a reliable night-time electricity supply, unless you buy a battery-operated model or improvise your own from a 12-volt battery. They are thought to be more effective than coils.

Sleeping under a ceiling fan or in an air-conditioned room keeps mosquitoes at bay – until the electricity goes off.

Limb against net. Clever mosquitoes may still find you. Buy a roomy net, and don't flail your limbs.

'Buzzers' have no effect on mosquitoes.

8 Deal with the source

Try to eliminate breeding sites near the house. These include thick vegetation, ponds, areas of stagnant water including animal hoofprints, rainwater tanks with poorly fitting lids, the axils of leaves, pots on the verandah and the tops of bamboo canes. Mosquitoes can fly at least a mile, but eliminating the breeding sites within the immediate area of the house reduces the number. This also helps prevent dengue fever.

Make sure that open water tanks are screened, using the same mesh size as for house screening.

Arrange for the government spraying team to visit your area. Consider stocking nearby ponds or paddyfields with larvicidal fish, e.g. guppy, or procuring polystyrene beads to put into wet pits and pit latrines.

Prevention tactic number two: taking antimalarial tablets

Malaria has reached high levels among travellers. This is partly because many travellers, especially those abroad longer term or on assignment, take no antimalarials at all, even in high-risk areas, and many more stop taking them after a few weeks.

Here are some *wrong and dangerous* reasons for not taking antimalarials:

- I/my friend took antimalarials and still got malaria (but did you miss a dose, or can't you remember?).

- If you take antimalarials, when you get an attack there's nothing left to treat it with (yes there is – at least three effective preparations).
- Everybody recommends a different tablet, so whom should I believe (your own adviser – *what* you take is probably less important than the fact *that* you take something).
- We're expats and have lived here x years and we know best (then why are expats one of the highest-risk groups?).
- I believe in garlic, vitamin B and yeast (there is no evidence that they work, just wishful thinking).

Here are some *good* reasons for taking them:

- They save lives – statistics prove it.
- Even if you get malaria it is less likely to kill you or be dangerous.
- Your health insurance may not cover you if you don't.
- If you don't, your compliant colleagues may swear behind your back as they rush you to the nearest hospital at midnight.

If you take the *correct* pills *without missing doses* you are much less likely to get malaria, and even if you do, research has shown that *it is likely to be less severe*, which will allow you longer time to receive proper treatment.

Gulliver, in his travels to Lilliput, was surprised to discover that civil war started over whether to open a boiled egg at the large end or the small end. Most expatriates soon find that the answers as to which is the best antimalarial is an equally divisive issue, the European, the Brit and the North American rarely agreeing. The advice in this book largely follows recommendations from the Malaria Reference Laboratory in London (1997), and the World Health Organisation (1998).

Whichever antimalarial you take, follow these rules:

Choose the recommended regime before you leave

Don't change or stop unless there is a compelling reason such as unacceptable side effects *or clear evidence that malaria is rare or unknown in your immediate area.* Advice from expatriates or nationals that pills are unnecessary, dangerous or useless should be treated with caution. So should pressure to change one type for another. An apparent absence of mosquitoes does not mean you cannot get malaria.

Don't forget your tablets

Try to take them at the same time each day (or week), and keep them in the same place as part of a regular routine. A bottle of pills on the dining-room table, above the housekey rack, under your pillow or with your toothbrush are favourite memory-jogging sites. Always keep a supply with you when you are travelling, plus a few extra for forgetful friends. *Do not forget antimalarials when on holiday.*

How to take your tablets

Take tablets with a drink after meals. In the case of proguanil, if two tablets together make you sick take one after one meal and the second after another meal on the same day. With chloroquine you can take one tablet one day and your second after three or four days if you cannot manage two on the same day. Doxycycline tablets must not be taken when lying down or immediately before lying down or the oesophagus can become sore.

When to start

Start antimalarials well before travelling. In the case of proguanil, chloroquine and Maloprim start one week before entering a malarious area. In the case of doxycycline start 24 hours before. In the case of mefloquine (Lariam) start three weeks before leaving. This is because about three out of four cases of side effects will occur within three weeks, giving you a chance to change to an alternative. Continue antimalarials for four weeks after you leave any malarious areas.

What to do if you vomit

If you vomit within two hours of taking your antimalarial, repeat it once (Maloprim and mefloquine are exceptions and should not normally be repeated). If you have severe diarrhoea at the time of taking proguanil (Paludrine), repeat it once.

Which antimalarials for which country?

Below are recommendations based on official information from the Malaria Reference Laboratory UK, 1997. Please read through the after-notes on special situations very carefully. Only countries where malaria is known to occur are included.

Country	Risk areas	Regimes	
		1st choice	*2nd choice*
Abu Dhabi	Very low risk	0	0
Afghanistan	Only below 2,000 m May–November	C+P	**
Algeria	Very low risk	0	0
Angola	Whole country	MEF	C+P
Argentina	NW corner only	CHL	PRO
Azerbaijan	S border areas only	CHL	PRO

DEFEATING MALARIA

Country	Risk areas	Regimes	
		1st choice	*2nd choice*
Bangladesh	All areas except Dhaka.	C+P	**
	Chittagong Hill Tracts worst affected	MEF	C+P
Belize	Rural (no risk Belize Dist.)	CHL	PRO
Benin	Whole country	MEF	C+P
Bhutan	S districts only	C+P	**
Bolivia	Rural areas below 2,500 m	C+P	MEF/MAL
	Amazon Basin area	MEF	C+P
Botswana	N half only November–June	C+P	MEF/MAL
Brazil*	Amazon Basin, Mato Grosso, Maranhao, 'Legal Amazon'.	MEF	C+P
	Elsewhere low risk	0	0
Brunei	Very low risk	0	0
Burkina Faso	Whole country	MEF	C+P
Burundi	Whole country	MEF	C+P
Cambodia*	Western Provinces high risk	DOX	**
	Elsewhere (low risk in Phnom Penh)	MEF	**
Cameroon	Whole country	MEF	C+P
Cape Verde	Low risk	0	0
Central African Republic	Whole country	MEF	C+P
Chad	Whole country	MEF	C+P
China*	Main tourist areas low risk	0	0
	present Hainan, Yunnan (Kunming free)	MEF	DOX
	Other remote areas variable risk	CHL	**
Colombia	Most areas below 800 m	MEF	C+P
Comoros	Whole country	MEF	C+P
Congo	Whole country	MEF	C+P
Congo (Democratic Republic, formerly Zaire)	Whole country	MEF	C+P
Costa Rica	Rural areas below 500 m	CHL	PRO
Djibouti	Whole country	MEF	C+P
Dominican Republic	Generally low risk	CHL	PRO
Ecuador	Below 1,500 m only	C+P	MEF/MAL
Egypt	Tourist areas very low risk	0	0
	El Fayoum June to October	CHL	PRO
El Salvador	Generally low risk	CHL	PRO
Equatorial Guinea	Whole country	MEF	C+P
Eritrea	Whole country	MEF	C+P
Ethiopia	Most of country. Addis central prob. safe	MEF	C+P
French Guiana	Whole country	MEF	C+P
Gabon	Whole country	MEF	C+P
Gambia	Whole country	MEF	C+P

Country	Risk areas	Regimes	
		1st choice	2nd choice
Ghana	Whole country	MEF	C+P
Guatemala	Below 1,500 m only	CHL	PRO
Guinea	Whole country	MEF	C+P
Guinea-Bissau	Whole country	MEF	C+P
Guyana	All interior regions. Georgetown low risk	MEF	C+P
Haiti	Medium risk	CHL	PRO
Honduras	Medium risk but variable	CHL	PRO
Hong Kong	Very low risk	0	0
India*	Whole country, except above 2,000m in north	C+P	**
Indonesia*	Bali and cities low risk	0	0
	Irian Jaya whole area	MEF	DOX
	Elsewhere variable	C+P	**
Iran	March–November only	C+P	**
Iraq	Rural north May–November	CHL	PRO
Ivory Coast	Whole country	MEF	C+P
Kenya	Whole country, central Nairobi prob. safe	MEF	C+P
Laos	Whole country (except Vientiane low risk)	MEF	**
Lesotho	Not normally present	0	0
Liberia	Whole country	MEF	C+P
Libya	Very low risk	0	0
Madagascar	Whole country	MEF	C+P
Malawi	Whole country	MEF	C+P
Malaysia*	Sabah	C+P	**
	Other deep-forested areas	C+P	**
	Other areas inc. cities low risk	0	0
Mali	Whole country	MEF	C+P
Mauritania	South all year, north July–October	C+P	MEF/MAL
Mauritius	Rural areas only	CHL	**
Mexico*	Most tourist areas	0	0
	Some rural areas	CHL	PRO
Morocco	Very low risk	0	0
Mozambique	Whole country	MEF	C+P
Myanmar (Burma)	Whole country	MEF	**
Namibia	Northern third November–June only	C+P	MEF/MAL
Nepal	Below 1,300 m. No risk in	C+P	**
	Kathmandu valley	C+P	**
Nicaragua	Medium risk but variable	CHL	PRO
Niger	Whole country	MEF	C+P
Nigeria	Whole country	MEF	C+P
Oman	Medium risk whole country	C+P	**
Pakistan*	Below 2,000 m	C+P	**

DEFEATING MALARIA

Country	Risk areas	Regimes	
		1st choice	*2nd choice*
Panama	West of canal	CHL	PRO
	East of canal	C+P	MEF/MAL
Papua New Guinea	Below 1,800 m	DOX	MAL+CHL
Paraguay	Rural areas October–May only	CHL	PRO
Peru	Rural below 1,500 m	C+P	MEF/MAL
Philippines	Rural areas below 600 m (no risk Cebu, Leyte, Bohol, Catanduanes)	C+P	**
Principe	Whole country	MEF	C+P
Rwanda	Whole country	MEF	C+P
Sao Tomé	Whole country	MEF	C+P
Saudi Arabia	Whole country except N, E, central provs, Asir Plat, W border, cities where low risk	C+P	**
Senegal	Whole country	MEF	C+P
Sierra Leone	Whole country	MEF	C+P
Singapore	No risk	0	0
Solomon Islands	Whole country	DOX	MAL+CHL
Somalia	Whole country	MEF	C+P
South Africa	Only low alt. N&E Transvaal, E Natal down to 100 km N of Durban	C+P	MEF/MAL
Sri Lanka	Whole country, except in and just south of Colombo	C+P	**
Sudan	Whole country	MEF	C+P
Surinam	Whole country, except Paramaribo and coast	MEF	C+P
Swaziland	Whole country	MEF	C+P
Syria	N border only May–October	CHL	PRO
Tajikistan	S border areas only	CHL	PRO
Tanzania	Whole country	MEF	C+P
Thailand*	Bangkok & main tourist centres low risk	0	0
	Rural areas including Ke Chang	MEF	**
	Borders with Cambodia, Myanmar	DOX	**
Togo	Whole country	MEF	C+P
Tunisia	Very low risk	0	0
Turkey*	Most tourist areas very low risk	0	0
	Plain around Adona, Side, SE Anatolia, March–November only	CHL	PRO
Uganda	Whole country	MEF	C+P
Utd Arab Emirates	N rural areas only	C+P	**
Vanuatu	Whole country	DOX	MAL+CHL
Venezuela	Rural non-coastal areas (Caracas free)	C+P	MEF/MAL
	Amazon Basin area	MEF	C+P

Country	Risk areas	Regimes	
		1st choice	*2nd choice*
Vietnam	Whole country except cities, coastal plain north of Nha Trang. Situation improving	MEF	**
Yemen	Throughout country	C+P	**
Zambia	Whole country	MEF	C+P
Zimbabwe	Below 1,200 m November–June	C+P	MEF/MAL
	Zambesi valley all year	MEF	**

Key to abbreviations used in list:

MEF	Take mefloquine 250 mg one tablet weekly. Max. time usually one year
C+P	Take chloroquine 150 mg (base) two tablets weekly *plus* proguanil 100 mg (Paludrine) two tablets daily
CHL	Take chloroquine 150 mg (base) two tablets weekly
PRO	Take proguanil (Paludrine) 100 mg two tablets daily
DOX	Take doxycycline 100 mg one tablet daily. Max. time usually six months
MEF/MAL	Take *either* mefloquine 250 mg one tablet weekly *or* Maloprim one tablet weekly
MAL+CHL	Take Maloprim one tablet weekly *plus* chloroquine 150 mg (base) two tablets weekly
0	No prophylaxis necessary. Report any fever
*	These countries have variable malarial risk. Obtain specific details after knowing your itinerary
**	No official second choice. Ask for specific advice if unable to take first choice

Notes on special situations

1 *Pregnancy*. Chloroquine and proguanil are safe. Avoid mefloquine in first three months of pregnancy and avoid pregnancy within three months of stopping mefloquine. Although mefloquine is safe in the middle and latter thirds of pregnancy, it is not practical as it is not recommended when breastfeeding. Maloprim is safe in the middle and latter thirds of pregnancy but not in the first three months. Doxycycline should be avoided in pregnancy. All pregnant women on antimalarials should take folic acid 5 mg daily.

2 *Breastfeeding*. Chloroquine and proguanil are safe. Avoid Maloprim until at least six weeks after birth. Do not use doxycycline or mefloquine when breastfeeding.

3 *Epilepsy*. Avoid both mefloquine and chloroquine if any past or present history of epilepsy. Except where proguanil alone is an alternative, take doxycycline. If you are taking phenobarbitone, phenytoin or carbamazepine you should ideally increase the dose of doxycycline as these anticonvulsants reduce its effectiveness. You could alternate doses by taking two doxycycline one day, and one the next, taking extra care not to get sunburnt (see page 106).

4   *Liver and kidney problems.*   With liver impairment chloroquine and proguanil are relatively safe. Other antimalarials (including mefloquine) should be avoided. With poor kidney function proguanil can build up in the blood and it is better to use a regime that does not include proguanil. Mefloquine and doxycycline can be used.

5   *Splenectomy.*   Use the drugs recommended, being extremely careful never to miss doses, and to avoid mosquito bites by using every precaution. Avoid the worst affected areas and report any fever at once.

6   *Dosages in children.*   See page 78. Mefloquine should not be used in children under two years old. Maloprim should not be used in children under six weeks old, and only after that age if a paediatric syrup is available (not available in the UK). Doxycycline should not be used in children under 12. Chloroquine and proguanil are safe at all ages.

7   *Antimalarials for those abroad longer than 12 months.*   There are not yet universally agreed guidelines. This is not through lack of trying – there is just no obvious answer so far. For areas where there is no resistance to chloroquine, the answer is quite simple. Take chloroquine if you can tolerate it, proguanil if not. For the most serious malarious areas, where chloroquine resistance exists (including sub-Saharan Africa), the answer is more difficult. You will need to discuss this with a travel health expert because your exact itinerary, lifestyle, job and state of health will help determine the answer. In summary, you have three choices:

– **Chloroquine and proguanil**   Generally safe to take long term, but only partially effective (50–70%) in the worst malarious areas, e.g. in much of sub-Saharan Africa.
– **Mefloquine**   The most effective, giving 90% protection or more. Side effects – real and perceived – are a problem for many. Only technically licensed for 12 months or less in the UK, but used for much longer by members of other nationalities. Most side effects declare themselves early.
– **Doxycycline**   Almost as effective as mefloquine. Expected to be licensed shortly in the UK for preventing malaria. Main drawback is greater tendency to sunburn, so less appropriate in the fair skinned, those who enjoy sunbathing or where your job keeps you in the open air. Has been used for periods exceeding one year by many without problems, but current advice is to use it for six months or less. Doxycycline is moving up the menu, given current concerns about mefloquine.

A strategy some are recommending is to choose two different regimes, using one for the worst risk times of the year or areas you visit, and the second for other times and places. This helps get round the problem that the most effective antimalarials tend to have the most troublesome side effects.

8   *Formulation of chloroquine.* The normal adult dose is two 150 mg (base) tablets. One tablet of chloroquine 150 mg base is equivalent to one chloroquine sulphate 200 mg tablet and to one chloroquine phosphate 250 mg tablet. This means that the normal adult dose for prevention for all these chloroquine formulations is two tablets weekly.

Where can you obtain antimalarials?

In the UK chloroquine and proguanil can be bought over the counter. Mefloquine, doxycycline, Maloprim, Fansidar, quinine and Malarone have to be prescribed by a doctor but are not available on the NHS. This means that doctors will give a private prescription for which they usually charge, and in addition you will need to pay the chemist.

Antimalarials can be bought from most travel clinics (see Appendix A).

The quality of antimalarials in many developing countries is variable. Unless you know of a good supply it is better to take a supply from home.

How do you treat malaria?

If you think you may have malaria, follow these steps:

1   See a reliable doctor or health worker and ask for a malaria smear. You should do this within eight hours of the start of fever or of other suspicious symptoms.
2   If the malaria smear is positive or the doctor believes you have malaria, make sure you receive treatment. If you are carrying your own standby tablets, show them to the doctor.
3   If the smear is negative or the doctor says you have not got malaria, self-treat anyway if *either* there is no obvious cause for your fever *or* your symptoms are not fully resolved within twenty-four hours with no recurrence.
4   If your symptoms continue or recur, whether or not you have treated for malaria or had a positive blood smear, make sure you get expert medical help as quickly as possible.

Although travellers off the beaten path should always carry standby treatment with them if in malarious areas, you are still recommended to see a doctor and get a blood smear, if possible.

There are two new tests for malaria, both of which depend on obtaining a finger prick of blood, applying it to a test-strip and then reading the results. Two current brands are the ParaSight F test and the ICT Malaria Pf test. It is likely that these and similar tests will become useful in travellers to remote areas who are trained in their use, but at the time of writing are not recommended for general use.

Malaria suspected or confirmed must be appropriately treated without delay.

Recommended standby treatment for malaria

There are two reasons for taking standby treatment (i.e. your own supply of tablets) to treat a suspected or confirmed attack of malaria.

The first is if you are more than 24 hours, ideally more than 12 hours, from a reliable health facility and you have symptoms of malaria. The second is to have treatment available if you attend a doctor for a blood smear in areas where antimalarials may not be available or you may be prescribed an inappropriate medicine.

In practice it is worth considering standby antimalarials for any trip longer than seven days in areas with a high malaria risk and unreliable drug supplies (e.g. much of sub-Saharan Africa). For trips of seven days or less, they are unnecessary as the incubation period for malaria is always seven days or more.

The first choice for standby treatment for most areas is quinine tablets 300 mg, two tablets three times a day for three days followed by Fansidar, three tablets together once.

Alternative choices:

1 *Malarone tablets* (atovaquone 250 mg plus proguanil 100 mg): four tablets together for three successive days if p. falciparum malaria is likely. Effective, low side-effects, but expensive.

2 *Artemesinin derivatives.* There are various choices, none yet licensed in the UK at the time of writing. One of the most effective is co-artemether (artemether 20 mg and lumefantrine 120 mg). One trade name is Riamet. Follow dosage guidelines and information on drug information leaflet. A slightly less effective alternative is dihydroartemesinin (Cotecxin). The dose is 120 mg on day one and 60 mg for a further four to six days. Dosages for children are according to manufacturer's instructions.

Special situations:

1 *Pregnancy and breastfeeding.* Use quinine alone, 300 mg tablets, two every eight hours for five to seven days. Avoid Fansidar. See a doctor.

2   *Areas definitely known to have no known chloroquine resistance* (i.e. areas where first-choice prophylaxis in the country list – see pages 68–72 – is either CHL or 0). Take chloroquine 150 mg (base) four together on days one and two, two together on day three. Total ten.

Please note: chloroquine is no longer recommended as a treatment for sub-Saharan Africa.

3   Alternative for those taking mefloquine as prophylaxis. Adult dose: quinine 300 mg tablets, two tablets three times a day for three days, accompanied by doxycycline 100 mg, one tablet twice daily for seven days.
4   *Mefloquine as treatment.* If there is *no* alternative. Adult dose: 250 mg tablets, two tablets followed by two further tablets after six hours. There can be troublesome side effects and it is better not to use this if you are taking mefloquine as a prophylactic.
5   *Halofantrine as treatment.* If there is *no* alternative, adult dose, 250 mg tablets, two tablets every six hours (total six), followed by identical repeat course after one week. Although halofantrine (Halfan) both as tablets for adults and syrup for children is widely available in Africa, this should only be used if the patient has no history of any cardiac problem *and* has had a recent normal ECG. Otherwise fatal heart problems can be caused in both children and adults. WHO has issued warnings about the use of halofantrine.
6   Special treatment regimes for resistant areas of South-East Asia – see details on page 80.

Malaria, pregnancy and breastfeeding

Pregnancy

An attack of malaria, in particular malignant (P. falciparum) malaria can cause severe symptoms in pregnancy, including miscarriages and stillbirths. Ideally, those who are pregnant should avoid areas where malignant malaria is common.

If this is not possible it is essential to take *prophylactics* without missing tablets, as well as full precautions to avoid mosquito bites (see pages 62–6). Pregnant women and children should avoid altogether travelling in western Cambodia or in the Thai border areas with Cambodia and Myanmar, as recommended treatment would not be safe for you.

Chloroquine and proguanil are entirely safe in pregnancy. Mefloquine and Maloprim are also considered to be safe except in the first three months of pregnancy. In addition, pregnancy should be avoided within three months of discontinuing mefloquine. Doxycycline should be avoided in pregnancy. Take folic acid 5 mg daily.

For *treatment* quinine is safe and is the treatment of choice.

Breastfeeding

Maloprim, Fansidar (or its equivalents) are harmful to newborn babies. They are also secreted in breast milk, and breastfeeding mothers should avoid both until at least six weeks after birth, using quinine for treatment instead.

Chloroquine, proguanil and quinine are safe during breastfeeding. Other antimalarial drugs, including mefloquine, should be avoided.

Malaria and children

Babies and young children can quickly become seriously ill with malaria. Moreover because their symptoms may not be typical, the diagnosis can easily be missed.

Ideally, children under six months should avoid areas where malignant malaria is common. If this is not possible they should start antimalarials from birth (ideal) or from six weeks (essential) and sleep

Giving Antimalarials to children is an acquired art

under a bed net impregnated with permethrin or Icon (see page 63). Babies under six weeks, if travelling in an area where Maloprim is recommended, should instead take proguanil (Paludrine) and chloroquine (see Tables 2 and 3). Under the age of two they should only take Maloprim if a syrup is available.

Table 2 Prophylactic dosages for children (i.e. for prevention)
(as fractions of the adult dose)

Age	Chloroquine Paludrine	Maloprim	Mefloquine
0–5 weeks	⅛	Not recommended	Not recommended
6 weeks to 1 year	¼	⅛ but only as a syrup	Not recommended
1–5 years (10–19 kg)	½	¼ but only as a syrup	Not used in the under-2s or below 15 kg; 2–5 years, ¼ adult dose
6–11 years (20–39 kg)	¾	½	½ (6–8 years); ¾ (9–11 years and up to 45 kg)
12 years or 40 kg or over	Adult dose	Adult dose	Adult dose

Doxycycline should be avoided in those under the age of 12.

Table 3 Treatment dosages for children

	Fansidar or Metakelfin:
Two months to 4 years	½ tablet (i.e. ⅙ adult dose)
5–6 years	1 tablet
7–9 years	1½ tablets
10–14 years	2 tablets
Over 15 years	3 tablets
	Malarone
Under 11 kg	Not recommended
11–20 kg	1 daily
21–30 kg	2 daily
31–40 kg	3 daily
Over 40 kg	4 daily

(all taken as single daily dose for three days)

Quinine: 10 mg/kg every eight hours for seven days.

Chloroquine is available in the UK as a syrup (Nivaquine syrup). Some children prefer this to a crushed tablet, others are deeply suspicious. Maloprim (Deltaprim) is available as a syrup in Zimbabwe and some surrounding countries.

Other antimalarial drugs are only available as tablets. They should be crushed and given on a spoon with jam, honey or something sweet, or flavoured with chocolate. Alternatively they can be dissolved with sugar in a little milk, or rolled in butter, peanut butter or a favourite salty savoury and placed near the back of the tongue. As a *last resort* a tablet can be crushed, added to sugary milk, drawn up in a clean syringe from which the needle has been removed and introduced slowly down the side of the tongue. Giving antimalarials to children is an acquired art.

Note: The dosages in Tables 2 and 3 follow the recommendations of the UK Malaria Reference Laboratory. These recommendations differ in some details from advice on the instruction slips that accompany some bottles of antimalarial tablets, and also from World Health Organisation sources. This is because there is not yet international agreement, though this is expected shortly.

Malaria after returning home

'Flu' may be malaria for any time up to at least one year and especially in the first three months. This is especially important if returning from sub-Saharan Africa. If you have been taking mefloquine it can delay the onset of malaria. Make sure you report any suspicious symptoms without delay, especially in children. You should either report to a GP or go direct to the accident and emergency department of a main hospital, explain you have come from a malarious area and insist you have a blood smear. If this is negative and the fever persists or worsens you should have a repeat test carried out, preferably at a tropical diseases centre. It is *not* safe simply to take chloroquine and hope for the best. Even if you have your standby of quinine and Fansidar you should still have a blood smear, but take the standby treatment with you and show it to the doctor.

Note that if you are in or near London you can go to the Hospital for Tropical Diseases at any time of the day or night, without a letter, if you think you may have malaria (see page 203 for this and other centres).

If you have had recurrent attacks of malaria and are now home for good or for a long leave, it is sensible to take a course of primaquine to eradicate the persistent forms of benign malaria that may otherwise plague you for months. You should discuss this at your tropical health check.

If you have been brought up in a malarious country, then come to study or live in the UK for more than twelve months, you may lose your immunity. This means you are at risk of getting malaria on return to a malarious area. It is worth taking prophylactics for six months after returning and being very careful then, and subsequently, to report and treat any symptoms that could be malaria.

Notes on commonly used drugs

When in the tropics, probably sooner rather than later the conversation will turn to malaria. Details of the latest therapeutic fashion mingled with advice, good, bad and indifferent, will soon fill the air. It is helpful to know basic information both about the medicines you may be using as well as those others are talking about. A large number of different trade names add further to the confusion. Here is a simple field guide.

Amodiaquine (Camoquin, Flavoquine, Florquine, Miaquine)
Uses: Was used for prophylaxis, now discontinued owing to risk of blood disorders. Occasionally still used for treatment in chloroquine-sensitive areas.

Artemesinin derivatives (Artenan, Cotecxin etc.)
These effective antimalarials are derived from the herb Artemisia annua, and have been used in China for centuries under the name quinghoasu. The main artemesinin derivatives are known as artemether, arteether dihydroartemesinin, and artesunate.
Uses: for treatment of malaria where other drugs are ineffective or not available. Two common forms are Cotecxin and Artenan. For dosage of Cotecxin as standby, see page 75.
Two recommended treatment dosages in areas of South-East Asia with high drug resistance are: artesunate 4 mg/kg daily for three days (approximates in adult to 200 mg daily) plus on day two, mefloquine 15 mg/kg and on day three mefloquine 10 mg/kg. Alternative regime without mefloquine: artesunate total dose of 12 mg/kg spread out evenly over seven days, plus doxycycline 200 mg daily for seven days. (These regimes kindly provided by Professor White of Bangkok.)
Warnings: these drugs are not yet licensed in the UK at the time of writing. Read any data sheets carefully before using, especially side effects and contraindications.

Chloroquine (Aralen, Avloclor, Chinamine, Delagil, Imagon, Malari-quine, Malarivon, Nivaquine, Plaquenol, Resochin, Sanioquin, Treso-chin)
Uses: For prevention and treatment as described in text.
Warnings: nausea, itching – and rashes especially in those with black skin. May make psoriasis worse. It should not be used in those with a history of epilepsy. Chloroquine is safe in pregnancy and during lactation. Best taken after food.

It is available from chemists without a prescription and from travel clinics.

Eyes and chloroquine: damage to the retina is not now thought by most experts to occur if weekly chloroquine *only* is taken. If however chloroquine is in addition used for treatment it may accumulate in the retina, in which case regular eye checks should be carried out. Some experts still advise checks if regular chloroquine at a dose of 300 mg (base) per week has been taken continuously for six years or more (see also page 161).

Savarine is chloroquine 100 mg (base) and proguanil 200 mg in a single tablet. The dose is one tablet daily.

Chlorproguanil (Lapudrine). An alternative to proguanil (probably slightly less effective) taken as 20 mg tablet twice weekly or, better, daily.
Warnings: as for proguanil.

Doxycycline (Vibramycin, Nordox)
Uses: as a prophylactic at a dose of one (100 mg) tablet per day for Cambodia (especially western) and Thai/Cambodia, Thai/Myanmar border areas. It is an alternative for other malarious regions and is being increasingly used. Can also be used as a treatment along with quinine if mefloquine is taken as a prophylactic (see page 76).

Warnings: should not be used in children 12 or under nor in pregnancy and breastfeeding. It can increase the risk of vaginal thrush, diarrhoea and sunburn, and if taking it you should avoid the sun or take extra protective measures. Take it with plenty of fluids and not just before lying down. Experience of side effects for periods of longer than six months is limited.

Fansidar (The trade name for sulfadoxine 500 mg plus pyrimethamine 25 mg)
Uses: for treatment of malaria as described in text. Should not be used for prophylaxis. There is increasing Fansidar resistance in Africa and other areas.

Warnings: generally safe if used for treatment. Should be avoided in those sensitive to sulphonamides or pyrimethamine, in pregnancy and during the first six weeks of lactation. Should not be used in children under two months. Sometimes causes skin rashes and allergic reactions.

Available on prescription and from some travel clinics.

Halofantrine (Halfan)
Uses: *should only be used under medical supervision*. It is an effective treatment against most forms of malaria, including chloroquine-resistant strains, but the course of six tablets should be repeated after one week to prevent recurrences. As Halfan syrup it is an effective treatment for children but it is not available in the UK.

Warnings: cases of serious cadiac effects, including deaths, have occasionally been reported. Halfan should only be used in travellers who have had a recent, normal ECG, and no history of heart disease. Avoid during pregnancy and delay conception for at least one month after completing a course of treatment.

It is not safe during lactation.

It should not be used for treatment unless no other medication is available.

Available on prescription only.

Maloprim (The trade name for pyrimethamine 12.5 mg plus dapsone 100 mg) (Deltaprim, Malasone)

Uses: for prophylaxis as in text; available only on prescription.

Warnings: unlikely to cause blood disorders if taken at normal dose of one per week. Avoid in liver or kidney disease, first three months of pregnancy and first six weeks of lactation. Those sensitive to sulphonamides sometimes develop an allergic reaction and should take it for a trial period of two weeks before deciding to use it long term. Those who are pregnant must take folic acid 5 mg daily in addition.

Malarone (The trade name for atovaquone 250 mg plus proguanil 100 mg)

Uses: an effective treatment where resistance to other antimalarials is likely. The dose is four tablets together as single dose with food or a milky drink at same time each day for three days (total 12 tablets). Children over 11 kg can take it at doses according to manufacturer's instructions (see Table 3, page 78).

Warnings: not suitable in pregnancy, or for vivax malaria. Read drug information leaflet carefully.

Malarone is licensed in the UK for treatment and will probably become so for prevention. It appears to be safe and effective, though expensive.

Mefloquine (Lariam, Mephaquin, Methaloquine)

Uses: for prophylaxis as in text. It gives better protection than any other drug in areas of chloroquine resistance. It can be used as a treatment if no other effective drug is available under medical supervision, and providing it has not been used as a prophylactic. The dose for treatment is 250 mg tablets, two tablets together, then two further tablets after six hours. (Mephaquin comes as 228 mg tablets in USA.)

Warnings: there has been a huge amount of discussion about mefloquine. Although side effects occur they have been exaggerated by the media. The result of the real and perceived problems with mefloquine have undermined confidence in its use, especially among long-term expatriates and aid workers. In fact only about one person in 10,000 suffers very serious side effects either physical or mental. However, moderate but unpleasant side effects, including depression, anxiety, hallucinations and nightmares, occur in between 25% and 40% of travellers. Other nuisances include nausea, dizziness, fine tremor, irritability and rashes. A recent UK survey of 875 people living for 12 months or more in malarious areas showed that only 3% used mefloquine.

Mefloquine should not be used by anyone who has previously had an adverse reaction when using it, nor in those with a history of any mental illness, including anxiety, depression, insomnia, significant mood-swings or a personal or family history of epilepsy. It should be avoided in the first three months of pregnancy, when breastfeeding and in those taking beta blocking drugs. Consult the drug information leaflet and read it carefully before using mefloquine.

No figures can tell us how many lives have been saved or debilitating attacks of malaria prevented by mefloquine. If you wish to try it, start three weeks before leaving because about three-quarters of side effects show up by that time, giving you an opportunity to change prophylaxis before going abroad.

Available on prescription and from some travel clinics.

Mefloquine should carry a social health warning: avoid excessive discussion of real or imagined side effects.

Primaquine (Neo-quipenyl)

Uses: prescribed by doctors to eradicate recurring attacks of benign malaria, usually after a course of chloroquine first. Usual dosage is 15 mg daily for fourteen days, but this sometimes needs to be doubled, especially in South-East Asia. Primaquine is occasionally used as a prophylactic.

Warnings: in those who lack an enzyme known as G6PD, it may cause a serious reaction. A G6PD blood test should be performed before treatment, ideally on everyone, and essentially on those of African, Asian or Mediterranean descent. May also cause rashes and other allergic reactions. Should be avoided in pregnancy.

Proguanil 100 mg (Paludrine, Chlorguanide, Lepadina, Palusil, Proguanide, Tirian)

Uses: for prevention of malaria as described in text.

Warnings: frequently causes mouth ulcers (continue if possible) and occasionally hair loss (in which case stop taking it). May also cause nausea and stomach discomfort, so should be taken after food, preferably in the evening. Safe in pregnancy and lactation, but pregnant women should take folic acid 5 mg daily. Can affect the dose of anticoagulants.

Available from chemists without prescription and from travel clinics. Proguanil is little used by those from North America.

Pyrimethamine (Daraprim, Chloridin, Malocide, Tindurin, Syraprim)
Uses: this was widely used for prevention of malaria but is no longer recommended as its effectiveness is very low.

Quinine (Quinimax, Quinoforme)
Uses: for treatment of all forms of malaria as described in text.

Warnings: may cause headache, tinnitus, dizziness, nausea and allergic reactions. Can be used in pregnancy and lactation if chloroquine is ineffective. Should ideally be used under medical supervision, especially if mefloquine has been used as a prophylactic. Quinine is generally considered a safe (though unpleasant) drug.

Available on prescription and from some travel clinics.

Other drugs and combinations sometimes used:

Azithromycin (Zithromax) is a reasonably effective prophylactic occasionally used.

Co-artemether is artemether 20 mg, lumefantrine (benflumetol) 120 mg and is effective at curing malaria in South-East Asia and other parts of the world with chloroquine resistance.

Daraclor is pyrimethamine and chloroquine.

Fansimef is sulfadoxine 500 mg, pyrimethamine 25 mg and mefloquine 250 mg, and is used for treatment under medical supervision as an alternative to Fansidar.

Lapoquin is chlorproguanil plus chloroquine.

Metakelfin is sulfalene and pyrimethamine and is used as an alternative to Fansidar.

Tetracycline (Achromycin, Cyclomycin, Panmycin, Tetracyn etc.) is occasionally used for treatment in areas where there is chloroquine and Fansidar resistance. In these cases a course of quinine is followed or accompanied by tetracycline 250 mg four times daily for seven days. It should not be used in those sensitive to tetracyclines, in pregnancy and in children under 12.

Summary

Malaria is a serious nuisance at best and a fatal illness at worst. You can think of defeating malaria according to these four steps:

A   **Awareness** Being aware of the risk and what you should do about it.

B   **Bites by mosquitoes** Taking action to avoid them through the use of impregnated bed-nets, insect repellent, cover-up and avoidance.

C   **Compliance** Deciding on the prophylaxis to take and never missing a dose.

D   **Diagnosis** Seeing a doctor or self-treating within eight hours of suspicious symptoms, both when in a malarious area and for 12 months after leaving it, including when returning home.

AVOIDING AIDS

What you need to know

The difference between AIDS and HIV

AIDS stands for the Acquired Immune Deficiency Syndrome. It is caused by the Human Immunodeficiency Virus (HIV), which attacks the immune system. Usually within three months of being infected with the virus, antibodies develop to HIV and the blood antibody test becomes HIV positive.

Infection with HIV usually leads to AIDS, though the length of time between becoming infected and developing AIDS is extremely variable, averaging about ten years. During this 'latent period' the person infected with HIV is largely free of symptoms but is infectious to others. Once AIDS has developed death usually occurs within two years.

Recent advances with anti-retroviral drug therapy have greatly prolonged the survival time for those in developed countries who can afford or have access to treatment and can tolerate the side effects.

The extent of the problem

Worldwide at the beginning of 1999, there were approximately two million confirmed cases of AIDS, with nearly 34 million adults and children estimated to be living with HIV/AIDS. This was a 10% increase within one year. Each day 16,000 new cases were occurring. In a few countries up to 25% of the adult urban population is HIV positive. AIDS is now the fourth commonest worldwide cause of death.

Most countries have now reported AIDS, and the number of cases from South and South-East Asia and parts of Latin America, as well as from Africa, is increasing rapidly.

How AIDS is spread

- Through *having sex* with an infected partner. Worldwide this is the main method of spread.
- Through receiving *infected blood transfusions* or blood-derived products.
- Through *dirty needles*, syringes, lancets, scalpels and dental instruments.
- Occasionally through *surface* spread (such as cleaning up blood spills) where infected blood and other body fluids are in contact with mucous membranes and injured skin (cuts, abrasions, chapping).
- *Razorblades*, shared toothbrushes and instruments used for ear-piercing and tattooing may cause occasional cases.
- Through spread from *mother to child* at or during birth.
- HIV infection can be spread from an infected mother to her child through *breast milk*.

HIV infection is *not spread* through normal social contact, even if close and prolonged. There is no evidence that insects, including mosquitoes or bed-bugs, can spread AIDS, nor do toilet seats, swimming pools, cutlery or shared communion cups.

By living in a country where AIDS is common you face a *potentially* greater risk of becoming infected than you would in your home country. *But by following a few commonsense rules* your risk of infection can become negligible.

What you need to do

These precautions will minimize your risk:

Before you go

- Complete *immunizations*.
- Have a *dental* check.
- Find out your *blood group* and keep a record with you.
- Take a supply of recommended *antimalarial* tablets and other recommended antimalarial equipment if going to a malarious area.
- Take a *needle and syringe* kit.
- Consider taking an AIDS *protection kit* containing an intravenous giving set and bottles of plasma substitute.
- Plan ahead if *pregnancy* is possible.

- *Decide to abstain* from casual sexual encounters.
- *Take condoms* with you unless you consider your principles, beliefs and defence mechanisms will *guarantee your safe behaviour even at times of stress or loneliness.*
- Resolve *not to get drunk* as many cases of HIV are contracted in an alcoholic haze.

While abroad

- *Avoid casual sexual encounters.*
  The only way of being certain to avoid HIV infection, and over 20 other diseases transmitted through sex, is to be permanently loyal to one partner who is known to be HIV negative. In practice this means that only if you abstain from pre- and extramarital sex can you be certain to avoid infection.
  As many as 75% of sex workers in some cities of the world are HIV positive.
  Women as far as possible should avoid situations, lifestyles and inappropriate clothing that might increase their risk of being raped, or misinterpreted.
- *Use condoms if you have sex with anyone other than a permanent partner known to be HIV negative.*
  Safe sex only means safer sex. Estimates on condom failure vary between 10% and 20% owing to carelessness, splitting and slippage, often aided by alcohol. At the Eighth World Congress on Sexology, 800 delegates were asked to indicate if, using a condom, they would have sex with a person known to be HIV positive. Only one indicated they would. At the Tenth World Congress the question was repeated to health professionals. Not one would have risked having sex, even using a condom, with a person known to be HIV positive. (A. Grazioli, *British Medical Journal* Vol 312, page 1478)
  These realities mean that abstinence and fidelity should move up the menu for methods of avoiding HIV infection, without denying the importance of using condoms correctly.
- *Treat genital ulceration.*
  If you develop any sores or ulceration in the genital area, get these treated at a good medical centre and strictly avoid sex until they are fully healed.
- *Avoid road accidents.*
  These are a major risk because serious accidents often necessitate medical treatment and blood transfusions. Please read the section on page 89.
- *Avoid blood transfusions from unknown or untested sources* (see pages 91–5).
  In case of an accident or emergency where serious blood loss is

occurring, you or your companion should follow the guidelines on page 91.

- *Avoid dirty needles and syringes.*
  Produce your own needles and syringes except in health facilities where you reliably know that sterile, sealed disposable needles and syringes are always used. Try to ascertain that the nurse actually does use the needle and syringe you provide. This will require tact and courtesy!
- *In addition*:
  Produce your own lancet for a malaria smear.
  Whenever possible *use medicines* that can be taken by mouth rather than by injection. You may need to be assertive.
  Avoid locally made gammaglobulin or other blood- or serum-derived products.
  Take full precautions to avoid malaria, as severe malaria increases the need for treatment by injection or blood transfusion.
  Plan any non-urgent surgery or dentistry for when you come home.
  Health-care workers will need more detailed advice. It is important they discuss through the full implications of working in an area where the risk of HIV cannot be entirely eliminated. They should consider taking a personal antiretroviral medical kit with them, for immediate post-exposure prophylaxis, starting within one or two hours of a high-risk incident.

On return home

You may start to worry that you have become infected with HIV. Unless you have been *knowingly* at risk the chance of becoming infected is extremely remote.

Anyone who wishes to have an HIV test is entitled to do so, either through their GP or as part of their 'Tropical Health Check' or at a hospital STD clinic. Confidentiality is ensured.

Because of new treatments that are prolonging the lives of those with HIV, it is a wise choice to opt for an HIV test if you have been at any risk at all. The earlier you start on antiretroviral treatment the greater your chance of long-term survival.

To be largely sure of any possible infection showing on the blood test it is worth delaying any final test until at least ninety days after any last possible exposure.

Provided the test is negative and you can record an occupational reason or specific non-recurring risk while abroad, you are extremely unlikely to be declined by an insurance company or charged a higher premium. If you are you can appeal. A statement of practice is available from the Association of British Insurers, 51 Gresham Street, London EC2V 7HQ.

Entry certificates

A few countries require certificates stating that you have tested HIV negative. A negative test carried out not more than ninety days before entry and accompanied by a doctor's signed and stamped certificate stating this was carried out in a WHO-accredited laboratory is usually sufficient, though some countries will expect you to have a test after arrival if you are planning to reside in that country. Check with the embassy of the country in question if in doubt, or with a specialist travel clinic.

Summary

AIDS in adults is largely a preventable disease. *It is better to be entirely safe than for ever sorry.*

PREVENTING ACCIDENTS

Road accidents

Road accidents are the commonest cause of expatriate death and head the list for emergency repatriations. Each year 700,000 people die in road accidents, 10% of these in India, and seven occur every day in Delhi alone.

Road accidents don't only kill, they maim, destroy families and lead to long-term disability. They increase the risk of becoming infected with HIV and hepatitis B and C because of the transfusion risk. Most road accidents are preventable if you regularly follow basic precautions:

- Fit and wear *seat belts* to both front and rear seats, and ensure that they are used by all, including children. *Wearing seat belts, even for the shortest journeys, is probably the single most important health precaution you can take when overseas (or at home).*
- *Keep your vehicle in good condition* by regular servicing, and make sure tyres are adequate, and brakes and lights working properly.
- Make sure any driver you employ, personally or for a project, is both licensed and competent to drive.
- Try to *avoid driving when tired*, or for prolonged periods, or overnight or without a co-driver.
- Never drink and drive or drive when taking medicines that make you drowsy.

- *Leave plenty of time* for journeys so you are not in a hurry.
- *Choose drivers, taxis and rickshaws with care*, and, as far as your ingenuity allows, make sure that lights, tyres and brakes are in good order before setting out. Ensure your driver is alert and not under the influence of drugs or alcohol. 'Close-face bargaining' can enable you to observe pupils, and smell breath.
- *Ride* in the safest part of the vehicle.
- Carry in the vehicle a *first-aid* kit, *torch* and *leather* gloves for pulling victims free.
- Motor cyclists should wear *crash helmets* (or change to a safer form of transport), even for the shortest journeys.
- When *crossing the road* remember the direction of traffic flow. Take special care of children if visiting a city after living in a rural area.

For the *procedure* to follow in a serious road accident, see page 94.

Swimming accidents

These are common overseas, both in the sea and swimming pools. Medical support to save life – and disability – is that much harder to obtain.

Prevent *sea accidents* by:

- only swimming in *areas known to be free from dangerous currents*, sharks, sea snakes, poisonous fish (e.g. stone fish, sting rays) and jellyfish (e.g. box jellyfish);
- *never going out of your depth*;
- always swimming *with a companion*;
- never swimming if you have been *drinking alcohol*;
- *avoiding sunburn*;
- *avoiding polluted* areas and not taking in water through your mouth;
- keeping a close watch on children, especially if using inflatables.

Prevent *accidents in swimming pools* by:

- *never running* along the edge of the pool;
- *never drinking* alcohol before or during swimming;
- never diving without first having *carefully checked the depth* of the water;
- never diving into a *cloudy pool*;
- avoiding *polluted pools*;
- *avoiding sunburn* and making sure any children are carefully protected from the sun.

Finally, after your swim or at any other time be careful on your *hotel balcony*. Several travellers die each year because of a low or weak balcony – often assisted by a high blood alcohol level.

Domestic accidents

This has been called the hidden epidemic. Overseas children are at high risk. So are older visitors or anyone new to the country. On arrival in a room, hotel or new home, carry out a risk assessment. Observe and imagine any possible hazards. If you have kids, try to see the house and its surroundings through their eyes, and at their height.

Here are some hazards to watch out for, especially if children are present:

- *Slips and falls* from balconies, windows, slippery marble floors or uneven staircases.
- *Electrics*: unsafe sockets, bare wires, unearthed appliances including immersion heaters, faulty wiring in showers.
- *Dangerous substances*, including medicines (especially if sugar coated) or fluids such as chemicals (e.g. bleach). Friends and neighbours may store dangerous substances in bottles or containers originally bought for food or drinks and still retaining an innocent label.
- *Fire hazards*: always check a possible way of escape, especially if windows are barred – consider using hotel rooms on the lower floors (unless security problems make this unwise).
- *Cuts from glass*, e.g. from doors or thin window panes.
- *Scorpions* and *poisonous spiders* lurking in dark holes, cupboards or shoes, and snakes in the bathroom.
- *Burns* from open fires, cookers and hot handles, and scalds from hot fluids.
- Running out *into the road*.
- *Cuddling dogs* and picking up cats, especially if unknown.
- *Being in a hurry* or in a stress.

KNOWING ABOUT BLOOD TRANSFUSIONS

Occasions when you might need blood

The commonest reason for needing a blood transfusion when overseas is because of a road accident. Other causes include: bleeding during an operation, blood loss before, during or after childbirth, severe malaria and a bleeding peptic ulcer. You can minimize these risks by commonsense precautions, a healthy lifestyle and planning ahead.

Serious blood loss – of more than 25% of the blood volume – means you will probably require emergency transfusion. However, for all but the most urgent situations you can start treatment using a plasma substitute to replace fluid lost until such time as you can reach a safe donor or obtain supplies of safe blood. Until recently plasma expanders such as Haemaccel were the best choice, but recent evidence shows that cheaper and simpler intravenous fluids such as Hartmann's solution work as well or better.

Making sure blood is safe

Any blood you receive must fulfil two conditions: first it must be free from infection, and second it must belong to the same or to a compatible blood group.

Blood should be free from infection

This includes HIV, hepatitis B and C, syphilis and malaria. When you go to a UK Blood Donor Clinic, tests are carried out on all the above except malaria, at which time your blood group is also ascertained. However, when you simply have a blood grouping arranged in a GP surgery, hospital laboratory or travel clinic, tests for infection are not necessarily carried out. Blood supplies in developing countries are often inadequately tested or not tested at all. They may be infected not only with HIV, hepatitis B, C and other viruses, but also with malaria and, in parts of South America, with Chagas Disease.

There are three ways to reduce the risk of receiving HIV-infected blood when overseas:

- Only accept blood that has been HIV-tested immediately before you receive it.
- Only receive blood from a donor whose lifestyle you trust. This is important because blood infected with HIV may still test negative for a period of three months after becoming infected, and during this 'window' period can still pass on HIV disease.
- Use intravenous fluids until you can reach a source of known safe blood (see below).

Blood should belong to a compatible group (see Table 4 on page 95)

Even when compatible blood groups are used, blood should still be cross-matched to further reduce the risk of serious reactions. In this test, drops of blood from the person giving and the person receiving blood are mixed together. Cross-matching should ideally be done just before the transfusion is set up. If you will be travelling as a team in dangerous situations with poor medical facilities, group members with the same blood group can arrange to have their blood cross-matched before departure.

REMEMBER: blood from an unknown or untreated source should be avoided except in life-threatening emergencies.

Practical steps you should take

1 Know your blood group before going abroad

If you will be living abroad or travelling extensively, make sure that you and all family members or group members know their blood groups. Each person should keep a written record with them at all times. Similarly, parents should keep a note of the blood group of all family members, and group leaders of all in their group.

Blood grouping can be arranged through your GP or local hospital; both will usually charge. Better still, you can become a blood donor and have it checked free of charge (see page 23).

2 Join a trusted donor group overseas

On arrival at your destination obtain a list of local, trusted donors, and consider adding your name. Most companies or projects employing expatriate staff will have such a list (sometimes known as a Walking Blood Bank), as will many British embassies or consulates. If they don't, you can set one up yourself.

You may not know, or trust, all names on this list. *This means that you should make a point of identifying two or three easily accessible expatriate friends or colleagues with a compatible group whose blood you would be happy to receive.* Make a note of who they are and their emergency contact addresses.

3 Consider taking an AIDS and hepatitis B protection kit

This is probably only necessary if you are doing extensive travel by road (or light aircraft) in areas where AIDS is common. If you do take a kit, make sure it contains one or more intravenous giving sets and at least two litres of intravenous fluid. If young children will be travelling with you, take one or more 'butterfly' needles. (See pages 201–2.) At the time of an accident the use of a kit does depend on someone being present who knows how to set it up, though simple instructions are usually included. If you take one abroad make sure you always have it with you on road journeys. It is no use having it under your bed if you've just had a road accident 100 kilometres from home. Plasma substitutes such as Haemaccel or Gelofusine should not be left for long periods in the boot of a car because of overheating. This is less important with simple intravenous fluids.

4 Know a transfusion procedure in case of an accident

This will include:

- *Giving/receiving* first aid, and prevention of further bleeding where possible (see Further Reading, page 220).
- *Setting up* an intravenous line as soon as possible and giving intravenous fluids if kit and health worker are available and if the injured person shows signs of shock (much blood loss – often concealed – with fast pulse, cold extremities, low blood pressure).
- *Admission* to a reliable health facility.
- *Arrangement for blood transfusion* if needed, as soon as available, and from a trusted donor or safe source. This could include contacting your health insurance emergency line or the Blood Care Foundation (see page 206).

Compatible blood groups

Everyone belongs to group O, A, B, or AB. In addition everyone is Rhesus (D) positive or negative. Blood has to be compatible for both the group and the Rhesus sign, otherwise serious reactions can occur with transfusions. It is ideal to receive blood from someone with an identical blood group to your own, or who is O Rhesus negative (universal donor). However, blood can also be given and received according to Table 4, providing cross-matching is carried out before the transfusion is given.

Table 4 Compatible blood groups

Blood group	Can give to	Can receive from
O+	O+, A+, B+, AB+	O+, O−
O−	All groups	O−
A+	A+, AB+	A+, A−, O+, O−
A−	A+, A−, AB+, AB−	A−, O−
B+	B+, AB+	B+, B−, O+, O−
B−	B+, B−, AB+, AB−	B−, O−
AB+	AB+	All groups
AB−	AB−, AB+	AB−, A−, B−, O−

COPING WITH STRESS
by Dr Ruth Fowke

Stress or Stimulus?

It sometimes seems that most people are either suffering from stress themselves or setting up seminars to help those who are. Stress is indeed an ever-present part of modern living, and few people will find that jumping on a plane for an overseas assignment will automatically lead them to a stress-free nirvana. Indeed, for many working abroad, levels of stress are high. This means that learning to recognize, prevent and deal with stress is one of the most useful lessons we can learn, both before and during our time overseas.

It is important to understand that a situation that is of little consequence to one person may be highly stressful to someone else, and for a third may be the very stimulus that leads to appropriate action. One answer to stress, therefore, is to 'know yourself' – and to learn what situations are stressful to you.

Stimulation is necessary for effective living. No stimulation generally means no achievement. The point in time or intensity when stimulation turns to stress is an individual matter. This means it is helpful for each individual and family to find out the optimum level of stimulation for their own well-being. In this way they are likely 'to have a good work-out rather than to rust out or burn out' (Figure 5).

Specific overseas stresses

Living together with other expatriates can often be the biggest stress factor of all. Remember that what stresses one person or family may merely amuse or stimulate another. These individual differences to

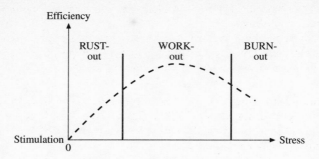

Figure 5 Personal efficiency curve

stress can in themselves cause tension, especially in those living and working in confined circumstances without the possibility of relief from one another's company. Just realizing this fact can in itself help the situation. Some can only recharge their personal batteries with plenty of people around them to join in the activity; others crave to be alone for a while. A routine lifestyle is essential for some; a random one is necessary for the health of others. Some people work best in sequential, even steps; others can only do so in bursts of energy with pauses between. The output of both may be similar, but the method of working is so different that each can mistrust and come to dislike the other. It is difficult for larks and owls to agree on the best time to start work. But even if they can't agree they can at least learn to accept that each has a different metabolism (and that God created them both).

Loneliness is a further cause of stress to many. It will strike people in various ways and at different times and is particularly hard to manage when the partner, friend or rest of the group seem to be adapting well. The operative words here are 'seem to', because gentle discussion often reveals that others too are having or have had the same symptoms. Just knowing that others feel the same brings considerable relief. It is helpful also to pre-plan activities, ideally with others, during any festivals, birthdays or anniversaries of personal importance.

Many people get stressed by feeling themselves to have *inadequate skills for the job assigned*, or having no clear role, job description or areas of responsibility (see page 119). Some are threatened by having no precedent to guide them, or conversely being expected to follow uncongenial or rigid procedures. Any of these factors contribute to stress, which is best relieved by identifying the problem and discussing it through with an appropriate person, even if such a person needs some

96

careful hunting out. Bottling problems up helps neither the newcomer nor the establishment.

For those working overseas there are further particular pressures that may push them towards the slippery slope. They generally have to do with living and working in an environment where:

- *Attitudes* are different, especially professional ones. You may be working to different standards and a different timescale in a place with different ethics and values. Recognize these things and talk them through with someone.
- *Privacy and autonomy* may be markedly reduced. To be the subject of continual scrutiny wherever you go, and yet not be free to go where you choose, can be very stressful. There are often small ways you can increase your range once you have recognized the problem.
- *Your role is very different*. It may be unclear, unfamiliar and perhaps uncongenial. To go from being an established leader to finding yourself an insignificant newcomer can be hard, especially if the skills you are bringing do not seem to be wanted or valued. Acknowledging this may help to take the sting out of it.
- *Your sense of identity may be shaken*. If you stay long enough to be at home in the culture you may not feel you belong to either the new or your previous one. Bilingual children may be more at home in their host country than the 'home' one, which can be a real stress for their parents. Talk it out with someone, don't bottle it up.
- *Violence*, police surveillance and political uncertainty are commonplace. To be living always in a state of maximum alertness is very hard on the nerves. Make sure you take all the 'R and R' you are entitled to.

Signs of stress

As stimulus turns to stress, work output gradually lowers, generally accompanied by a compulsion to keep working. Guidelines for healthy living, especially those regarding recreation and leisure time, are ignored 'just for once' or 'until I catch up'. Often, however, the person never does make up lost ground and a vicious circle develops.

Healthy and unhealthy life patterns can be represented by the two triangles in Figure 6.

A person who slides into the second type of lifestyle continues to work harder and put in longer hours with less overall effect. Those who continue in this way are likely to lose concentration, have memory lapses and seem 'less alive'. They may become irritable and humourless, even anxious and depressed. They become more rigid in thought

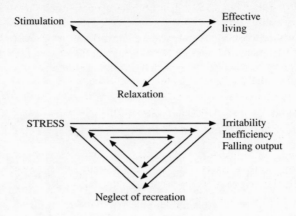

Figure 6 Stress triangles

and behaviour, have a narrowed focus and seem to lose their normal elasticity and the ability to recover when pulled apart. All these things may be more easily detected by their friends than by themselves. More than this, their whole immune system may be weakened so that their resistance to infection, including malaria, is lowered.

If at this stage no break is taken, a return to normal can only be achieved by total removal from the situation and a period of lengthy recovery. Fortunately, you can avoid a decline into burn-out or breakdown by taking time away from work and the demands of others, and by absorbing yourself in some quite different activity.

Lifestyle review

Learn to recognize when your personal efficiency curve begins to decline, and then give your lifestyle a shake-out to prevent burn-out.

The aim of reviewing lifestyle is to help you generate options so that you can make appropriate choices and take charge of your life. It is designed to get you off that slippery slope and back towards peak performance. Look at the following:

- *Your lifestyle.* Are your basic needs being met, do you get enough sleep, exercise and food? Have you any time for friends and fellowship – and don't forget to include some fun too. Is finance a problem?
- *Your relaxation.* What do you do to 'switch off'? Chances are you have dropped your hobbies and interests – take them up again, quickly!

- *Work satisfaction*. If you are reasonably content with 70% of your work time you can probably cope with the other 30%. If the ratio is worse, try making some adjustments, and also consider in what other area of your life you can find some fulfilment.
- *Relationships*. Are they kept in good repair? You may need to give more time and attention to some of them.
- *Your expectations* of yourself and of others. Perhaps you need to go for what is 'good enough', rather than perfect. This does not mean accepting slip-shod standards but simply doing things in a way that is adequate, i.e. good enough for the purpose of the task.
- *Areas of uncertainty*. Check out any information that seems ambiguous or unclear. Make clear statements and requests yourself. Tell the relevant people that you are stressed – don't assume that they know – and tell them plainly.

Stress strategies

Just as one person's stress can be another person's stimulus, so patterns of relaxation differ greatly between different types of people. What one person finds relaxing may seem boring – or incomprehensible – to someone else. The answer is to discover your own coping strategies and find out what forms of relaxation will be both effective and possible in your overseas location. Some will have to train themselves to become detached from the 'Protestant Work Ethic'. Others won't find this difficult at all once they 'have permission', or can quote doctor's advice.

Here are some further practical suggestions:

- *Avoid* self-medication with 'leisure' drugs, tranquillizers, nicotine or too much alcohol, coffee and caffeine-containing drinks.
- *Do* get enough sleep, change of occupation and exercise.
- *Do* talk your situation and feelings through with someone.
- *Do* develop an absorbing hobby or interest outside your work.
- *Don't*: carry on working if you get sick – better to rest up before you get really laid up; *don't* delay taking time off; *don't* neglect your friendships; *don't* forget to laugh – it's a good way of defusing stress; *don't* forget to take exercise – that regular walk, jog, hour in the pool or game of volleyball can help to unjangle your nerves.

And finally . . .

Someone has worked out that we ourselves can help to solve 50% of our problems, another 30% can be eased if we have the courage to ask for help, and only 20% will remain despite what we do. Although we can't alter this 20% we can change our own attitude by a combination of acceptance, prayer or spiritual discipline. When our attitude alters, our stress diminishes – especially if we take appropriate steps to deal with the 80% we can do something about.

Most important of all is to keep a sense of proportion, to nurture a sense of humour, to avoid fatigue and to remember to switch off regularly by switching on to some form of recreation and relaxation. Even taking time to slow down, to do some deep breathing and to stretch, then relax every muscle group from toe to head is beneficial, as are more formal relaxation tapes, at least for some people.

Anyone who has never been stressed has probably never lived life to the full. Only by living to our particular limits do we know what these limits are, but wise and healthy people, having discovered these, do not often, or for long, *push themselves or allow others to push them beyond their threshold.* Learning to say No (in an appropriate way) to whatever requests put you over your personal stress level is the best way of coping with it.

Finally, with the subject of stress so topical in our culture, we need to make sure we do not get stressed about being stressed, or worry we are about to have a nervous breakdown. Some gentle humour, self-detachment and remembrance of friends who have been able to tough it out when circumstances demanded it, can help us to keep things in perspective, and tide us over difficult times.

If despite all this you really feel that stress is getting the better of you, do let someone know. It is much quicker to put things right at this stage than to let them drag on. Consider having a personal debrief on returning home (see page 145), and remember that it is no disgrace to be 'honourably wounded' when you are serving abroad, or at home, and that wounds do heal.

HEIGHT, HEAT, COLD, SUN

Altitude

Many travellers can't resist the temptation of climbing a near (or distant) mountain peak or fitting in a high-altitude trek while the opportunity is there. Although the rewards are great, so are the potential risks, especially if your time available is short, your preparation and equipment limited or you don't want to appear a wimp by failing to keep up with your companions.

Mountains carry several hazards. The risk of *accidents* is greater, most of which can be prevented by careful preparation, common sense and not being in an undue hurry. The risks of exposure to *sun*, *wind*, and *cold* are also greater (see pages 103–8).

Acute mountain sickness (AMS, altitude sickness)

A common condition in mountains is *acute mountain sickness* (AMS). This does not just affect the elderly and unfit. Indeed, the young volunteer, able to climb fast and hoping to do a quick ascent before returning to the UK (or before the weather turns) is at the greatest risk.

AMS in its milder forms affects about 50% of unacclimatized travellers at 3,500 metres and 80–90% at 5,000 metres. The danger of AMS is that it can progress quickly and unpredictably to life-threatening High Altitude Pulmonary Oedema (HAPE), which mainly affects the breathing, and to High Altitude Cerebral Oedema (HACE), which largely affects the brain. HAPE, especially, may come on with little warning.

As a general rule, watch out for AMS in any journey to above about 3,000 metres, especially if you have not acclimatized for a day or two at an intermediate altitude. Symptoms may be delayed and not become apparent for twenty-four to forty-eight hours. A minority of people are affected from about 2,000 metres upwards.

If you are planning to trek or climb above 3,000 metres you should familiarize yourself with the symptoms of Table 5.

Table 5 Acute mountain sickness

Benign form	*Severe form*
	High altitude cerebral oedema (HACE)
Headache	Pounding headache unrelieved by pain-killers
Loss of appetite/nausea	Drowsiness, confusion or hallucinations leading to coma
Dizziness	Unsteady, staggering walk
Disturbed sleep	Double vision
	High altitude pulmonary oedema (HAPE)
Breathlessness on mild exertion	Breathlessness at rest
Irregular 'sighing' breathing	Cough with or without sputum, possibly bloodstained
	Blue lips, sometimes with mild fever
ACTION:	ACTION:
Stay at same (or lower) altitude for 48 hours. Descend if symptoms worsen	Descend without delay to lower altitude until symptoms substantially improve

Prevention of AMS

- Before travelling to heights above 3,000 metres, stay for one or two days at that height or just below. *Then make a slow ascent.*
- Above 3,000 metres spend each *night* not more than 300 metres above the last. One full rest-day should be allowed every two or

three days or every 1,000 metres. Where overnight shelters do not allow this, take extra care. Mount Kilimanjaro (5,895 metres) is a case in point.

- Try to follow the maxim 'climb high, but sleep lower'. Symptoms often come on at night and can be masked by tiredness and exhaustion and not be noticed by your companions.

- Drink plenty of extra fluids, as dehydration quickly occurs at high altitude.

- Acetazolamide (Diamox) helps to prevent and treat AMS. It can be started at any time, but consider taking it if you are travelling straight to a height of 3,000 metres or are starting to climb from that altitude. Carry it on any high-altitude trek. The dose is either 250 mg twice daily or one 500 mg slow-release tablet daily. Start one day before travelling and continue while climbing. Take this before flying into any high-altitude airport over 3,000 metres including La Paz, Cuzco and Lhasa. Diamox makes you pass more urine than usual and you should avoid it if sensitive to sulpha drugs. It has to be prescribed by a doctor.

- Leaders of high-altitude tours and expeditions must follow the above guidelines and set a pace that the slowest member can keep to. Speak up early if the speed or rate of ascent is more than you can manage.

Treatment of AMS

- If signs of benign AMS develop, remain at the same altitude until symptoms resolve. Take paracetamol. If there is no clear improvement over the next few hours, descend at least 500 metres. *Never continue to climb higher if you have symptoms of AMS.*

- *Descend* as quickly as possible if symptoms of HAPE or HACE are suspected (see Table 4). Whether by staggering at the side of a companion or being carried on an improvised stretcher, descend to an altitude where symptoms largely disappear.

- In HAPE and HACE, in addition use oxygen and a hyperbaric chamber (e.g. Gamow or Certec Bag) if available, but don't delay descending. Give dexamethasone 8 mg, then 4 mg every six hours in HACE, and nifedipine (Adalat) 20 mg slow-release four times daily in HAPE. Seek urgent medical advice.

Special situations

- *The elderly.* Those over about 70 and anyone with known heart or lung problems or taking beta blocking drugs: get detailed medical advice before travelling over 2,000 metres, and go back down the hill if symptoms get worse.

- *Asthma.* Asthma is unpredictable at high altitude, but most do well: fewer allergens makes it better in some, cold dry air occasionally worse in others. Asthma does not make AMS more likely, but an asthmatic attack (or chest infection) in addition to AMS will add to the overall risk. Those with asthma need medical assessment if travelling above 3,000 metres, and should always have inhalers with them.

- *Children.* Children are probably no more likely to get severe symptoms than adults, but younger children cannot explain the way they are feeling. Sensible guidelines include: children under two on treks should not sleep above 2,000 metres; children two to seven should not sleep above 3,000 metres; children over seven should be watched with extra care for signs of AMS. Diamox should not be used in children.

- *Headache and insomnia* at high altitude. Current research suggests that paracetamol and aspirin are safe for headache, and temazepam 10 mg safe for insomnia on all but the highest expeditions.

Table 6 Heights in metres above sea level of some high-altitude cities and airports

Lhasa, Tibet	3,900
La Paz, Bolivia	3,700 (airport 4,000)
Cusco, Peru	3,300
Toluca, Mexico	2,900
Quito, Ecuador	2,800
Cochabamba, Bolivia	2,600
Addis Ababa	2,600
Bogota, Colombia	2,600

Cold

Cold injury usually occurs either when there is a strong wind or you are wet through or both. It can occur rapidly if you are injured or immobilized at high altitude. Minor degrees are common if you expose your skin to the sun when climbing in the hills during the day, then become chilled overnight. Blood becomes diverted to the inflamed skin so further reducing your body temperature.

Hypothermia occurs when the core body temperature falls below 35 °C. Thin young men, children and the elderly are at greatest risk.

Symptoms and signs that your body is seriously cooling down resemble drunkenness. They also include a feeling of intense cold, uncontrollable shivering, tiredness and listlessness. When walking it takes increasing effort to keep going and to avoid stumbling. There may be slowness in responding to the comments and questions of companions, angry or confused responses, or denial that anything is amiss. Be alert for any companion who has stopped, rested or apparently fallen asleep.

Signs of *frostbite* are intense pain at the site – usually cheeks, chins, ears, nose, hands and feet – followed, on the cheeks, by hard whitening of the skin. Check any area that has registered pain as soon as possible.

Frostnip, which can quickly lead to frostbite, causes numbness and whitening of the skin (most commonly on the cheeks) that may pass almost unnoticed.

Prevention

Keep dry. Do this by wearing a waterproof outer layer, which will also protect against the wind. Prevent excessive sweating on the inner layer – best done by wearing cotton or string underwear and leaving the neck and wrists open for ventilation, unless the temperature is far below freezing.

Wear several layers of clothes, each one being larger than the one below so that there are no tight fits. In this way layers of air are trapped, so increasing insulation, and any dampness from outer or inner layers tends to spread less. Cover your head using a hat with ear-flaps, wear a scarf and use warm mittens rather than gloves.

Set up a 'buddy system' where each of a pair watches out for warning signs in the other.

Treatment

Treatment of hypothermia consists of *gradual but sustained rewarming without delay*. Remove your companion from the wind or wet, take off any wet clothes, give a warm sugary drink and share your body heat in a sleeping bag. Do not give alcohol. Supervise for at least twenty-four hours. If symptoms are severe (e.g. incoherent with clouded consciousness), medivac without delay and with extreme care.

Treat *frostnip* by rewarming, e.g. with warm breath in a gloved hand, but do not rub the skin. Treat *frostbite* by protecting the affected part, rapid rewarming in water at, but not above, 40 °C and evacuation as soon as possible. Avoid using dry external heat sources such as stoves. Strong painkillers will be needed, especially as rewarming starts.

Heat

Your body normally takes fourteen to twenty-one days to get used to a hotter climate. During that time the sweat glands become more efficient and water and salt regulation improves. In these first two to three weeks, risks and discomfort are greatest. This is especially the case in the elderly or those who are overweight or unfit. Risks are obviously increased during strenuous physical activity in the sun, or in a hot and humid atmosphere.

Quite apart from heat injury (see below), hot climates can cause or worsen constipation, and kidney stones are more likely to develop. But these problems can be *minimized* if you regularly *keep up your fluids*.

Remember that coffee and alcohol tend to cause rather than cure dehydration, so keep to clean water or soft drinks.

The normal body temperature is 37 °C (98.6 °F) or slightly below. The normal fluid intake of an adult in a temperate climate is 2–2.5 litres per day. This can increase to at least 12 litres per day in a very hot climate.

There are two forms of illness caused by heat. *Heat exhaustion* is common and easily treated; *heat stroke* (also known as sunstroke) is rare and much more serious.

Table 7 Types of heat injury

	Heat exhaustion	Heat stroke
Symptoms	Weak, exhausted, poor concentration, thirst, headache, possibly muscle cramps	Confused, drowsy, vomiting, sometimes convulsions, may lead to coma
Skin	Flushed, moist	Hot, usually dry
Temperature	Normal or slightly raised	High, usually above 39 °C
Pulse	Normal or slightly raised	Fast, e.g. 100 per minute or above

Prevention

This is mostly common sense:

- Don't 'rush the tropics', i.e. take life at an easy pace.
- Wear cool, cotton, loose-fitting clothing, plus a hat in the sun.
- Keep up your fluid intake, so that your urine remains pale. This may mean drinking 3, 4 or 5 times more than usual.
- Add salt to your food (but don't take salt tablets).
- Consider using ORS (see page 50) when it's very hot or humid.
- Be cautious with exercise and don't spend long hours walking in the heat until confidently acclimatized.
- Stay in the shade whenever there is an option.
- Take extra care with children, including having adequate fluids and methods of shading in tropical traffic jams.

Immediate treatment

Ensure that you (or the victim):

- are placed in the shade, wearing the minimum of clothes;
- are gently fanned or sponged with a cool wet cloth;
- drink as much as possible without this causing nausea (soft drinks are ideal, plus one or two packets of ORS);
- have the body temperature monitored;
- receive emergency medical care if not improving or if coma develops.

Remember, heat stroke is a *medical emergency*.

Finally, also remember that certain infectious diseases, especially malaria, can mimic or worsen heat injury.

Sunburn

On returning from an assignment overseas, friends and acquaintances may show more interest in your sun tan, or lack of it, than in what you have actually been doing. Most expatriates soon realize that the sun is largely something to be avoided, except when carefully controlled. However, sunburn is still common, both on holidays and outdoor work projects, or in the case of children, forgetful or distracted parents.

Too much sun, apart from causing sunburn in the short term, also leads to an increased risk of skin cancer in the long term. Experts tell us that getting sunburnt, having irregular high exposure to the sun and being strongly exposed as children are the three main risk factors for melanoma. You should therefore avoid *both* getting sunburnt *and* any prolonged exposure, which ages and damages the skin. It's a cause of regret to many that 'The bronzed beauty of today is the wrinkled prune of tomorrow.'

Sunlight contains two main forms of ultraviolet light. UVB is largely what causes sunburn, as well as some forms of skin damage, including thickened skin patches (solar keratoses) and non-melanoma skin cancer (see page 187). The other form, UVA, appears to be the main cause of melanoma.

Most sun lotions protect against UVA and UVB, but always check, especially with brands you buy in developing countries. One word of caution: experts are not yet convinced that sun creams, even those that protect against both UVA and UVB, are very effective at protecting against skin cancer, even though they reduce sunburn. So the message remains: avoid getting sunburnt, and avoid prolonged exposure even if you use sun creams.

As far as holidays go, you should be able to develop a modest tan without unduly damaging your skin provided you take a few common-sense precautions. The famous Australian mnemonic 'Slip, Slap, Slop' is a good start:

- Slip on a shirt.
- Slap on a hat.
- Slop on some sun screen.

Guidelines for skin protection

Remember that:

- *The power of the sun* increases rapidly the nearer you get to the equator, the higher the altitude at which you are living and the nearer it is to the middle of the day. Most burning takes place between 10 a.m. and 3 p.m.

- *Reflecting surfaces*, including water, *greatly* increase the burning power of ultraviolet light, meaning you can still burn on a cloudy day. This applies to sand (beaches and deserts), sea and snow.

    Ultraviolet light strongly penetrates water, meaning you are not safe swimming or snorkelling.

- *Expose yourself gradually* – starting with fifteen to twenty minutes and increasing by a few minutes each day. If the skin starts to look red or feels sore, go into the shade at once.

- *Note danger times for sunburn.* Snorkelling: wear a shirt and use a water-resistant sun lotion. Travelling in small boats without shade, or the backs of lorries or on motor bikes: remember to cover up, not forgetting your neck. Any situation when you are in the sun, and a cool, seductive breeze blows against your skin: you are just as much at risk.

- *Apply sun lotion every one to two hours* and again after swimming or heavy exercise. Apply the lotion thoroughly, evenly and frequently, especially if you swim or are sweating a lot. If your skin is very fair, start with a protection factor of 20 to 24, otherwise 15 to 18 will be sufficient. Preferably use a water-resistant brand if you intend to swim, snorkel or do water sports. Always use a cream that protects against UVA and UVB.

- If you frequently have to walk or work in the sun, *wear a wide-brimmed hat* or use an umbrella or headscarf, keep your arms covered and apply sun cream to your face and lips. These precautions will also help to protect against the long-term effects of the sun. Finally, don't forget your arm resting out of the vehicle window!

- *Children* on tropical beaches or at swimming pools, especially if fair or freckled, *need careful protection*. It is sad when a child's only memory of the holiday-of-a-lifetime is the agony of sunburn. Spend time explaining why protection is important so that you are working together on the problem.

- *Babies* should never be placed in direct sunlight.

- *Certain parts of the body* need extra protection, especially the lips, any depigmented patches or areas only rarely exposed.

- *Wear sunglasses.* Check that they protect against ultraviolet light and have a British Standard Label or Kitemark – or the equivalent for the country you buy them in.

- *Some medicines* increase the tendency of the skin to burn, especially tetracyclines, doxycycline and certain diuretics. So do some cosmetics.

- *Treat severe sunburn with calamine*, rest and aspirin (those over 12) or paracetamol. Keep blistered areas clean. See a doctor if the burn is very severe, or blisters start to get infected. Avoid the sun until the skin is thoroughly healed.

- If you suffer from *cold sores on your face*, the tropical sun can make them worse. Use plenty of sun lotion, including lip-salve. If they start to develop, apply acyclovir cream (Zovirax) at the first sign of trouble.

CREATURES THAT BITE AND STING

Snakes

Serious snake bite is rare among travellers. Comparatively few snakes are poisonous, and more often than not only manage to inject a small amount of venom. Even if venom has been injected, serious symptoms usually take hours, not minutes, to develop. A poisonous bite will usually show two fang marks, quite separate from a row of small tooth marks, which are not dangerous (see Figure 7).

Prevention of bites

By following a few rules snake bite can almost always be prevented. Snakes attack when provoked, virtually never attacking if you keep still. One exception is sleeping on the ground in rural areas (especially in South Asia), when snakes may seek out your body warmth. If living in areas where poisonous snakes are known to live, follow these precautions:

- When walking outside, especially in long grass or thick undergrowth, carry a stick to beat the path in front of you. Wear boots or strong shoes and trousers. At night, carry a torch as well.
- Keep the grass and other vegetation short around your house.
- Never put your hand into holes, onto or under rock ledges or anywhere you cannot easily see if a snake is lurking.
- Wear gloves to collect firewood or logs if snakes are known to be common.
- Avoid climbing trees or rocks covered in dense foliage.
- Take care walking under overhanging trees or bushes.
- If camping in an area where snakes are common, try to sleep on a bed or raised platform, at least one foot off the ground.
- Avoid swimming in rivers matted with vegetation, in mangroves or muddy estuaries (because of sea snakes).
- Inside the house, check dark corners before reaching into them.
- If you come across a snake, stay absolutely still until it slinks off.
- Never handle snakes even if they appear harmless – or dead.

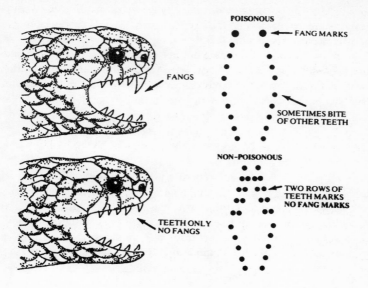

Figure 7 Poisonous and non-poisonous snakes: telling the difference

Symptoms of snake bite

Everyone who thinks they may have been bitten by a snake is extremely anxious, and signs of anxiety mimic the symptoms of certain forms of snake bite. Signs that suggest venom has actually entered the body include the following: bleeding from the nose, or areas distant from the bite; blood-stained vomit; dark urine; swelling spreading up the limb from the bite; drooping of the eyelids; difficulty swallowing or breathing; slow, irregular pulse or falling blood pressure; paralysis, marked drowsiness or unconsciousness.

Treatment

Give maximum reassurance and keep the affected body part *as still as possible*, preferably below heart level. Any remaining venom should be wiped off the skin. In the case of a bitten limb apply a firm, broad bandage along its entire length, splinting the limb if possible. This should not be too tight in the case of snakes that cause local swelling such as vipers and rattlesnakes. The limb should not be moved or exercised. A good technique is to apply a pad, ideally of rubber, over the bite and under the firm bandaging. Only if this is really impracticable should you apply a tourniquet, and only then if you are sure the snake injected a neurotoxin (i.e. cobras, kraits, mambas, sea snakes). This must be tight and be slowly released after twenty or thirty minutes under medical supervision.

Go to the nearest health facility known to have antisnake venom, taking the dead snake if possible but not handling it directly. The anti-venom should be given intravenously by an experienced health worker only if there are one or more signs of definite envenoming as listed under symptoms above. Adrenalin must be on hand in case of an allergic reaction. Pain should be treated with paracetamol, and not aspirin, which may worsen any bleeding tendency.

You should avoid cutting, sucking, electric shock therapy and traditional remedies such as the 'black stone'.

It is only worth taking anti-venom with you if you are going on an expedition or living in a remote area where poisonous snakes are known to be common. Even then you must be sure it will be effective against the snakes you are likely to come across, meaning it is usually best to obtain it in-country or from a regional manufacturer. See Appendix D, page 202 for sources of information.

Leeches

These are common in jungle areas and monsoon forests, usually lying in wait by the path. The writer, when inexperienced, once had fifty leeches attached at one time when trekking in monsoon Nepal. Leeches are dangerous only when attached in numbers over a period of hours, when they can cause marked loss of blood.

Prevent leeches from biting you by wearing stout footwear and trousers tucked in at the ankles to boots or thick socks. Apply a *DEET*-containing insecticide to your skin and soak trousers and socks in *DEET* or permethrin before going out. Salt or industrial spirit will cause a leech to detach itself in anguish, but the wound bleeds and itches for some time afterwards and occasionally gets infected if the biting part of the leech remains in the skin. Avoid swimming in forest lakes or rivers where water leeches are known to occur.

Poisonous fish and jellyfish

Some fish have poisonous spines that can detach if you brush against them (e.g. when diving in coral reefs) or tread on them (as with sting rays in shallow seas). Fragments of tentacles can become painfully embedded after brushing against poisonous jellyfish, with potentially fatal results in the case of sea wasps and box jellyfish (commonest in northern Australia and the Philippines).

Prevent these hazards by getting expert local advice when swimming, snorkelling or scuba diving in unfamiliar areas. Assess risk factor by location, time of year and weather conditions. Consider wearing Lycra stinger suits. Avoid sting rays by shuffling rather than stepping in sandy water where they are known to occur.

The *symptoms* of envenoming include sudden severe pain, swelling and, in more serious cases, diarrhoea, vomiting, sweating or difficulty breathing, which spells urgent transfer to hospital.

First-aid treatment is important. Immerse stings from rays or other fish in water as hot as you can stand. In the case of spines and tentacles from fish and jellyfish, remove these with tweezers, having urgently applied vinegar or dilute acetic acid first. In the case of box jellyfish, CSL Chironex anti-venom must be given immediately.

Sea urchin fragments can easily become embedded in the sole of your foot in tropical seas. Smaller ones gradually absorb and disappear; others can be removed by forceps after paring down the skin, having first softened it with salicylic acid.

Scorpions and spiders

These usually bite only if annoyed. Avoid reaching into unlit corners, and shake any shoes before putting them on. Don't walk barefoot in the house or anywhere else if scorpions are known to be present. Check your bedding.

In scorpion-infested areas, camp sites should be checked and cleared of scorpion tunnels before pitching tents.

Most scorpion bites are very painful; only a few are dangerous, Central and South American, North African and some Indian species being the most notorious. An injection of local anaesthetic (e.g. lignocaine 2%) or a strong painkiller can be given. EMLA cream, a local anaesthetic cream available on prescription in the UK, reduces the pain. Children or anyone seriously affected should go to hospital.

Spiders, with a few exceptions such as the Black Widow or Australian Redback, are rarely dangerous. Prevent and treat in the same way as for scorpions.

Bees and wasps

There are two potential dangers for travellers. One is the rare attack by swarms of bees, usually in thundery weather (run fast or dive into water). The other danger, more common and easier to deal with, is the single sting if you are hypersensitive to bees, wasps or hornets.

If in the past you have had a severe reaction to a sting or have developed progressively worse reactions, take and keep with you at least two self-injectable ampoules of adrenaline (epinephrine) such as Epipen, or Epipen Junior for children, available in the UK on prescription. Also wear a Medic Alert bracelet or pendant (arrange through your local chemist or phone 020–7833 3043).

Nettle rash accompanied by swelling of the lips or tongue or wheezing are signs that you should use adrenalin straight away. In addition take a double dose of an antihistamine (e.g. chlorpheniramine, Piriton).

Fleas

Fleas are small jumping creatures 2–3 mm long, compressed sideways. They cause itchy bites, often in children, and are found anywhere on the body but commonly around the ankles. They are usually found in association with domestic pets.

Prevent flea bites by applying flea powder regularly to dogs and other domestic mammals. Where living accommodation is infested with fleas, carry out the following: apply flea powder to all areas where fleas are found; air all bedding and mattresses, and if severe soak your sheets in permethrin; sleep at least two feet above floor level having first checked your bedclothes, body clothes and body surface for fleas. Treat any animals: be patient – flea populations detached from their animal hosts eventually die out.

Jiggers

These fleas are found in many parts of Africa and parts of South America. They cause symptoms by burrowing into the toes or feet and forming pea-sized swellings that may ulcerate.

You can prevent them by wearing good shoes or boots when walking in areas where they are known to occur. The treatment is to ask someone experienced in dealing with them to remove the jigger with a sterile needle. Apply antiseptic after removal to prevent infection.

Lice

Lice are crawling insects 2–3 mm long found in the scalp, body hair or pubic region (crab lice).

They lay eggs, and the empty eggshells, known as nits, are dandruff-like objects attached firmly to the hair shafts. Head lice are very common in the tropics, often affecting expatriate and local children.

Head lice can be treated with permethrin 1% lotion. After washing and drying your hair, apply according to maker's instructions, leave for ten minutes then rinse and dry. In the UK and some other areas, lice have developed resistance to permethrin. Good alternatives are malathion or carbaryl. Whichever you use, re-treat after seven days.

For pubic lice use malathion or carbaryl. Apply to all body hair, not just the pubic area; include the beard but exclude the scalp. With all these preparations, avoid contact with eyes and mucous membranes.

Lice are *prevented* by good personal hygiene and by avoiding intimate contact with those infected – not, of course, easy to ascertain in advance!

Lice on clothing can be dealt with by washing the clothes in hot water (over 55 °C) or sealing clothes in a bag for two weeks, when all the lice will die out.

Ticks

If you notice a small nodule or dusky-coloured bump on your skin not apparently there a few hours or days before, this could be a tick. They attach themselves to the body, usually after you have been walking through vegetation or in close proximity to animals. Ticks feed on blood, gradually enlarging and eventually falling off.

They can, however, cause disease (tick-borne encephalitis, tick-borne relapsing fever, typhus and Lyme disease). Where they are known to occur, check your skin or that of your companion each evening. *Remove* them by tweezers using the following technique: grasp firmly, press inwards, rock slowly from side to side, and gently detach taking care not to leave the head behind.

Prevent tick bites by using insect repellent on the skin or soaking trousers and socks in DEET or permethrin. Tuck your trouser legs into thick socks.

Mites (causing scabies)

Mites are tiny creatures causing this common skin condition, frequently caught by expatriate children who go to a local school or by health workers and others in close contact with the local population. *Symptoms* include severe itching, especially at night. Scabies quickly spreads to other family members.

Treat it by applying permethrin 5% dermal cream or an 0.5% malathion preparation. Apply to whole body up to neck line, leave for 12 to 24 hours, then wash off. Avoid contact with eyes and mucous membranes. Benzyl benzoate may be the only preparation you can buy in remoter areas. Use it in the same way but remember it can sting, especially if the skin is chapped or cut. A single dose of ivermectin 0.2 mg/kg (the same drug used to treat river blindness) is effective in scabies. All sheets, blankets, linen and clothes with which your skin has been in contact should be washed in hot water and dried if possible in full sun. Itching may persist for up to two weeks after the scabies is cured. If it still continues, treat again or see a doctor.

Bed bugs

These usually bite at night, often leaving a scattering or a line of intensely itchy bites on exposed parts of the skin. They also hide in benches, for example at railway and bus stations, leading to a line of bites on the back of the thighs.

Prevent them by choosing clean accommodation. Bed bugs gradually disappear if you put your bed in the sun or outside during the day. Keeping a light on at night discourages them from biting, and sleeping under a well-tucked-in permethrin-impregnated bed-net will stop them from reaching you. *Treat* bites by *not scratching* them and with an antihistamine by mouth (e.g. chlorpheniramine or terfenadine; see page 198). Bed bugs do not spread any serious diseases.

Tumbu fly (mango fly, putsi fly)

If living in tropical Africa or, less commonly, in South America (the home of the similar bot-fly) and you develop the symptoms of a painful boil, make sure there is no maggot inside it. This first betrays its identity by two black dots near the boil's surface. The larva enters the skin from eggs laid by tumbu flies on clothes that have been left outside to dry.

This condition is *prevented* by hot-ironing all clothes left outside to dry in those parts of the tropics where it is common or, better, drying clothes inside or on a clothes line in full sun.

It is 'cured' by placing a drop of oil on the boil overnight and gently squeezing out the maggot. The squeamish do best to wait in the next room.

Other biting insects

Here are a few more that can cause grief to travellers:

- *Assassin bugs* (kissing bugs, cone-nosed bugs, vinchucas). These cause Chagas disease in South America (see page 157).
- *Chiggers* (not to be confused with Jiggers). These are small red mites that cause skin irritation. They are common in East Asia, the Pacific Islands and South America. They can cause Scrub Typhus (see page 193). Use DEET insect repellent and tuck trousers into socks where chiggers are known to occur.
- *Nairobi fly*. This insect (actually a blister beetle) is common in East Africa in the rainy season. It is about half a centimetre long and is red, black and dark green. You should flick it off the skin and not crush it because it can cause intense skin irritation when squashed on the skin, especially near the eye. Apply calamine lotion or mild hydrocortisone to the skin and take antihistamines. Seek medical advice if the eye is severely inflamed.
- *Sandflies*. These small insects cause intensely itchy bites in hot climates. They spread leishmaniasis (see page 175), and the less serious sandfly fever.
- *Tsetse flies*. These spread sleeping sickness (see page 187).

HOW TO SURVIVE AN OVERSEAS ASSIGNMENT

Hopefully you will have read the section on preparing for an overseas assignment (page 23), which discusses culture shock. There is supposed to be a grave in India with the following epitaph: 'Here lies the body of a person who tried to hurry the East.'

Perhaps the main secret of coping with a new country is to identify an appropriate pace to life, and then adapt your personal rhythms accordingly. This will be based on your own happy mean between the laid-back fatalism of the local population on the one hand, and the reasonable goals and expectations of your job, expedition or travel plans on the other.

Take shopping, for example, or getting a visa or even buying petrol. This may take half a day or even longer. You have a choice of staying on home time, being a frustrated foreigner and upsetting those around you, or just switching into a different gear, allowing the adrenalin to drain away and sitting or standing (un)comfortably, with a book and supply of safe drinks until your turn comes. You may make two or three new friendships before the day's finished – perhaps just as important as the project proposal or letter home you haven't finished writing yet.

Here are some survival tips.

The climate

When first landing at a tropical airport children sometimes wonder why the pilot hasn't turned the aircraft engines off, only to discover that the blast of hot air comes from the country, not the plane. It takes two to three weeks for your body to partially adapt to the new temperature, longer if the climate is humid. Even then you are unlikely to be able to maintain the pace of life you are used to. So allow much longer than usual for normal physical and mental activities.

When first arriving in a hot country you will obviously lose large amounts of fluid through perspiration. This means you must replace both fluid and salt by drinking large amounts, more often, and adding salt to your meals. A good alternative is to make up your own rehydration solution (see page 50). Although this is normally used to replace fluid lost in diarrhoea, it can be very reviving during a long, hot tropical day, especially in the absence of safe, soft drinks. You should avoid using salt tablets.

Wearing appropriate clothes can also help you to acclimatize. They should be *loose fitting*, so allowing air to circulate; *absorbent*, so allowing you to cool more easily (100% cotton is ideal, silk for the rich and famous), and *pale in colour* so they reflect rather than absorb the heat. Acclimatization is slower in the elderly, the pregnant, the overweight or if you are very exhausted. Men acclimatize slightly quicker than women, in whom undiagnosed anaemia can slow the process further.

Language

There is nothing so frustrating as not being able to communicate with the people whom you have left home and luxuries to live alongside. Only the lucky few can fully learn a new language on the job. If you are going on an overseas assignment of say two years or more you must ensure adequate time for language study before starting any official tasks. During this time language learning should take priority over everything else. Even after this phase is over language slots must be built into your timetable so that you are able to continue studying. It is worth discussing this in detail with your sending organization at an early stage, so that everyone has the same expectations. A Linguaphone or BBC course can help *before you go*, as can getting hold of a phrase book or user-friendly language manual.

Some survival tips

• *Take time off/out.* Within the first week of arriving, work out a method for safeguarding your leisure. Set priority-time for rest and recreation and write it into your diary, giving it equal priority to meetings and work deadlines. Establish a balance between your work and your time off. Draw boundaries so that work does not gradually take over everything else.

For those working overseas the very minimum time off should be one, preferably one and a half days per week, one long weekend in six, five weeks per year. In refugee and civil war situations the weekend should become a week taken completely off-site. Of course this advice may be tricky to arrange if work is very heavy, you are single and there is no obvious travelling companion, or it takes hassle, danger and 48 hours to get anywhere you can really relax. But the hidden dangers of just keeping going may in the end cause you more trouble.

If there is no obvious place to escape to, and nothing to do when off-duty or away from work it is even more essential early on in your assigment to devise ways of relaxing on-site and constructing a bolt-hole. Devise a system of protecting your personal privacy.

Expats who work all week, then use Sunday for church or voluntary activities, are high-risk candidates for burn-out. Even back-packers and travellers will need at least one 'domestic' day per week, or the delights of the road and new travel experiences will irritate rather than stimulate.

Leisure time needs to be built into both your contract and the understanding of your senior colleagues – even if it may not be understood in the local culture. It also needs to be programmed into your personal and family expectations. Mothers (and fathers) of young children are a priority sub-group!

Unless you give top attention to time out, exhaustion and burn-out will eventually occur, even though they may take time to declare themselves, often after a period of unproductive guilt-driven activity.

Here are three tendencies that spell 'caution, take action': becoming an *alcoholic* (see below); becoming a *workaholic* – only too easy in the absence of any obvious alternative; becoming a *computerholic* – when on coming home in the evening you nod to the spouse and kids and then disappear into your 'cave' to play computer games or surf the Net till midnight.

- *Have varied social contacts*
  In isolated postings it is common for everyone to work, play, relax and even pray together. Sooner or later (usually sooner), relationships and personal contentment begin to break down.

  Cultivate friendships outside your immediate circle, with local families and acquaintances and with expatriates who hold differing viewpoints or interests. Try to *make it possible* to take time out from the compound, campus or immediate surroundings.

- *Discover leisure interests.* Many birdwatchers and stamp collectors have first developed their interest overseas, as have mountaineers, geologists, novelists and painters. The customs, culture and art forms of many developing countries are a rich mine of interest. Board games, reading, the BBC World Service, or BBC World TV, CNN, joining or starting a Scottish dancing club, reading the *Guardian Weekly* or the *Sunday Observer* help to keep you fresh and integrated, as does watching funny videos sent from home.

- *Take part in regular sport.* Swimming is often ideal, crocodiles and bilharzia allowing. Walking, tennis, volleyball, squash and badminton may be possible. Some expatriates go jogging, despite the looks of surprise from the local population. Regular physical exercise, ideally at least once or twice a week, not only helps you to keep fit but also reduces stress.

- *Become a writer.* Some people find that at times of severe frustration, difficulty or excitement, adopting the mindset of a novelist or journalist can be helpful. Half-day waits in the visa office or close shaves at an armed roadblock or street demo become prime source material.

- *Accompanying spouses.* For partners with no specific job description, expatriate life can at times become frustrating and boring. Caring for the children and the home may in large part be carried out by others, friends and relatives are on another continent, and you may have no official job or role. Moreover your partner may be busy and fulfilled (and therefore insensitive to your needs) or very frustrated with an assignment that is not working out (and therefore in need of you on which to offload aggro).

Apart from following the common-sense tips above, a few other points may be helpful:

- *Before* you go, as far as possible define, discuss through and clarify your likely role overseas with your sending agency, field leader and partner. You may be able to draw up a specific job description, task or appropriate expectation. If your role is to be left vague or you are to 'wait and see how things develop', this should be through an informed, planned decision and not simply by default.
- Develop your own outlets away from home, cultural patterns and visas allowing. This may mean voluntary help in the local community – through a church, voluntary organization, school or hospital. Many have discovered that their contribution in the informal sector is just as valuable as if they had gone out with a specific job description or role.
- Invite friends from home, or elective students and expatriate volunteers living nearby to stay or share meals.
- Determine to become really proficient in the local language. This is the best way of reducing social isolation.

- Learn about a new subject, either informally or by correspondence or through the Open University.
- Learn or re-learn to play a musical instrument.
- Resist the delights and dangers of too much booze, whether local or brought in from outside (see page 121).
- Be open with your partner, who will need to understand the realities of your own life and the way you feel. Be proactive in establishing time off as a couple and as a family.

Professional update

For many working or serving overseas, professional opportunities can be exciting and challenging. Keep notes of interesting or significant discoveries, events, cases or ideas. Make sure you receive professional journals from home. When on home leave try to fit in some professional update, course or conference. Consider writing a paper or travel article or book. How about doing some research?

Medical facilities in developing countries

These will vary greatly between one country and another and between cities and rural areas. The best may rival our teaching hospitals, the worst be places to avoid at all costs. Although excellent doctors and good hospitals may exist, you will probably be alarmed by the crowding, lack of hygiene and difficulty of communicating. Two further hazards are the mercenary attitude of some doctors – and less than brilliant nursing standards. Here are some survival tips:

- Minimize the need to see doctors by setting up a healthy lifestyle, being fully immunized and health-briefed before leaving, taking measures to prevent 'accidents', using antimalarials and sleeping under an impregnated bed-net. All these measures have been proved to greatly reduce danger and illness overseas – and the need to visit doctors or hospitals.
- On arrival (or preferably before), find out about the nearest reliable hospital, doctor or medical facility. Resident expatriates and the British Embassy or consul are good sources of advice, and your own organization may well have details. Knowing what is available (and what is not) is essential, especially if you have young children. Many countries have Western or Western-trained doctors in their academic institutions, mission hospitals or private practices. Check them out as soon as you can.
- Take your own first-aid kit with needles and syringes in case you need an injection, and gently insist that this is used unless facilities

are known to be reliable. This is especially important in Africa. Also take any other recommended kits, such as an AIDS protection kit.

- Women and men should be aware that doctors in any country may occasionally fail to follow considerate or ethical practices. Be prepared to say No to an examination you feel is unnecessary or inappropriate.
- For guidelines on pregnancy abroad see pages 124–30.

Medicines and injections in developing countries

There is enormous variation in the availability of useful medicines. Although essential drugs may sometimes be hard to obtain, brand products are often in abundance. In most of Asia and Latin America and in the larger cities of Africa many medicines are available without prescription from roadside pharmacies.

Before buying or using medicines overseas:

- Check they are made by a reputable company, preferably a multinational, and that they look genuine. Fake drugs are common, especially in West Africa and South Asia.
- Check the expiry date.
- Check the generic or scientific name (usually found somewhere on the bottle or packet, though in small print) to make sure it really is the preparation you want.
- Avoid preparations that contain steroids (e.g. prednisolone) unless this is definitely what you need. Never use eyedrops with steroids unless prescribed by a doctor skilled in eye diseases.
- Avoid blood- or serum-based products, including locally made gammaglobulin. They can spread HIV infection.
- Avoid injections, intravenous glucose and other widely used remedies *unless really indicated*. In many countries health workers, from doctors to traditional practitioners, use injections even for mild self-limiting illness. Often no treatment is needed at all, or medicines by mouth will be just as effective. If an injection is essential, go to a reputable health worker and provide your own needle and syringe.
- If you suspect you have malaria take your self-treatment kit with you in case an appropriate treatment is not available (see page 75).

Alcohol

In some countries or particular communities, alcohol is forbidden or strongly discouraged. If this is the case it is only worth accepting a drink if this is both legal and acceptable with those among whom you live and work.

WEEKLY UNITS

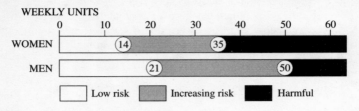

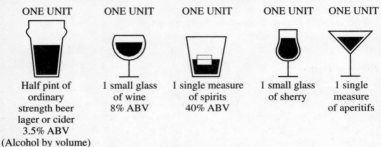

Figure 8 Units of alcohol

A greater problem is often the free availability of alcohol, including home brew – which added to tiredness, loneliness or stress can bring to light a past, or new, drinking problem.

It is worth setting yourself high standards, as prevention is far easier than cure. Consider keeping a drink diary if you find it hard to keep your drinking under control. In this you list *when, where, how much* and *with whom* you drink each day of the week.

Sensible rules include: never exceeding the recommended limit (21 units per week for men, 14 units per week for women – see Figure 8), keeping three days per week alcohol-free, practising ways of saying No, never getting drunk, drinking alone, or drinking before sundown. Avoid making a habit of 'needing' a drink every evening in order to wind down. Never binge-drink. If this means avoiding mixing with certain people, so be it. If you ever feel the problem is getting on top of you, tell someone appropriate and ask for help before it becomes known in the community or passes beyond your control.

Security

Although this varies widely, security is a problem in many parts of the world, as are the dangers of robbery, rape, kidnap and getting caught up in a local disturbance.

A few common-sense rules can greatly minimize your risks:

Personal possessions

Avoid ostentatious dress and gadgetry – wear clothes appropriate to the local culture. Travel with as little cash on you as possible. Wear a money-belt, preferably inside your clothes, or use a tubigrip to keep cash or tickets on the inner side of your leg. Watch your possessions with great care in crowds, on public transport, especially night trains, and on beaches. Be on guard for pickpockets, especially in well-known tourist areas. In areas where mugging is common, consider keeping a small amount of local currency, dollars or pounds where you can easily hand them over.

Personal safety

Try to grasp the basic rules of how people relate and the words and mannerisms that cause offence or could be misunderstood. Especially important is to gauge the degree of intimacy between sexes that is considered acceptable. What might be considered a gesture of friendship in Latin America might cause great offence in Pakistan. Keep a low profile, understandably difficult for blondes in Africa or giants in East Asia. Avoid dark or lonely areas in city or country. Keep to well-worn routes. Act confidently as though you know where you are going. If a car stops near you and asks instructions, or beckons for you to approach, act with extreme caution. Try to travel with a local resident who knows the best routes to take and how to cope with any difficult situation. Try not to use maps in public, but study the route in advance of setting out. Get to know your neighbourhood, the telephones that work, your nearest police station. Avoid excessive alcohol. If you find yourself on the edges of a disturbance or demonstration, beat a hasty retreat.

You can get detailed advice on the safety of travel in any country of the world by phoning the Foreign Office on 020–7270 4129/4179.

Driving

Except in areas known to be safe, follow these rules. Never pick up a stranger. Avoid roads infrequently used. Try not to drive alone at night. Take extra care when your car is stationary and try to adjust your speed so you don't have to stop at traffic lights. Always stop at road blocks, do what you are asked without arguing and try to avoid eye contact; never lose your cool. Make sure someone else knows your destination and the route you plan to take. In built-up areas keep the windows closed and the doors locked. When a car takes you home, ask the driver to wait until you are safely inside.

Domestic safety

Assess the likely risk of robbery, armed or otherwise, and take appropriate precautions. This may mean keeping a guard dog, building a perimeter fence, having an intercom with another nearby resident or employing a watchman. Consider using a time switch for lights or radios, calling a loud goodbye as you leave an empty house, fitting security locks and window bars and keeping a whistle handy. If your house looks as though it has been broken into, do not go in alone – summon help first. Only sleep with an open window if it is difficult to enter from the outside, or if there are bars or grilles in place.

Thieving is often opportunistic, meaning you should not leave things lying around your garden or an open house, and that you should secure all doors and windows with care whenever you go out at night. Only employ domestic staff after making sure, preferably by reliable references, that the person is of good reputation.

Hotel safety

(Double) lock your room, keep valuables with you, and retain your key when leaving the building. Don't leave precious things lying around in your room. Remember that your passport may have a high value on the black market.

If your door has a safety chain, use it, and never admit anyone unless you know their identity. Keep your door and balcony locked and curtains drawn. Avoid rooms that are easily accessible from the outside.

PREGNANCY

Parents-to-be often wonder if it is safe to travel or live in a developing country when pregnant. Before deciding on this it is helpful to understand the level of risk during different times in the pregnancy, and then set this alongside your travel plans. Your doctor or obstetrician will probably be able to advise you, and if you are going with a company or agency their medical adviser may have guidelines.

It is helpful to think of pregnancy overseas under three separate though related headings:

- safety of travel during pregnancy;
- safety of living in a developing country when pregnant;
- safety of having a delivery overseas.

Safety of travel during pregnancy

Simply travelling during pregnancy carries small additional risks owing to the greater likelihood of fever, dehydration, accidents and distance from good health care when away from home.

If you do have to travel in the first three months, try to arrange at least one antenatal appointment before going abroad, at which time you can discuss any concerns you have with your doctor. You may just be able to fit in your first scan.

The middle three months (mid-trimester) are generally the best time to undertake a journey. In this way you can complete basic antenatal investigations, including blood tests and scan, before you leave, and be in place for any problems that may arise towards the end of the pregnancy.

You should think carefully about travel if any of the following apply to you. They would not necessarily stop you but you should discuss them with your doctor:

1 You have had a *medical condition* that adds to the risk of pregnancy. This would include heart disease, diabetes, significant anaemia, asthma or chronic lung disease, previous deep venous thrombosis or pelvic infection. It might also include any other serious or long-term illness, especially if you are taking medication for it.

2 You have had a *problem in a previous pregnancy*. This would include a previous actual or threatened miscarriage, ectopic pregnancy, known complication of childbirth, Rhesus incompatibility or raised blood pressure. Include any other condition that caused you to have extra appointments or treatment in your last pregnancy.

3   You have *problems in your present pregnancy*. This would include any vaginal bleeding, marked abdominal pain, raised blood pressure, presence of twins or a known low placenta.

Safety of living in a developing country when pregnant

This will vary greatly depending on the country and your exact location.

Although most overseas pregnancies will pass without difficulty, if problems do arise or a tragedy does occur you will want the reassurance that you took an informed choice based on the knowledge of possible risks. It is therefore worth considering what the commonest risks are:

Miscarriage. There is an increased risk of this in the tropics because of fever, especially malaria, and possibly severe dehydration.

If you do have a miscarriage and continue to bleed, medical facilities such as those for Dilatation and Curettage (D and C) may be less reliable – and less hygienic. Safe blood may be harder to get in the rare event of needing a transfusion.

Malaria, especially malignant malaria, which is common in sub-Saharan Africa and South-East Asia, increases your risk of anaemia, premature labour, miscarriage and stillbirth. A severe attack could put your life at risk, especially if you have not been taking antimalarials. The baby may be born with malaria. You can reduce the danger by taking strict precautions, but some risks for both mother and baby still remain.

You should avoid travelling in western Cambodia and the Thai border areas with Myanmar and Cambodia when pregnant as the only effective treatment is not safe in pregnancy. You should think carefully before living in any country where there is a high risk of chloroquine-resistant malaria, which now includes most of sub-saharan Africa.

Hepatitis E. This form of hepatitis is spread like hepatitis A (see page 171). In some countries, such as Nepal, it is very common, in others apparently much rarer. We do not yet have a very accurate idea of just how widespread it is. Hepatitis E is very dangerous in the second half of pregnancy. If you are in a country where it is known to be common or there is reliable evidence that it is about, take even more care than usual with food and water hygiene.

Medicines. Many medicines, including most treatments for diarrhoea, bowel infections and worms, are best avoided in pregnancy, meaning you may need to delay treatment until the baby is born. A bewildering number of drugs is available in many developing countries, either by prescription or over the counter. You should only take medicine both if it is essential and you have checked it is harmless to the baby. Table 8 lists drugs that have been *shown* to have adverse effects.

Table 8 Medicines, pregnancy and breastfeeding

First 16 weeks of pregnancy	Weeks 16 to delivery	Breastfeeding
Avoid	Avoid	Avoid
Carbamazepine	ACE Inhibitors, e.g. enalapril	Amiodarone
Danazol	Anti-thyroid drugs	Aspirin
Lithium	Barbiturates	Barbiturates
Phenytoin	Benzodiazepines, e.g. diazepam	Benzodiazepines
Retinoids	Beta-blockers, e.g. atenolol	Carbimazole
Sodium valproate	NSAIDS, e.g. ibuprofen	Combined oral contraceptive pills
Warfarin	Tetracyclines, e.g. doxycycline	Cytotoxic drugs
	Warfarin	Ephedrine
		Tetracyclines

Please note: 1 If taking any of the above, discuss with your doctor before stopping. 2 This list is not a complete one. 3 Check the data sheet of *any* drug you take during pregnancy. 4 This list was compiled from Fortnightly Review, *BMJ* Vol. 317, Nov. 1998.

Premature labour. Although in the absence of malaria this is little more likely in Honduras than in Hampshire, access to adequate treatment, such as safe blood for the mother and extra support for a premature baby, is greatly reduced.

You can minimize health risks during pregnancy by trying to set up an ordered lifestyle, taking regular exercise and allowing more time than usual for rest, relaxation and routine tasks. Avoid high-altitude trekking, scuba diving, horse-riding and skiing.

Safety of having a delivery overseas

There is potentially a greater danger from complications at the time of delivery in a developing country, unless you are within access of a known centre of excellence. Generally facilities both for routine and for emergency care are less reliable. You will need to make an informed choice, not through a romantic haze of optimism but based on a cool look at what would happen in the worst scenario.

The following are suggested *minimum* requirements for an overseas delivery:

- A maternity unit, easily accessible at all times of the day or night and at all seasons, with 24-hour cover from an experienced doctor able to carry out forceps and vacuum deliveries and Caesarean sections.
- High standards of hygiene, fully trained midwives and the guaranteed use of sterile instruments.

- The ready availability of safe blood from a trusted donor with the same or a compatible blood group.
- Resuscitation facilities for the newborn.
- The absence of any serious pregnancy-related problems in this or previous pregnancies, including Rhesus incompatibility.
- A personality that can cope with the added risks and anxieties of having a delivery away from your home country, with its high-tech back-up and family support.
- A partner or family member who can give practical support at the time of delivery, including overseeing travel arrangements.

In coming to your decision you should visit the maternity unit, meet the doctor and midwife likely to carry out the delivery and thoroughly check out the facilities. Make sure the doctor(s) is not away for long periods of time (or a golf fanatic!), or is not about to go on home leave. Talk with other expatriates who have had local deliveries, and with the medical officer of your organization.

Even if the minimum requirements are in place, the balance may still be tilted in favour of you coming home if:

- *either* this is your first delivery;
- *or* you are working in a country where HIV disease or malaria are common;
- *or* there is political instability, unreliable transport or the likelihood of heavy rains that could delay you getting to hospital.

If you decide against going home you may opt to move nearer the capital or a large city two weeks or more before the delivery date. Alternatively, you might decide to move to a nearby country with better health facilities.

If you do not feel comfortable about having a pregnancy overseas you should make sure you discuss this with your sending agency or medical adviser. Equally, if you are very keen to have an overseas delivery, make your wishes clear.

One final point: if both baby's parents and/or two or more grandparents were born overseas, check citizenship rules with the Home Office.

After the birth of the baby make every effort to breastfeed, not bottle feed, but don't allow yourself to be guilt-ridden if this really isn't possible.

Air flights and pregnancy

Most international flights will be unwilling to carry a passenger known to be 35 weeks pregnant or beyond, but many domestic flights make a cut-off point at 36 weeks. Check the exact regulations with the airline concerned and leave a margin of two weeks in case of last-minute changes of plan or cancellations. It's worth having a medical certificate giving the expected date of delivery, especially if flying near the airline's cut-off point or if you look about to give birth!

Air travel is generally safe in pregnancy. Make sure you keep your fluid intake up, and avoid alcohol. Your feet may swell more than normal. In order to prevent clots in the legs walk around at least once every hour and avoid sitting in a cramped-up position. Eat a fibre-rich diet throughout pregnancy and especially at the time of air travel. Travel sickness may affect you more than usual. Avomine is effective and safe.

Check the details of your travel insurance as most policies will not cover delivery or complications of pregnancy.

Immunizations and antimalarials in pregnancy

Although the risk of damage to the foetus from any vaccine given in pregnancy is extremely rare, like all medical decisions risks and benefits have to be matched up.

Plan your immunizations plenty of time ahead so that you can still have essential vaccines before you become pregnant. Tetanus, and gammaglobulin for hepatitis A are safe; other vaccines are best postponed, especially live vaccines (see page 3 for list). Immunizations are safe when breastfeeding.

Make sure you have had measles and rubella immunizations – usually through MMR in childhood. If in doubt, a blood test can tell if you have protection.

If you are going to a malarious area you must take antimalarials as well as strict precautions to avoid bites (see also pages 58–85, especially 76–7).

Rhesus incompatibility

There is a risk that rhesus-negative mothers who carry rhesus-positive children can have their own blood sensitized by their baby. The mother then develops rhesus antibodies that can adversely affect future babies.

The use of Anti D immunoglobulin helps prevent rhesus illness in the newborn and is recommended for rhesus-negative mothers in the following situations:

- For use within 72 hours of birth. If facilities abroad allow the blood group of the newborn baby to be tested and the baby's blood group is confirmed rhesus-negative, an injection of Anti D immunoglobulin is not necessary. If the blood group is positive or testing is not possible, Anti D immunoglobulin should be given to the mother, whether or not any Anti D was given during pregnancy.

- For use within 72 hours of a miscarriage or threatened miscarriage including vaginal bleeding.
- For use within 72 hours of external version, antepartum bleeding, trauma to the abdomen, amniocentesis or chorionic villus sampling.
- In some countries, guidelines recommend that rhesus-negative mothers should receive Anti D immunoglobulin at 28 and 34 weeks of each pregnancy. This is not currently recommended by British experts, one reason being that there is a worldwide shortage of safely prepared vaccine.

The vaccine should be kept between 2 °C and 8 °C, but can be taken in hand luggage during a flight, provided it is refrigerated on arrival. It should not be frozen. Rhesus-negative women who may have further pregnancies overseas should consider taking Anti D globulin with them.

CHILDREN

Most children enjoy living overseas, and many find returning home to the UK after several years in a tropical country harder than going out in the first place. Where problems do arise overseas they are usually caused by illness, times of separation or parents so involved in projects and programmes that their children do not get the quality time they need. This can of course happen just as easily in the UK.

Before leaving home

Give kids the vision! Enable older children to share 'ownership' of what you as a family will be doing. Involve them in your arrangements, excite them by what you will be involved with. In doing this, be careful not to raise false expectations or expect them to share the burden of making important decisions.

You can prepare very young children by selectively reading aloud about the country you are going to, showing them photographs, slides, films or videos. Older children can be encouraged to do a project on the country, ideally at school. If the class teacher is involved and makes this a class project it can help to maintain links between children and their classmates over the coming months.

If you can meet up with a family who have recently been to the place you are going to, so much the better, especially if they have children.

Usually, it is worth keeping plans to go abroad under wraps until they are reasonably firm. Continue normal school and family routines for as long as possible.

Children of all ages will need continuity with home throughout their time overseas. Encourage them to keep up friendships, send e-mails or even write regular letters. Favourite toys, cuddlies and books can make all the difference to the happiness of children during their first weeks overseas. Make sure there's space for toys, books and that favourite teddy. Keep a back-up trunk of other favourites not taken overseas for opening at home when you come back on leave or for a visiting relative to bring at a strategic moment.

When overseas, try to arrange visits from friends, relatives and grandparents. These, if appropriately timed and not too long, can be enriching times – and give children a valuable sense of continuity. They can also be an opportunity (or an excuse) for an exciting family holiday.

If your assignment is remote and long-term, take extra sets of baby clothes of progressively larger sizes. Also take with you appropriate birthday and Christmas presents for at least a year ahead.

Some children worry about whether they will like the food overseas. Reassure them and take care that meals and mealtimes are enjoyable, and that you don't introduce too many new tastes and smells all at once. There is some value in alternating European-style and local-style meals.

Finally a word about how to handle any doting, anxious or elderly relatives or friends you will be leaving behind. They may think you are crazy or irresponsible to be going abroad, especially with children. It's worth spending time talking this through, reassuring them, giving them carefully thought-through information and making sure you have phone, fax and e-mail connections sorted out to reduce the fear of isolation and what to do if 'something happens'. At the magic moment, suggest a trip so that they can come and see where you are living (if appropriate!).

Education overseas

Before confirming an overseas assignment, do careful research into school options and assess how suitable they will be for the likely duration of your time overseas. You will need to talk to other families who have had recent experience of the area you are going to.

A local school has many advantages for younger children as it helps them to feel part of the scene. This may be overshadowed, however, by variable quality of teaching and a sense of cultural isolation if your children are not accepted as ordinary members of the class. Home schooling is an option that suits some families well, but definitely not others. Check it out carefully, looking at different systems, preferably choosing one compatible with British educational requirements. World Education Service (WES) is one of these.

Children of secondary school age may do better at international schools, even if this means boarding. Boarding is hugely popular with some children, loathed by a few and agreeable to most. If children do board, visit as often as possible and be sensitive for any stress or unhappiness, which may arise from bullying, loneliness, overstrict teachers or rare cases of abuse. Most international schools offer a first-class education, but try to find one that can prepare children for GCSEs and A-levels, or the exams used in your country.

If children board in the UK, make sure they have guardians whom both they as well as you approve of and like. During holidays be especially careful to make them feel wanted and affirmed. This will mean pre-planning so that one or both parents have time free. Children who go to boarding school may subconsciously equate this with rejection, meaning that holidays or special visits are of great importance. Decisions by longer-serving expatriate families regarding when to come home are really important, and need to be thought about in advance on the basis of well-researched data.

Health care before leaving

Children will need appropriate immunizations, including BCG, and some courses started in the UK may need to be completed overseas. DPT, polio and measles are likely to be available, others may need to be taken. Discuss this with your travel health adviser.

Remember to start antimalarials one week before leaving. Make sure you know your children's blood groups. Arrange medical, dental and eye checks for older children or if your sending agency or company requests them.

Living overseas

Allow plenty of time at the beginning so you can get to know and understand your new environment together. Encourage your children to make friends with local children and families, but at their speed, not yours. Some children will react to the new situation by withdrawal and shyness. Give them space to develop relationships in the way and at the speed with which they feel comfortable.

If more serious withdrawal occurs, give additional home support and less contact with unfamiliar or frightening aspects of the culture around them. They may in addition be missing friends at home but may not always say so.

After a period of withdrawal, gently encourage new friendships with other children and introduce them to enjoyable aspects of life in your new location.

If there are local customs that frighten young children – cheek-pinching in South Asia is a common example – explain that this is the normal way of greeting children and is not an act of hostility.

Monitor your children's experience of the schools they go to, making sure they are not getting academically behind compared to their contemporaries at home, and also that no unusual customs or patterns of discipline are causing unspoken anxiety.

You can help family bonding by making sure that each member is familiar with what the others do and the places where they work and study. In many cases, children will take an active and informed interest in the work you are involved with if you share it with them and give them a sense of ownership and involvement. If you travel out from the home base as part of your work, try to take the children with you from time to time.

Make plenty of time for family activities. Many children brought up overseas retain lifelong memories of family picnics, visits to safari parks, tropical beaches and mountains, or just simple family days together. Holidays can take on new dimensions overseas, so never jettison them in favour of worthy schemes and work schedules. Workaholics often come into their own when abroad – to everybody's disadvantage, especially their children's.

Finally: when travelling with small children take special care they don't get lost while they (or you) wander off to investigate the latest sight, sound or animal.

Feeding children overseas

It is worth breastfeeding for one or even two years. Apart from all the other benefits it makes diarrhoea less likely.

Try to prepare feeds for the baby yourself (using carefully washed utensils), rather than leave it to the cook, houseboy or ayah unless you have carefully trained them. It is better not to feed any reheated food to very young children (see pages 35–8).

Give children, and especially babies, *boiled* water. Make sure there is a cool supply at all times so that children, when arriving home thirsty, don't have to make secret visits to the tap or well.

Because of the heat, children may have less appetite than in the UK. This means that a balanced diet is especially important. Include a good source of protein – either eggs, meat, fish or lentils – as well as regular fresh fruit and vegetables. Keep a growth chart for children under five to monitor weight gain. These are usually available from the local clinic or health centre – it does not matter too much if they are not in English. Take seriously any unexplained fall in weight or flattening of the curve.

Illnesses abroad

By leaving Basildon or Basingstoke you do not necessarily leave behind sore throats, earaches, snuffles and coughs. As a parent you may worry that ordinary symptoms are caused by extraordinary illnesses. Usually, with the exception of malaria, they are not.

Nevertheless, young children are more likely to become ill overseas than older children and adults. This means that if you are planning a long stay, one of your first jobs is to identify the best local health facility (plus an appropriate back-up and better-equipped referral centre). Visit, meet the staff and find out what level of care they can give. Then when illness does strike you will have Plan A and Plan B, which will reduce your fear and anxiety.

You should take special note of the following symptoms and situations:

- *Fever*. This may be caused by malaria (see below) or by any common childhood illness. High fever should be treated by undressing (under a mosquito net), tepid sponging and paracetamol. High fever or any fever that persists for more than eight hours, especially in a malarious area, means you should see a doctor. If this is not possible, treat for malaria as any delay can be dangerous. You must then seek advice if symptoms are not definitely improved within 24 hours. Avoid aspirin in those under 12 years old (see also pages 167–9).
- *Headache* accompanied by vomiting or stiff neck. With or without a rash this spells immediate referral to a doctor – it may be meningitis (see page 176).
- *Cough or difficulty breathing*. Beware of pneumonia, which you should suspect if the respiration rate reaches 50 or more per minute or if there is indrawing of the ribs or flaring of the nostrils on breathing. See a doctor if possible, and start antibiotics, such as amoxycillin or erythromycin at the correct dose for age. Asthma is common in children, and may start for the first time when you are overseas. Any severe attack of wheezing needs skilled treatment

quickly. Croup is common in children and can be serious, especially between six months and three years (see page 159).

- *Abdominal symptoms.* Only the luckiest child (or adult) will escape diarrhoea. Start ORS at once (see page 50); breastfed babies should continue to take breast milk. Giardia is common in children, and may be the cause of persistent diarrhoea or flatulence in any member of the family. Threadworms causing itchy bottoms are common, and all family members over the age of two should be treated with mebendazole (one, twice daily for three days) if *any* family member has symptoms. In fact it is good practice to deworm the whole family every six months using the same dose. Abdominal pain, especially if it persists, is accompanied by fever and settles into the right lower abdomen, could be appendicitis. See a doctor.
- *Infected cuts and grazes.* In hot and especially in humid climates, minor injuries easily get infected. Clean all breaks in the skin with care (removing all dirt and foreign bodies), then use antiseptic cream and keep covered with a light non-adherent dressing frequently changed until the skin is healed over (see page 184). Boils are common (see page 184). Especially when outdoors, children should wear appropriate shoes to protect against both injury and acquiring hookworm. They should, preferably, wear shoes indoors as well.
- *Scorpion and snake bites.* Scorpions like dark places. Teach your children to check their slippers and shoes before putting them on and to take care when putting their hands into boxes or into any dark place. If snakes are common, set up a family drill on how to avoid them and deal with them (see page 108).
- *Dogs and animals.* A family pet is often a vital member of the overseas family. Make sure the dog's rabies injections are always up-to-date (see page 45). Actively discourage your children from ever approaching, touching or stroking an unfamiliar dog or any other unknown animal.
- *Sunburn.* The combination of sun, light or absent clothing, excited children and distracted parents spells danger. Allow your children's skin to acclimatize gradually, starting with fifteen minutes' exposure only, using high-factor sun lotion. When swimming or on seaside holidays, take a long-sleeved shirt and stay in the shade during the middle of the day. If sunburn does occur, blame yourself and not your child, apply calamine and watch out for any infection (see page 106).
- *Accidents.* These are among the greatest hazards overseas. A few days after arrival, make a tour of the house and its environs and assess it creatively for any obvious or potential risks, never forgetting the family medicine shelf, probably groaning under a heavier weight than back home. Check the cooking area carefully,

making sure that hot handles cannot be easily reached and pans pulled off the stove. Crossing roads in a developing country is a skill children should only acquire at the side of an adult, especially if driving is on the right, you live in a city or are visiting one from up-country.

- *Sleep problems.* Children, like adults, may suffer from disturbed sleep when going to a new environment, especially if it is hot or there are unfamiliar smells and noises. Heat, the whining of mosquitoes or prickly heat may add to the problems. In addition it is easy for children to be stimulated or alarmed by new and bewildering experiences. Often the best remedy is to allow the child to talk and play, even if it is beyond normal bedtime – extra contact with parents may be all that is needed. If this and other remedies fail, or if you are desperate for sleep, then promethazine (Phenergan) or trimeprazine (Vallergan) for a few nights at the recommended dose for age can help to break the cycle. Occasionally this stimulates rather than sedates. If you have children three or under, give a trial run in the UK, then take a small supply with you.
- *Medicines.* For all but the shortest trips it is worth taking one or more courses of antibiotics, an antihistamine, travel sickness pills etc. (see Appendix A). Make sure you avoid medicines that are unsafe in children, and use the correct dose for age by consulting the patient information leaflet or instructions. In a malarious area never run out of prophylactics, and keep a standby with you for treatment (see pages 75–8).

Returning home

Periods of leave at home need to be so arranged that children do not feel squeezed out or of secondary importance. Make sure they see the people *they* want to, and do at least some of the things they want to do. Help them to understand the way their own country ticks so that when they finally come home they are not strangers in their own land. In the event of an extended leave, one or two terms at school can be very beneficial.

If your children have had more than one or two years abroad it is not advisable to bring them straight back into the first GCSE or A-level year without a prior year to get adjusted. Teenagers usually find re-adaptation to their home country difficult, and will need the most favoured opportunities possible for re-entry. Schools in the UK will need to have explained to them in detail the background, both academic and cultural, from which your children have come, otherwise they may be seriously misunderstood.

Children returning from a length of time overseas will often come across as different and be seen as outsiders by their new peers. They will probably feel outsiders themselves. Some of their experiences may not be believed or, even worse, be mocked or ignored. For older children who return to the UK it can be very helpful to meet up with recently returned expat families with children and share experiences. Also, church youth groups and Sunday schools, as well as the wider family (including grandparents) can be very helpful in giving children added security.

Returning home for good can be bewildering for the whole family, not least for children. Peer pressure in schools, especially during teenage years, is strong, and wearing current styles of footwear and knowing the right fashions, pop songs and slang can greatly reduce isolation and embarrassment. The more you have encouraged children to remain bicultural overseas the easier will be their eventual reintegration.

Health on return

Along with other family members, children should have a medical examination if they have lived in a developing country for longer than a year. This should include a stool test. It is sensible for all family members over the age of two to take a final course of worm medicine – mebendazole, one, twice daily for three days. If children have swum in areas where bilharzia is known to occur they should have a blood test (or urine/stool test). Malaria commonly occurs weeks or even months after coming home. Untreated malaria in children is *dangerous*. If you have been in a malarious area, do report any unexplained fever at once and ask for a blood smear.

DISABILITY

Provided you choose your destination and means of transport with care, physical handicap does not disqualify you from serious travel. Inhabitants and hosts in many countries are often very helpful. An 80-year-old relative of the writer recently made a three-week journey to a remote part of western China four months after a severe stroke had left him completely paralysed down one side and temporarily without speech. His secret? – determination, a sensitive travelling companion and careful pre-planning with airlines and accommodation.

A wheelchair should be robust, foldable, lightweight and as narrow as is comfortable. It should be well tested before the journey, and accompanied by a few simple repair tools. Battery-driven chairs are probably best avoided. A strong and considerate travelling companion for all but the hardiest is essential.

By prior arrangement with the airline, assistance can be provided at all stages of the journey, a suitable seat procured in the plane near the disabled toilet and the wheelchair accommodated on deck. For many airlines provision tends to be all or nothing. This means if you say you are disabled you will probably be supplied with full assistance at each stage of the journey. However, check out with care any special claims made by airlines or hotels.

During the flight it is important to exercise or massage the legs to prevent clot formation. Those on regular diuretic pills should continue to take them. All medication should be kept in your hand luggage to avoid anxiety and in case of delays. Keep a list of any medication you are on, with a duplicate for your travelling companion or contact at home. Make sure you take out full travel insurance, even if it means paying extra premiums.

Travellers with severe hearing disability will need a companion who can pass on advice and information and interpret needs to hosts overseas.

Information about wheelchairs can be obtained from Wards Mobility Services on 01892 750686, and on any aspect of travel for the disabled from The Disabled Living Foundation, 020–7289 6111 and RADAR, 020–7637 5400. Consider reading the book *Nothing Ventured*, a collection of travel vignettes by disabled globetrotters (see Further Reading).

DIABETES

Many diabetics manage to travel with little danger, provided they are well controlled, well advised and well supplied. However, you should discuss any trip outside Europe, or any overseas assignment, with your GP or specialist. If you use insulin you would need to be in reach of good medical facilities, preferably in the company of an informed companion. Have a doctor's letter with you giving details of the insulin dosage, wear a Medic Alert bracelet and if insulin-dependent obtain an Insulin User's Identification Card from the BDA (see below).

On the flight it is probably better not to order a diabetic meal but to pick and choose from normal food, using any extras you may have taken with you. If you are crossing time zones you should discuss a detailed action plan with your diabetic adviser. If crossing more than three time zones your health adviser may ask you to make a few changes. Travelling east to west, when days are lengthened, you may be advised to take an extra meal and cover it with extra insulin. Travelling west to east, with a shorter day, you may be advised to reduce the amount of carbohydrate and insulin. Test your urine or blood frequently both while travelling and for some days after arriving, altering your insulin dose accordingly. Running 'a bit high' is unlikely to cause any harm for two or three days.

In cases of *illness, fever or diarrhoea* you will probably need more insulin and should test your urine, or blood, at least four times daily. See a doctor *early* if you become less well or vomiting persists. As a diabetic you should take extra care to avoid preventable illnesses, in particular malaria and diarrhoea. Take special care of your feet, treating any fungal or other infections immediately. Keep your toe-nails short. Wear-in new shoes before travelling. Take special care not to get sunburnt, and avoid walking barefoot on the beach. Insulin may be absorbed more quickly in hot climates.

Take all necessary *supplies* with you until you have personally checked out their availability where you are going. This includes insulin, needles, syringes and testing equipment. Divide your supplies between two cases, and remember to keep all insulin in your hand luggage as the hold will freeze. While overseas keep your insulin in the non-freezing part of the fridge or in as cool a place as possible, out of direct sunlight. Insulin that has been above 25 °C for longer than a month may lose its effectiveness. Take double the quantity of tablets or insulin that you might expect to use, in case you need to increase your dose or you get delayed.

Always carry a form of *sugar* with you in case of hypo attacks. If going to a remote area or prone to attacks, also take glucagon or Hypostop. Make sure your travelling companion knows how to recognize hypo attacks and what to do about them. They may come on very rapidly while travelling, though they are uncommon during actual air travel.

If you are a *non-insulin-dependent diabetic* continue testing as you would at home, remembering there may be slight changes owing to differences in food and climate. It is important to keep near your target weight and to be regular with any tablets you are taking.

Further details can be obtained from the British Diabetic Association, 10 Queen Anne Street, London W1M 0BD (020–7323 1531). It publishes details of insurance schemes, advice for tourists and availability of health care and supplies in over 70 countries.

SECTION 3
WHEN YOU RETURN

ILLNESS ON RETURN HOME

On getting back home you may continue to have medical symptoms or concerns about your health. This is more likely if you have been living in a remote or humid location and if you have been in close contact with the local people. Countries in sub-Saharan Africa, South and South-East Asia are perhaps the most likely to leave you with a legacy of fevers, diarrhoea, weight loss or other symptoms.

Those who have been on shorter, hurried trips abroad, especially if working for hard-pressed aid agencies, not infrequently arrive home exhausted or unwell.

Illnesses that show themselves on return

Some illnesses may show themselves for the first time after you get home, while others may have started abroad but become worse or more obvious when back in this country. Important illnesses to be on the lookout for include the following:

Fever/malaria. A sensible rule is to assume that after returning home from a malarious area, any fever is malaria until proved otherwise. This is especially important in the first three months, when malignant malaria commonly recurs or even appears to occur for the first time, but benign forms may recur for months, occasionally years after returning from the tropics. Sometimes malaria can recur for the *first* time after returning home.

If you develop a fever or symptoms that you think could be malaria, follow the advice given on page 79. Although fever may have a variety of causes, *it is dangerous to ignore symptoms of fever after returning from a malarious area.* Sometimes a mild virus or even a cold may trigger malaria, and symptoms are often atypical, without the classic phases of shivering or sweating. Dengue fever, now found in most of the developing world, can mimic malaria; so can typhoid.

Diarrhoea. Attacks of diarrhoea that started overseas may continue in the UK. Symptoms occasionally occur for the first time. There are many causes, including dysenteries (bacterial and amoebic), Salmonella, Campylobacter and Giardia. The last often causes persistent diarrhoea with flatulence. Diarrhoea usually disappears without treatment, but you should see a doctor and take a fresh stool specimen *either* if it persists for longer than ten days after returning home *or* if there is any blood or mucus in the stool. Continue to report symptoms until either your stomach has returned to its normal pre-travel state or you feel suitably reassured.

If certain organisms such as Salmonella, Shigella or Cryptosporidium show up on your stool test, you may be asked to have three clear tests before being allowed back into full social circulation. This especially applies to schoolchildren, but practices vary from one part of the country to another.

Persistent diarrhoea, especially after returning from South Asia, may be a sign of malabsorption, in which case there is usually weight loss and frothy, floating stools. It is often associated with milk intolerance. This is easily treated, but you must report your symptoms to a doctor, preferably one with tropical experience (see page 202).

Sometimes repeated bowel problems abroad can trigger an irritable

bowel syndrome – a common and benign condition with irregular motions and abdominal pain. Again this should be diagnosed by a doctor rather than by yourself.

Remember that diarrhoea or bowel symptoms after you get home may have nothing to do with your travels – see a doctor if abnormal symptoms persist.

Worms of various sorts may first come to light on return home (see pages 173–5).

Cough or chest symptoms. Chest infections often hit expatriates during or just after their return home. If this is the case you should see a doctor, who will probably give you antibiotics. Make sure also that you report any cough that persists for more than a month (see pages 192–3). One rare but important cause of chest pain is a blood clot in the lung. This may cause sudden pain or shortness of breath, usually seven to 14 days after a long flight. The small clots develop in your legs, meaning one of your calf muscles will usually feel sore if you press it (see page 30).

Skin problems. Report any unusual skin symptoms. Groin itch, athlete's foot and other fungus infections are common. Persistent rashes, sores, ulcers or suspicious moles must be checked, as should any roughened skin patches in long-term tropical residents (see page 187). If you develop a sore that does not clear up and ulcerates, this could be cutaneous leishmaniasis from a sandfly bite. This is becoming commoner, especially in North Africa, the Middle East and Western Asia (see page 175).

Bilharzia. If you have had any contact with fresh water in areas where this is known to occur, you may later develop symptoms. Katayama fever (acute schistosomiasis) causes fever and usually wheezy cough, itching and diarrhoea. It needs treating without delay. Bilharzia can also produce blood in the urine or stool – or not give any symptoms at all (see page 154). Blood tests usually only become positive at least 40 days after you got infected (see page 157).

Persisting ill health, weight loss or unusual symptoms. If in doubt, check it out. Ill health of any sort starting during an overseas trip or persisting after return should always be investigated.

AIDS and HIV infection. If you have been involved in health care or had any other risk factor for HIV, you may want an HIV test on return. This is more important than it used to be because drug treatment used early can greatly delay the onset of AIDS. So if you've been at risk, it's worth having an HIV test.

Many people worry about jeopardizing future insurance cover. Having an HIV test is unlikely to affect your premium, provided it is negative (see page 88).

An HIV check can be included as part of your tropical check-up either by your GP or in a tropical diseases centre. Alternatively, it can be carried out at an STD (sexually transmitted diseases) clinic, probably the best place if you are worried that you may have picked up another form of STD in addition. Before having an HIV test carried out you will be given appropriate counselling and have the right to full confidentiality.

Psychological problems. Coming home can often be a time of stress, especially after a long or difficult assignment. A tropical check, if the doctor has time, can be a good opportunity to talk about any bad experiences. Certain events overseas are known to make adjustment more difficult or to increase the risk of flashbacks or other unpleasant symptoms. For this reason we would recommend personal debriefing (see page 145).

Career blank. It is very common after taking a year out, or after exciting or significant experiences abroad, to feel really confused about what you should do next. In this case it is worth arranging a career interview, either with your local careers service or privately (see page 204).

HAVING A TROPICAL CHECK-UP

Who carries them out?

If you are unwell or have symptoms, you should be carefully checked, preferably by someone with experience of tropical illnesses. This could either be your GP, university health centre, NHS tropical diseases unit or other centre specializing in travel medicine (see Appendix D). For any NHS referral you would normally need a letter from your GP.

Who should have one?

If you are well with no symptoms, opinions vary as to whether a medical is necessary. Many people are worried that they may have some hidden illness that will declare itself with mortal results, months or years later. Although this is rarely the case, you would probably benefit from a medical if you come into one of these categories:

- If you are unwell or have any persisting symptoms, including unusual tiredness.
- If you may have picked up an illness that only shows itself later. Bilharzia is by far the commonest (e.g. from Lake Malawi). TB, HIV

disease, Chagas' Disease, sleeping sickness, hepatitis B and filarial infection are all much rarer.

- If you have lived in a developing country for more than 12 months.
- If your style of travel has put you at special risk. This includes any prolonged stay or adventure travel in remote or primitive locations, or work in refugee, famine or war situations.
- If you or your family continue to be worried that you 'have picked something up'.
- If you continue to feel unduly stressed or depressed for more than a few weeks after returning home.
- If your company, mission or aid agency require it.

What does it consist of?

A tropical check-up usually takes this form: detailed questioning about any illnesses experienced, areas visited or health concerns you may have. There will be an examination, which includes listening to the chest, checking for any enlargement of spleen, liver or lymph glands, feeling the abdomen, a careful check of the skin and an examination of the ears, eyes and mouth.

At some centres (including InterHealth) there is also a chance to talk through any difficult overseas experiences.

Investigations usually include a stool and urine test and, where appropriate, a haemoglobin and full blood count (including percentage of eosinophils – a useful marker of parasitic infections). Tests can also be arranged on the liver and for bilharzia, filaria, Chagas' disease (parts of South America only), HIV or any other condition you or your doctor are concerned about. Chest X-rays and ECGs are only rarely necessary. The most useful 'tropical tests' are stool examinations and full blood counts.

If you are returning overseas you can also have your hepatitis A antibodies checked, unless you have had hepatitis A vaccine. If these are positive you have immunity and will not need immunization with hepatitis A vaccine or gammaglobulin. If you are a health worker or have previously had a course of hepatitis B immunizations, you can have your blood titres measured to see whether you need a booster.

It is worth remembering that a single negative stool test does not mean your gut is necessarily free of parasites. If symptoms continue you should have at least three stool tests, preferably with fresh stools taken to the laboratory within two hours. Many doctors recommend in addition that all those returning from an assignment in developing countries, either permanently or for prolonged leave, should take a course of mebendazole for worms (one, twice a day for three days for adults or children aged two and over).

Personal debriefing

Any difficult, dangerous or frightening experience overseas, either short-term or long-term, may have various effects that you only feel after returning home. So can the cumulative hassles from petty frustrations or endless efforts to get on well with your colleagues (or friends). These effects may make adjustment more difficult, lead you to feel anxious or depressed or cause gloomy thoughts, flashbacks or disturbing dreams that don't seem to go away. Occasionally they can lead on to a more serious condition known as Post-traumatic Stress Disorder (PTSD) or bring to light underlying tension or conflict that may have been present before you went overseas. Many of these problems can be greatly lessened by a chance to talk about any bad experience in a free-ranging debriefing interview on return home. If you have been on an assignment your sending organization will normally arrange an *operational debrief* (make sure you have one).

In addition, however, it is helpful to have a 'psychological' or *'personal debrief'*, during which you can talk about your feelings, fears and experiences.

The best time to do this is probably two or three weeks after arriving home – which gives you time to reflect but not enough to start endlessly recycling your experiences. If you've had a really traumatic experience, you should fix your debrief much earlier.

These debriefs give you a chance to talk in a relaxed setting with a trained debriefer or counsellor. You can talk freely about any aspect of your overseas experience. Debriefs are confidential and are distinct from counselling, though at the end of the session you may mutually agree that a series of counselling sessions might be helpful.

If you have been with a group of people who have all suffered a similar traumatic experience, a group debriefing for two to three hours can be very helpful. Ideally this should take place as soon as possible after the incident (this is known as Critical Incident Debriefing).

Debriefing is best thought of as a chance to talk about 'normal reactions to abnormal situations'. We suggest you consider arranging one of these if you come into one of the categories below:

- You have been working in a situation of famine, war, conflict or danger.
- You have experienced actual or threatened kidnap, rape, assault, armed robbery or other frightening experiences.
- You have had any serious or long-standing personality conflicts with colleagues.
- You have had an assignment that has been cut short, has been especially difficult or has not worked out as expected.

Finally, it is worth mentioning that some people find their religious faith challenged or threatened by experiences overseas, especially any that have involved seeing severe or mass suffering. In this case it is really worthwhile seeing a spiritual counsellor, chaplain, pastor or minister for prayer and discussion. Many people find that once they develop a well-thought-through 'theology of suffering', their faith can grow rather than falter (see Appendix D).

GPs, DENTISTS AND OPTICIANS

Registering with a doctor

If you handed in your medical card on going overseas you should now re-register with a GP. If you are not sure how long you will be staying at your address you can register as a temporary resident for up to three months, during which time you enjoy full NHS access. When registering permanently, your doctor or the practice nurse will want to see you for a brief medical, but this does not take the place of a tropical check-up. If you have previously been registered with either the same practice or a different one, it may take at least six weeks for your old notes to be retrieved. As a temporary resident your previous notes would not normally be sent for.

NHS eligibility

On return to the UK you will be entitled to NHS treatment if

- *Either*   You have had ten years' continuous residence in the UK and have *either* been working abroad for not more than five years *or* have been taking home leave in the UK at least once in every two years *or* have a contractual right to do so *or* have a contractural right to the cost of your passage to the UK at the end of your engagement.
- *Or*   You have been in the UK for the previous 12 months.
- *Or*   You have come to the UK to take up permanent residence.

For more details see *National Health Service Hospital Charges to Overseas Visitors: Patient's Guide*, May 1999. NHS Executive A–PH15 Quarry House, Quarry Hill, Leeds LS2 7UE.

Seeing a dentist

At the time of writing an increasing number of UK dentists are no longer taking on new NHS patients. For this reason it will often be worth seeing a dentist known to you from before or who is known to any relatives with whom you are staying.

Seeing an optician

As a general rule it is worth having an eye check at least every five years, and more often if you wear glasses or have any personal or family history of eye disease, including glaucoma.

Eye checks are free for those 60 or over, under 16, those with diabetes or a family history of glaucoma. If you are over 40 or there is glaucoma in your family make sure you have your eye pressures measured, each year in the case of glaucoma running in the family. Let the optician know if you have been taking chloroquine regularly for more than five years.

Being referred to a specialist

Those coming home on short leave are having increasing difficulty getting specialist referrals within the National Health Service.

If you need a specialist referral, follow this procedure:

See your GP as soon as possible after getting home or, if you know your GP, write from overseas; explain the problem and your limited timescale, being sure to mention if you are serving with a charitable organization. If there is likely to be a delay, write a courteous note to the consultant to whom you have been referred, marked for personal attention; ask the medical adviser of your sending agency or company to write a supporting letter to either your GP, the consultant or both. If an appointment still cannot be arranged, consider seeing the consultant privately. If you have a medical at InterHealth and need a referral, this can be arranged, though not usually through the NHS. Any Anglican clergy or past or present mission partners of an Anglican missionary society are entitled to free specialist referral at St Lukes Hospital, London and its associated consultants.

REVERSE CULTURE SHOCK

> We shall not cease from exploration
> And the end of all our exploring
> Will be to arrive where we started
> And know the place for the first time.
>> *T.S. Eliot*

Even if you are one of the lucky ones who can quickly adapt from one culture to another and feel as comfortable after ten days back in

Taunton as during your ten years in Timbuktu, it may still be worth
reading this.

The problem

Many people get thrown by the effects of coming back home,
especially after any long, difficult or meaningful experience abroad. It
may seem even more of an issue than the culture shock you
experienced, or didn't experience, when you first went abroad. You
may have assumed that the comforts of home, your favourite luxuries
and friends eager to hear of exploits in remote corners of planet earth
are bound to make you feel good.

And when you first arrive home and start to recount exciting
experiences as the hero, or tramp, returning home, you probably *will*
feel pretty good. But after a while this gradually seems to change. For
no apparent reason you start feeling listless, anxious or depressed; you
don't want to get up in the morning; you start losing your enthusiasm,
even your self-confidence; you feel angry at the materialism and
pettiness of people's lives; you feel confused about yourself and about
your future. Perhaps for the first time in your life you find yourself
crying in your room – or really losing your cool. What can possibly be
the matter?

Probably nothing. You have the normal condition of reverse culture
shock. You have left a country and its people whom you came to enjoy
and appreciate. You have left a job or travel experience that despite its
frustrations was often fulfilling – and sometimes exciting. You have
lost a role and a clear place in the scheme of things. Now you are
mourning the loss of all this, you are missing the good friends,
favourite places and significant experiences. 'Last week at this time I
was ... now I am looking out of a rainy bedroom window in
Birmingham.' If you have ever lost a close friend or relative you may
recognize the similarity of some of your feelings now.

Apart from sadness at what you have left behind, you may be
shocked by what you find at home. As an outsider coming in to land
and then acting as a detached observer, you can see the way the country
really is, the aloofness of the British, the apparent indifference of the
people around you to the real issues of the world. You may feel like a
messenger from outer space with insights and understanding no one
will listen to.

Further, you find yourself in a dilemma. On the one hand you need to
reintegrate into the society you've returned to; on the other you do not
want to compromise all that you've learnt (and become) by being
swallowed up by the culture at home and becoming like the people you

feel you have moved beyond. Staying an outsider may be painful, but you wonder whether it isn't better than taking on the values of the people around you. It seems as though you have moved on in your personal development, whereas your friends seem either to have stayed the same or moved in a completely different direction from yours.

And what about these friends? To start with, they all seem so busy. They no longer seem to talk about important things (did they ever?). Even those who should know you well ask daft questions about why you are not more suntanned. They quite forget which country you have been living in, and out of ignorance or embarrassment ask hardly any questions about the real things you have been doing, or too many about certain things you would like to forget. They seem more interested in the latest fashions than in the concerns of the poor. And when you do find someone genuinely interested, you are so relieved that you go on talking for too long.

Life seems bewildering. Take shopping. Why are there so many things on the shelves? Is it morally justified for supermarkets to sell 47 different types of breakfast cereal? Before leaving for overseas you felt at home in the streets, now you no longer do. Even going to the post office requires undue concentration to avoid saying something silly or coming away with the wrong denomination of stamps.

You may become annoyed or intimidated by friends and family continually asking what you are going to do next or enquiring when you are going to settle down – as though your overseas experience was some blip that nice people don't talk about.

Perhaps you first went abroad because one chapter in life was drawing to a natural close or because you felt a strong urge – or call – to do so. Now you are home, this chapter has closed, but the pages in the rest of the book seem blank. Careers? New jobs? You are hardly able to cope with yourself – how can you possibly cope with making decisions, writing a CV, being interviewed, starting a new course or job, earning a living?

Some possible solutions

If you can identify with some or all of these feelings, relax – you're normal. If you can't, don't worry either. Those with certain personality types can cope with change much more easily than others. Of course you may feel it later.

Here are some suggestions that may help:

Recognize – and don't deny – the feelings you have. Writing them down may help. Choose one or two friends with whom you can share your feelings, preferably those who have travelled or lived abroad or been out to visit you. If you have been employed or on an assignment, make the most of any debrief your organization offers, getting anything off your chest that you need to. If you have been in a tough location or had a difficult experience, seriously consider also having a personal debrief shortly after coming home (see page 145). Equally, if your relationship with a partner or spouse seems to have taken a nose-dive (common overseas and on re-entry), try to arrange some joint counselling. Try not to leave any unfinished agenda with your sending agency or company. Ask for a further session if you need it. If money is an issue or you sense that you were let down or sent out with the wrong expectations, talk about it.

Keep in touch with overseas friends and projects. There are useful things you can probably do for some time to come, which will give continuity and a sense of purpose until the future becomes clearer. Join any group where others who have returned meet to discuss, pray, or raise support for people and projects you are familiar with. Go to any reunions, reorientation weekends or get-togethers. Keep up with friends now in the UK you have known overseas. You, and others, will benefit from setting up a bridge from your past life to your new one.

Be patient. Let the process of integration take its own, appointed time. Gradually you will be able to adapt without feeling your overseas experiences have to be wasted or gently forgotten about. This will happen as you come to see people as individuals, not stereotypes, situations as dynamic and not static, and one day's challenges at a time as all you are asked to cope with. You will learn the knack of accepting the good, avoiding the bad and recognizing what you can usefully do to help bring change within the limits of your gifts and energies.

Dare to admit your ignorance about many of the things you used to know about but no longer do – how things are done, the latest fashions, celebrities, TV programmes, the names of the English football squad. You are unfamiliar with some of the customs and culture of the country you now find yourself in, so admit it, put on your anthropology hat and find out about the strange inhabitants of your home country, just like you did with the new people you encountered when you first went abroad. Wander in the shops, familiarizing yourself with prices, brand names and what is available. Make the *Radio Times* or some equivalent a study project. Take note of what people are wearing, what the new banknotes look like and the value of unfamiliar coins. Find a good and long-suffering friend and question him or her about things you want to find out about, especially unfamiliar words you keep hearing and that people expect you to know. Your knowledge about all matters materially trivial but socially important will grow, and so will your confidence.

Join a social group where you will feel comfortable and where you have a shared interest. It may be a church, an evening class, a club or a parent-teacher association. As you become used to one group, so other situations will become less daunting.

Get some careers advice if you are unsure about your future. Your local careers service can supply you free and relevant information about courses and jobs. They can explain about retraining schemes, eligibility for further education grants and accreditation of prior learning. You are entitled to use their library, and usually their computerized list of courses throughout the UK (see Appendix D).

Although it may help your peace of mind to know when your next job or course is going to start (and when the cheques will start coming in), don't necessarily be in too much of a hurry. Go at *your* pace rather than that of well-meaning friends eager to know what you are going to do next. Get to know yourself and what you really want to do, now that you are home. Your interests, outlook and viewpoint may start to change over the first few weeks – or months – that you are back in the UK, especially if you have been abroad for some time. Don't necessarily take the first job that comes your way simply out of desperation. It may be better to wait until something more appropriate crops up. In the meantime, get someone to help you prepare a well-written CV that maximizes the value of the experiences you have had. Don't be intimidated by a period of unemployment, but do show you have used the time constructively. As an unemployed person you are in the company of many others, including top executives.

Take a holiday if you have been on a tough or lengthy overseas assignment. You may have been caught up in the 'Protestant Work Ethic'; now enjoy the 'Leisure Ethic' and 'God who gives us all things to enjoy richly'. Don't take on too many assignments and speaking engagements until you have had a proper break, your slides have been developed and you've spent time with your family and friends. This may mean some pre-planning before you come home with any agency you have been with, and should be based on what you know you can comfortably cope with, rather than what you feel you ought to be doing. You may feel the need to have a time of personal reflection or, if a parent, time as a family – or just as a couple.

Know when to shout. If any feelings of doom and gloom persist unduly or are very severe, and if your appetite and sleep pattern become markedly disturbed, don't hesitate to see someone who can help. Some sympathetic counselling, along with temporary medication, will normally hasten a cure. If your assignment has been especially difficult or if you have had to come home early, these feelings are more likely to affect you. It is *not* a disgrace to be 'honourably wounded' when doing something useful overseas (see page 221).

Downhill from now on, or slipway to a richer life? With time and practice it is possible to build on your overseas experience, whether it has lasted six months or six years. Your time abroad, whether rich and hard to leave behind or bleak and hard to understand, will always be potentially enriching, provided you really integrate the experience. Who knows? – it may be the gateway for a longer time abroad in the future, the means of helping you to understand those of different cultures within this country or just a way of enriching your life. It may even help you to introduce your family and friends to the excitement of overseas travel – or service.

SECTION 4
NOTES ON IMPORTANT CONDITIONS

BACKACHE AND SCIATICA

Backache and sciatica can cause travellers much concern. The effect of lifting heavy luggage, sleeping in unfamiliar beds, needing to restrain or carry young children and being tense and hurried, all put the back at greater risk. This can be compounded by springless buses, rickshaws striking potholes or years bumping across bad roads in vehicles with decaying seats and groaning suspension.

If you have ever had a severe back problem, slipped a disc or had persistent sciatica *you should discuss this with your doctor before leaving* or when next back home. If necessary, ask to see a specialist or osteopath. If your bouts of backache are unpredictable, severe or slow to return to normal, give careful thought to where, and how, you should travel.

Preventing backache is much easier than treating it. Follow *with extra care* the techniques you know to be important for your own back. The cardinal rules include: standing and sitting up straight, keeping your back straight when lifting, putting a small cushion to the small of your back when sitting, and doing any regular exercises that have proved beneficial.

One of the most important ways of both preventing and treating a bad back is to have a satisfactory bed with a firm, but not over-firm, mattress. If you wake in the morning with your back worse than when you went to bed, it is likely that your bed is contributing to the problem. It is fine to use a soft mattress a few inches thick, provided it is on top of a completely firm unsagging wooden base. The floor is a good alternative. Treat with suspicion any spring mattress unless it is new.

Treating a bad back is the same in the tropics as anywhere else, though there is often little medical back-up if your back finally 'goes'. Bed rest is often the only treatment available to you, though a friendly physiotherapist has come to the rescue of more than one stranded volunteer. Current advice is that we should get up and move around gently as soon as we can. Taking an anti-inflammatory such as ibuprofen 200 mg, one or two tablets three times a day, can ease the pain.

There are certain *warning signs* that you should report at once. These include backache associated with difficulty passing urine, weakness in the feet or legs, sciatica and numbness down one leg that worsens despite treatment, and pain or numbness down both legs at the same time. Any of these symptoms may indicate that pressure, usually from a slipped disc, is building up on the spinal cord and that urgent surgery may be needed to prevent permanent damage. These more severe symptoms are rare, however, and 'back awareness', coupled with common sense, will enable most of us to survive.

BILHARZIA (Schistosomiasis)

What is it?

Bilharzia is caused by parasitic flatworms, known as schistosomes, with pretty smart life-cycles. They take up residence in the blood vessels surrounding the bladder or large intestine. Here they spend their time producing eggs that, when released, cause irritation of the bladder or bowel before being excreted.

Eggs from those infected who pass urine, or defecate, into fresh water are taken up by snails that soon release larvae into the water that in turn penetrate human skin (occasionally causing you to itch). These travel through the body, usually via the lung, before settling down into the dark interior. It is at least four to six weeks, often longer, before any symptoms develop, and many infected people have no symptoms at all.

Where is it found?

Main risk areas for travellers are sub-Saharan Africa, the Nile Valley, north-east Brazil and the Far East (see Figure 9). Lakes Victoria, Malawi, Kariba and Volta are known trouble spots, but any fresh water, including lakes, rivers, ponds and irrigation canals, may be affected. Slow-flowing or stagnant water, especially if snails are present, is the most likely to cause trouble. Sea water is safe, as is any water either chlorinated or stored in a snail-free environment (e.g. a swimming pool) for forty-eight hours.

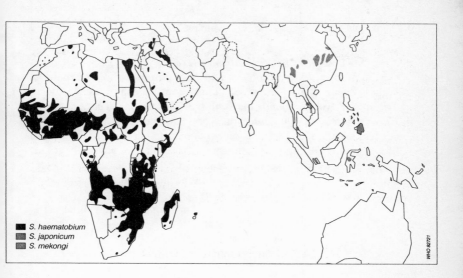

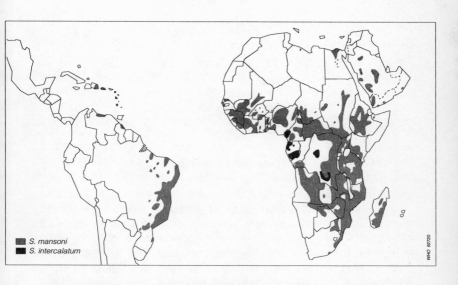

Figure 9 Areas where bilharzia (schistosomiasis) is found (WHO 1999)

155

What are the symptoms?

The disease can take one of two courses:

- *Acute schistosomiasis or Katayama fever*. Symptoms, which often start 40–60 days after exposure and may mimic typhoid or malaria, include fever, itching, wheezy cough, muscle ache and diarrhoea. The spleen, liver or glands may enlarge. This needs urgent treatment.
- *Chronic infection*. One common type of bilharzia (S. haematobium) causes irritation or blood when you urinate, or makes the semen blood-stained (or lumpier than usual). Anaemia can gradually occur, and after many years severe untreated infections can lead to bladder cancer. S. mansoni can cause blood in the stool, and many months or years later sometimes affects the liver.

Many people, however, have no symptoms, and their bilharzia is only discovered by tests at a tropical check-up (see page 143). Many, but not all of these will eventually self-cure. A few travellers told they have ME, in fact have undiagnosed bilharzia.

How is it prevented?

By avoiding any contact with infected water in areas where bilharzia occurs. This means you should avoid: swimming and washing in infected water; pushing vehicles or wading through rivers; water sports in affected areas; drinking infected water. If exposure cannot be avoided wear waterproof boots, dry the skin immediately after getting wet, cross up-stream from villages and get tested (see below). The shores of lakes are far more affected than open water farther out.

How is it treated?

By taking praziquantel (PZQ) 40 mg/kg daily in two divided doses. This can only be obtained at specialist centres in the UK (including InterHealth). Some doctors treat for one day, others for three. For adults of average weight this usually works out at praziquantel 600 mg tablets, two twice daily. PZQ sometimes causes nausea but is generally safe. Taking PZQ before you dive into that alluring lake, or shortly afterwards, is useless. If you go ahead and swim against medical advice you can take PZQ about 40–60 days later, or if you are a swimming or sailing addict, e.g. on Lake Malawi or Victoria, you can self-treat once yearly as per national control programme guidelines. But it's much better to avoid getting it.

Tests for Bilharzia

The most accurate test is to look for ova in the urine or stool, but they are not always easily found. On a blood test bilharzia is one cause of a raised eosinophil count (one of the white blood cells). Probably the most useful test is a bilharzia ELISA blood test, which only becomes positive at least 40 days, and often much longer, after being exposed. It is best to delay having a test until about 60 days after your last swim, splash, wade or wash in fresh water. After treatment the test can take at least 18 to 24 months to return to normal, but it is worth having it rechecked every 6–12 months until it returns to normal levels.

BRUCELLOSIS

Brucellosis is mainly a disease of cattle, goats and sheep, and humans usually catch it through infected milk, cheese or butter. It is common in West Asia, the Arabian Peninsula and other parts of the Middle East, and scattered areas around the Mediterranean and in Africa. Agriculturalists, development workers and adventure travellers are at greatest risk.

Symptoms are variable and often vague, usually starting at least one month after exposure. At first there may be fever, general weakness and pain in muscles, back and joints, sometimes lasting a few weeks. Many cases then get better on their own but some continue, with intermittent (or 'relapsing') fever leading to profound tiredness, further muscle and joint pain and depression. In this form it can mimic chronic fatigue syndrome (see page 162), or a depressive illness.

It is *prevented* by making sure all milk (and milk products) are either politely refused or only drunk if pasteurized or boiled for ten minutes.

It is *diagnosed* by tests on blood serum and *treated* under medical supervision with doxycycline and either rifampicin or streptomycin.

CHAGAS' DISEASE
(South American trypanosomiasis)

Though rare in travellers, this is a serious disease found in Central and South America, where it is spread by infected 'assassin' or 'kissing bugs' (see Figure 10), creatures that live in mud walls and bite at night, commonly on the face. It is a risk for aid workers, adventure travellers and volunteers who sleep in mud or adobe huts in rural or poor urban areas, especially where chickens are common. Chagas' disease can also be spread through blood transfusions.

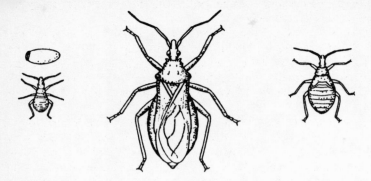

Figure 10 The Cone-nose bug, also known as the Vinchuca, Assassin or Kissing bug, responsible for spreading Chagas' disease (1–4 cm long).

The bite is usually obvious, and the first *symptom* is a reddish nodule at the site of the bite, often with swelling of an eyelid. Fever commonly develops and lymph nodes become swollen. Symptoms may, however, be slight or non-existent, but serious disease, especially heart failure and swelling of the colon or oesophagus, may occur years later.

Prevention involves sleeping away from the hut or, if this is not possible, in the middle of the hut away from the walls. A mosquito net if thoroughly tucked in gives protection. Local blankets and rugs should not be used. Search your bed for hidden insects and apply insect repellent to your face.

Treatment, under medical supervision, needs to be started as early as possible. This means that anyone who may have been exposed or has had an unscreened blood transfusion in South America should request an ELISA blood test at the time of their tropical check-up.

COUGHS AND COLDS

Some people are surprised when told they can still catch a cold when living in a tropical climate. As in the UK, the majority of colds get better on their own, but those working long hours or following hectic international schedules frequently develop chest infections, especially at the end of an assignment or on returning to the UK.

If a cold fails to clear up after a few days, and if in addition you are run down or have a tendency to *bronchitis* or *sinusitis*, see a doctor and start on antibiotics such as amoxycillin, 500 mg three times a day for seven days (see Appendix A).

Pneumonia, especially in children, may develop fast, particularly after a cold or when very tired. You will usually feel ill, be coughing and have pain in your chest on breathing. A respiratory rate of over fifty breaths per minute in a child is strongly suggestive of pneumonia. Call a doctor if you can, and otherwise start on antibiotics at the correct dose for age.

Any cough that persists longer than a month should prompt you to have a medical check, as very occasionally it may be caused by *tuberculosis* (see page 192). Anyone who has had frequent or persistent coughs while working in a developing country, especially with unexplained loss of weight, should be thoroughly checked on return to the UK, and should have a sputum test, tuberculin test and chest X-ray. This especially applies to health workers.

Asthma occasionally starts for the first time when overseas, especially in any children who have a family tendency for eczema, asthma or hay fever. If someone in the family develops severe or persistent wheezing or a stubborn night-cough, consult a doctor. Any episodes in a child should be discussed at your next home medical, to make sure you are recognizing and treating it in the best way. Wheezing is occasionally caused by tropical parasites, for example roundworms or bilharzia.

Croup can also hit for the first time when overseas. If a child develops difficulty on breathing in, remain calm, hold your child confidently and reassuringly in an upright position, remove any pets and try to steam up the room, for example by boiling a kettle or saucepan, using an umbrella or sheet as a canopy. Most attacks will gradually subside, but remain within earshot for the rest of the night as the attack may recur. If symptoms continue to worsen and you have a good local health facility, seek medical help as soon as possible. Discuss any attack of croup at your next leave medical.

DENGUE FEVER

Dengue (pronounced *deng-ee*) is a nasty viral illness with a serious agenda for world domination. Transmitted by the Aedes mosquito, it is spreading rapidly throughout the tropics, and in many areas is second only to malaria as a cause of severe fever in travellers. The worst affected areas are tropical South America, the Caribbean, Pacific Islands, South and South-East Asia and, increasingly, Africa.

Dengue tends to be worse in urban areas and usually comes in epidemics, though scattered cases occur much of the time. There are four different dengue virus sub-types, and getting one actually makes it more likely that one of the others will hit you harder if you're unlucky enough to get it again. No vaccine is available – yet.

There is a severe form of dengue, called dengue haemorrhagic fever (DHF), where the temperature (see symptoms below) goes even higher (e.g. up to 41 °C) and bleeding starts to occur from the nose, gums and other organs because the number of blood platelets collapses. This is extremely rare in travellers, though many people get very worried about it. DHF tends to affect local children in poor areas.

Symptoms often start with sudden fever, headache, pain on moving the eyes and vomiting. There is frequently severe joint, muscle and back pain ('breakbone fever'). A rash often develops between the third and fifth days, usually starting on the trunk and spreading to the face and limbs. Recovery follows, but commonly a second bout of illness with further pain and fever develops ('saddleback fever'). You may feel tired and weak for a surprisingly long time, but dengue is very rarely fatal in travellers.

Prevent dengue in two ways. First, make sure the surrounds of your house are free from standing water – flower pots, tyres, air conditioner outlets and the tiniest puddles will be all the Aedes mosquito needs to breed. Second, if you hear of local cases or are in an area where it is known to be common, cover yourself well and use plenty of insect repellent. Aedes tends to bite during the day, especially two hours after dawn and two hours before sunset, after which Anopheles, which spreads malaria, takes over the evening shift.

Dengue is *treated* by rest, patience and sympathy. However, because it can mimic malaria it is sensible first to get a malaria smear if you can, or self-treat for malaria if in doubt. Dengue commonly affects short-term travellers in the first week after their return from an at-risk area.

EYE PROBLEMS

Eyes are at greater risk in hot climates, especially if the air is dry and dusty or if you wear contact lenses. You can prevent most eye infections by regularly washing your face with soap and water, which reduces the number of germs that can enter your eye.

Conjunctivitis is the commonest problem. The eye becomes red, feels gritty and is sticky or stuck down on wakening. The treatment is antibiotic eye drops, e.g. chloramphenicol applied every two hours until symptoms clear. Make sure the drops or ointment do *not* contain steroids unless prescribed by a competent doctor.

Dry eyes. Sore, dry, gritty eyes are often caused by lack of tears. Obviously they can get worse in a hot, dry climate or in the plane. Use artificial tears, e.g. Hypotears, as often as you need to.

Yellow eyes. If in the sober light of day you think your friend's eyes look yellow, it could be jaundice. You could have yellow eyes too, of course, but if you've read page 3 and had your hepatitis jabs, it's much less likely.

Styes are not uncommon, especially if you are tired or run down. They are caused by organisms that cause boils in other parts of the body. Warm compresses can help the pain; antibiotic eye drops or antibiotics by mouth sometimes speed up the natural healing. Styes should not be squeezed.

Contact lens wearers should discuss their trip with their contact lens practitioner, and take sufficient solution with them, using only sterilized water as additives. At the first sign of any pain or irritation, the lens should be taken out for at least *twenty-four hours*. Any persistent or severe discomfort needs medical advice. Take extra contacts with you, plus ordinary glasses, plus sunglasses, which can protect against sun, dust and wind. In unhygienic conditions, and in particular with soft lenses, an infection called *Acanthamoeba* can *seriously* damage the cornea. In dirty or dusty situations you would do better to wear glasses or at least take out your contacts at night.

Glasses. Take at least one spare pair, and make a note of the prescription in case of loss. Glasses are often stolen.

Eyes and *chloroquine*. It is rare for any permanent changes to occur until a cumulative total of 100 gm of chloroquine has been taken – equivalent to a prophylactic weekly dose for about five years. Experts increasingly believe that no harm will occur if chloroquine is *only* taken for prophylaxis – harmful amounts only building up if in addition courses are taken for treatment.

Early signs of reversible damage are blurring of the vision and haloes around lights. More permanent changes affect the retina, leading to deteriorating vision. It is worth having regular eye checks, including examination with a slit lamp (from a medical eye centre or ophthalmologist) if you have been taking long-term chloroquine for both prophylaxis and treatment, or if you have suspicious symptoms.

Very high altitude or *polar conditions* may lead to snow blindness; prevent this by wearing goggles. Wear sunglasses for protection in very bright light.

Eye check before you leave the UK. It is worth having this done before any long-term assignment (and during regular leave).

If you are over 40 or there is glaucoma in the family, have your eye (intra-ocular) pressure checked as well. You will need to ask your optician to include this.

Report any symptoms that do not clear quickly. Eyes, especially if infected, can deteriorate rapidly in a tropical climate. See a doctor, preferably an eye specialist, if in doubt.

FATIGUE AND CHRONIC FATIGUE SYNDROME (ME)

Why am I so tired?

Feeling tired is extremely common in those living overseas (and at home). Overwork, worry and failing to take regular time off are probably the commonest causes. You may have trouble getting on with a colleague, have frustration at work and too much, or too little, to do. You may be bored or homesick, losing sleep, or beginning to suffer from stress without realizing it. If the reason is not obvious to you, ask your friends, who may have better insight than you.

A number of physical conditions can also make you tired. Anaemia is a common one, often caused by heavy periods, not eating enough iron-rich food, having frequent attacks of malaria or suffering from untreated hookworm or other bowel conditions.

Bilharzia (see page 154) can make you feel tired, as can brucellosis (see page 157), Lyme disease and sleeping sickness, though these are rare. Occasionally, more serious, non-tropical diseases can start with tiredness, such as diabetes and thyroid problems; so can a depressive illness.

Viruses are also a frequent cause. Two common ones are hepatitis before, during, and sometimes months after the illness, and glandular fever and related viruses, common in younger travellers and often very persistent.

If you feel abnormally tired or it seems a long time since you had your normal amount of energy, take the trouble of having an unhurried talk and examination from a doctor who understands your culture. Various blood tests can be arranged that usually exclude serious or treatable causes, and glandular fever is usually shown up. However, many viruses are not revealed by normal blood tests.

You should not diagnose chronic fatigue syndrome in yourself, but leave this to a sympathetic doctor who has made sure there are not other, commoner causes for the way you are feeling.

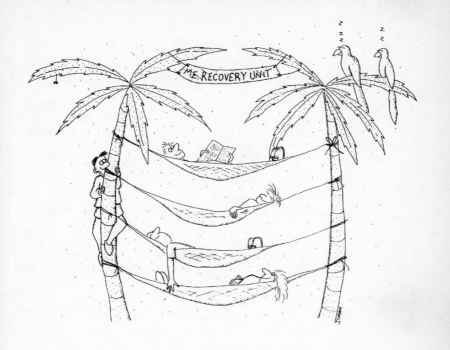

What is CFS?

CFS is a puzzling and frequent illness that has become well known over the past decade. It goes under a variety of names, including myalgic encephalo-myelitis (ME), yuppie disease and the post-viral syndrome. Quite apart from its debilitating symptoms, those who have it often face further problems with doctors, friends and colleagues who may be ignorant or unsympathetic. CFS patients therefore often have to run their own 'public relations bureau'. This can be especially difficult among expatriates and overworked colleagues. Estimates suggest that at least 1% of the population have CFS, and fatigue states of various types are common in travel and tropical clinics.

The symptoms of CFS

The chief symptom is profound tiredness and a sense of weakness or aching in the muscles, especially of the arms and legs. It has been described as 'flu minus the fever, which doesn't go away'. These features usually date from a specific time, most often from a virus infection or flu-like illness whose symptoms persisted.

Mental exhaustion, poor concentration, memory loss and changes in sleep pattern are also common features. Vigorous or unaccustomed physical or mental exercise causes a relapse of symptoms. Because recovery is slow and cannot be hurried, those with CFS often develop symptoms of despondency or, less commonly, an actual depressive illness.

Normally CFS is only diagnosed in those with typical symptoms that have persisted for at least six months. It is different from a simple state of chronic tiredness or exhaustion (Tired all the Time, or TATT syndrome).

The causes of CFS

CFS is commonly thought to be caused by a virus. The Epstein-Barr virus responsible for glandular fever is probably only one of several viruses normally rapidly fought off by the body's immune system, but that on occasions can persist, leading to CFS.

Recent research has shown that patients with typical symptoms of CFS often have a reduced number of special blood cells known as CD8 suppressor cells, thus giving scientific support to the fact that CFS is a distinct and valid physical illness, a fact only too obvious to those suffering from it. Further research describes a biochemical way of differentiating CFS from primary depression. This gives medical evidence that CFS is distinct from depression, even though the symptoms of CFS may on occasions lead on to it.

However, many CFS patients are found to have been living stressful or very energetic lifestyles at the time their illness started. Often this is through the outward circumstances of a difficult assignment or because past problems are reactivated by the stress of a tough overseas placement. Experience suggests that the presence of stress, or persistent overworking, reduces the body's ability to fight off infection. For this reason some, but not all CFS sufferers find that a course of counselling or cognitive behavioural therapy hastens their recovery.

The duration of CFS

Full recovery from CFS usually takes place, but may take many months, occasionally several years.

The treatment of CFS

See a doctor

Identify and then regularly consult a sympathetic doctor. If you think your symptoms fit into this category you should see a medic who has time, experience and sympathy with the condition, and access to laboratory tests. A hurried consultation with an uninformed and unsympathetic doctor should be avoided! This may mean waiting till you return to the UK, and even then doctors will need to be chosen with care.

Some other illnesses, including some tropical diseases, can mimic CFS, and it is important both medically and for your peace of mind that these are discussed and excluded, if necessary by further tests or a specialist referral.

A regular review and discussion of how you feel can be very helpful as two heads may be better than one in both planning an appropriate lifestyle and assessing progress.

Accept your diagnosis

Once CFS has been confirmed as your diagnosis, accept this without guilt or shame. Recent research has confirmed the existence and 'respectability' of CFS.

You will, however, need to get used to explaining your illness and symptoms to others. The use of a simple handout or article can be helpful. The term CFS, or post-viral syndrome, is preferable to ME, which may cause subconscious confusion with multiple sclerosis (MS), a totally different and far more serious condition.

Set up an appropriate lifestyle

Balance: The key to recovery is learning to balance input (rest, encouragement, support) with output (physical and mental exercise and other activity). This in turn depends on learning to identify and carry out the maximum activity that does not worsen your symptoms over the following days. The amount of activity takes careful working out, and to start with it may be surprisingly little. It will also vary from day to day.

Your output will need to include the core priorities of life, plus any other activities you are able to add in without causing excessive tiredness or delaying your progress. Overactivity, often brought on by frustration, false guilt, an obligation carelessly agreed to or the expectations of others, can set you back days. Equally, underactivity can lead to further weakening and atrophy of the muscles.

Sleep: In the early days of CFS, many feel a need or even a hunger for sleep. At this stage extra sleep or rest is an essential part of treatment. It can include a long lie-in, an afternoon nap or early night. If night-time sleep is a problem it is worth first reducing the amount of daytime sleep you take and/or gently increasing your amount of daily exercise. If that fails, consider short-term medication to help you sleep at night. As recovery starts, it may be necessary to start rationing the amount of sleep you have, particularly during the day, or at least combining it with a gradually increasing exercise programme.

Work: Work and responsibility need to be removed or reduced to a level at which gradual recovery is possible. This means that reduced hours, or time away from work, is usually necessary to begin with. You will also need to avoid situations where you need to pre-plan activities or make diary entries that may be hard to cancel. It is hard to predict how you will feel one day, week or month in advance, and it is helpful not to take on irrevocable commitments. As recovery takes place you can practise a lifestyle into which a gradual return to work can be slotted. Initially this should be for a few hours, once or twice a week, with a gradual increase as energy levels allow. *Do not rush this stage.* You will need your doctor's advice, and, if necessary, explanation to help your employer understand your needs and provide flexibility in your working arrangements.

Exercise: It is important even from the earliest days to take some exercise so as to keep your muscles in trim. Walking is obviously sensible, to which swimming and a gentle exposure to a favourite sport can be added. Absorption in a sedentary hobby, reading or studying will provide useful mental exercise.

A golden rule: try to invest a proportion of energy in 'the bank' every day, rather than going till you drop.

Medication

Sometimes the symptoms of CFS and the change from a normally active lifestyle can cause clinical depression, in which case antidepressants can hasten recovery. Recent reseach shows that the drug sertraline, starting with 50 mg or less daily, then increasing the dose under medical supervision, helps restore energy in a number of people. Short-term, mild sleeping pills may help to break any serious sleep disturbance.

Solidarity with other CFS patients

Find others with CFS with and from whom you can share experiences and receive mutual support. Some but not all find the ME Association is helpful. Avoid allowing solidarity to develop into an obsessional interest in your condition. Don't allow CFS to take over your life, your conversation or to dictate your friendships. Avoid the common tendency of slipping into a negative way of thinking.

Counselling and prayer

As already mentioned, counselling can sometimes hasten recovery, especially if you are aware of unresolved tensions. It is usually better to start it only when your energy levels have begun to recover. A counsellor needs to be chosen with care and should be someone who understands CFS and who is in full sympathy with any religious outlook you may have. Many have found various forms of prayer ministry helpful. Cognitive behavioural therapy arranged through CFS clinics undoubtedly also helps some sufferers.

Avoid too high expectation from 'magic remedies'

Some individuals claim that special diets or other inputs will help to bring recovery. Try these extras if you wish, but do not be disappointed if they are not as successful as you hoped. An increasing number of CFS sufferers claim a daily cold bath improves their energy levels.

An unexpected bonus

Many have found that being forcibly set aside with CFS has deepened their spiritual life or helped them gain other valuable insights. Many active people need red traffic lights. It may, however, only be after your recovery that you begin to see the benefits of your illness.

FEVER

Fever in the tropics, unless mild or quickly self-limiting, should be taken seriously, even though most fevers will turn out to be neither serious nor 'tropical'. If living in or coming from a malarious area, consider fever to be malaria until proved otherwise.

Common or important causes of fever

In practice, many fevers in developing countries, as in the UK, are caused by viruses: they usually cause short, sharp rises in temperature and rarely last more than three days. They are common in children.

Other familiar diseases often start with a fever. Here is a checklist: measles, chickenpox, mumps; tonsillitis and upper respiratory infections including flu and related viruses, throat, ear infections and sinusitis; pneumonia or bronchitis; glandular fever; tooth abscess, boils and cellullitis; appendicitis, pelvic infection and, one of the commonest of all, cystitis, which does not always give typical symptoms (see page 194). Blood poisoning may cause a high, swinging fever and a rare cancer called lymphoma occasionally causes recurrent fevers.

Certain *serious tropical diseases* can cause fever, and sometimes there will be few other symptoms, especially to start with.

- *Malaria* is probably the commonest (see pages 60–62), followed by
- *Typhoid* and related fevers (see page 57).
- *Dengue fever*, usually of 'saddleback' type (see page 159).
- *Hepatitis* may start with fever (see pages 171–3).

Other illnesses with fever include:

- *Acute schistosomiasis* (bilharzia) – mainly in sub-Saharan Africa (see page 156).
- *Tick-borne relapsing fever* – especially southern and eastern Africa (see page 188).
- *Typhus* – usually trekkers in Africa and Asia, commonly with a rash (see page 193).
- *Sleeping sickness* – visitors to game parks, agricultural workers in eastern and western Africa (see page 187).
- *Meningitis* – usually accompanied by severe headache, stiff neck and a non-blanching rash – no time to lose (see pages 176–7).
- *Dysentery*, with bloody diarrhoea (see pages 48–9).
- *Amoebic liver abscess* – severe pain in the liver (see page 52).
- *Tuberculosis* – recurrent evening or night fever, usually with cough (see page 192).
- *Lassa fever* – severely ill, usually with ulcerated sore throat and muscle pains, rural areas of western Africa – get home fast.
- *Heatstroke* (see pages 104–6).

Dealing with fever

It is important to find the cause for *any* very high fever or one that persists or recurs, remembering that children often spike high fevers with simple viral infections. If possible you should consult a doctor, and meanwhile cool the patient by undressing and giving cool fluids and paracetamol. This is especially important in children, despite the subconscious urge of many to cover with blankets.

If you are in a malarious area (or have recently come from one), see a doctor or health worker within eight hours and get a blood smear. If this is not possible, self-treat for malaria (see pages 74–6).

If there is no rapid improvement, then typhoid becomes more likely and you should treat for this (see page 57). Treatment for typhoid will deal with several other causes of fever as well, including some pneumonias, urinary infections, and bacillary dysentery.

Suspected liver abscess can be treated by a full course of metronidazole or tinidazole (see pages 52–3).

If you or your children are not quickly responding to treatment, see a doctor. If you have had severe or recurrent fevers abroad, especially if these have been undiagnosed, it is important to have a tropical check-up as soon as possible on your return.

GYNAECOLOGICAL PROBLEMS

These can be a real worry overseas because of the reluctance to accept medical advice from unknown doctors. Before leaving for any long overseas trip, all women between 25 and 65 should have a cervical smear (pap smear), except possibly those who have never had a sexual partner. It is worth checking on your smear result by phone. Smears should be repeated every three years if normal, and according to your doctor's advice if not fully normal.

Period problems

When travelling or going to live in a strange place, periods may get lighter or stop altogether, sometimes for months. This is very common, and no action needs to be taken unless pregnancy is a possibility or if you or your friends notice that you have lost a lot of weight.

Periods may also become irregular, abnormal or prolonged. If such problems persist you should see a doctor. If this is not possible, and you are definitely not pregnant, it is possible to take the combined oral contraceptive pill (for example Eugynon 30, Norinyl 1 etc.) at a dose of four tablets a day for seven days. The period should stop during treatment and come again within the week after finishing the seven-day course. You should only do this if you have recently had a clean bill of health and can see a doctor if abnormal bleeding is not cured by this treatment.

To delay a period, take the combined oral contraceptive without pill-free gaps. You should only do this for two or three cycles.

It is worth reporting any prolonged, heavy bleeding as soon as possible whenever it occurs, not least because of the increased risk of needing a blood transfusion. Also check any persistent changes from your normal cycle when you next come home.

Remember that it is better not to be menstruating during wildlife safaris, or while swimming where sharks may be lurking.

More important still, you should avoid entering mosques when you have your period; also certain temples unless a reliable local informant tells you it's okay.

Vaginal discharge

This is often commoner in the tropics, especially in hot and humid conditions and if you wear tights or jeans.

'Thrush', usually causing an itchy discharge, is especially common. If you suspect this, use clotrimazole (Canesten) suppositories nightly for six nights, or nystatin. An alternative is to take itraconazole 100 mg oral tablets two in the morning and two in the evening for one day. This should not be taken if there is a possibility of pregnancy or if you are also taking antihistamines such as terfenadine (Triludan).

Trichomonas is a common cause of discharge, often offensive. The treatment is metronidazole 200 mg tablets, two twice daily for seven days (again avoid if possibility of pregnancy and also avoid alcohol). See a doctor if your symptoms persist.

Sexually transmitted diseases (e.g. gonorrhoea or chlamydia) can cause a discharge, and if you think there is a possibility of an STD, try to see a reliable doctor. If this is not possible, self-treat as described on pages 183–4.

Family planning

If you are on the pill, take ample supplies of the preparation you are used to until you find out whether a reliable brand name of identical composition is available locally (see also pages 14–15).

For couples who have definitely decided not to have more children, it is worth giving serious thought to a permanent form of contraception (tubectomy or vasectomy) well before leaving or early on in your next home leave. This reduces one form of stress that is at least largely under your control.

HEPATITIS

What is hepatitis?

Hepatitis is an infection of the liver caused by a virus, usually leading to jaundice in which the eyes and skin go yellow. Hepatitis A and B are preventable by immunization, and as far as travellers are concerned *should* be diseases of the past.

Types of hepatitis

There are at least five different forms, of which hepatitis A, B, C and E are important illnesses for travellers to know about.

Hepatitis A

This is the commonest form of jaundice in travellers, found almost worldwide and most often picked up in the Indian subcontinent, East Asia or tropical Africa. It is spread by the faeco-oral route – in other words, germs from the faeces of an infected person contaminate the food and water drunk by another. It is therefore common wherever personal or public hygiene are poor. Those with hepatitis A nearly always make a complete recovery, even though it may take time. The interval between becoming infected and developing first symptoms (incubation period) is two to six weeks. The infection tends to be more severe the older you are.

Hepatitis B

Also known as serum hepatitis, this is a less common but more serious form. It is 100 times more infectious than HIV but is spread in a similar way to AIDS, i.e. by having sex with a hepatitis B carrier or through infected blood and dirty needles. However, especially in young children it can also be caught by prolonged close contact with a carrier. Health workers are also at special risk. Hepatitis B often leads to permanent liver damage, and in the long term can cause liver cancer. The incubation period is six weeks to six months. Ten million cases of hepatitis B are caused by dirty needles every year. The World Health Organisation has signed up over 100 countries for universal immunization programmes. The UK is not yet one of them. Increasingly recommend travellers to seriously consider having hepatitis B vaccination (see below).

Hepatitis C

Though only discovered in 1989 this is common worldwide. Like hepatitis B it also causes liver cancer, but is spread largely through infected blood transfusions, injections and body piercing – less often through sex. There is no vaccine.

Hepatitis E

This is similar to hepatitis A both in the way it is spread and the symptoms it gives – with one big exception: it causes one woman in five to die who catches it during the middle and latter thirds of pregnancy. Being almost as common as hepatitis A in some countries, this spells extreme caution with food and water hygiene for anyone who is pregnant. Your hepatitis A jab will not protect you, and there is not yet a vaccine (see page 126).

Symptoms of hepatitis

All forms of hepatitis tend to start in a similar way – with headache, fever, chills and aching. Nausea or sickness usually occurs, often triggered by the smell of food or cigarette smoke.

There may be pain over the liver (the upper right side of the abdomen). The urine darkens and the eyes and skin usually become yellow.

At this stage it is common to feel very ill, exhausted and nauseated. After days or sometimes weeks the symptoms gradually improve, though full health may not be restored for up to six months.

Children and some adults may have a much milder illness, or even have hepatitis without knowing it. Those with hepatitis B are usually more seriously ill and symptoms persist for longer.

Treatment of hepatitis

As with most viral illnesses, there is no specific treatment. The key to recovery is *adequate rest*, usually in bed to begin with. Provided the body rests sufficiently it is usually able to fight off the illness. Those who fail to rest or who return to work (or looking after their children) too quickly risk a longer illness or a relapse. Parents with young children will need maximum support, and in some situations unaffected partners *will need to take time off work to look after the family.*

Plenty of sweet drinks, especially those containing glucose, are claimed to ease the nausea. Intravenous glucose or fluids should be avoided unless vomiting makes it impossible to take fluids by mouth. There is no real evidence that special diets either help or hinder recovery.

Women who are on the pill are usually recommended to avoid it for about six months (and use alternative contraception!). It is also sensible to avoid alcohol until health has returned completely to normal.

Blood tests that monitor liver function (LFTs) can usually be arranged; though useful, they are not essential except in severe illness. In some centres it is possible to confirm whether hepatitis A, B, C or E is the cause of the infection. Alternatively, this can be done at a routine medical examination back home.

Prevention of hepatitis

Hepatitis A and E are prevented by good personal hygiene, and by following the advice on pages 35–46. Hepatitis B and C are prevented by following AIDS prevention advice.

Immunizations are of great value. All those aged five or over (or younger children at very high risk), unless known to have hepatitis A antibodies on a blood test, should have a course of hepatitis A injections (or gammaglobulin) if going to a developing country (see pages 209–12).

All health workers serving in developing countries, and all expatriates, especially children, residing or travelling for longer than three months should receive hepatitis B immunization. If in doubt, discuss this with your travel clinic or a specialist in travel medicine.

Patients with hepatitis A are at their most infectious before the jaundice develops (i.e. during the incubation period), and are thought to stop being infectious within two weeks after the jaundice starts. They can mix freely after the jaundice has faded. Those with hepatitis should use separate utensils and towels and take special care with personal hygiene. There is no need for strict isolation. Family contacts not known to have immunity or who have not received gammaglobulin in the past six months, or been immunized with hepatitis A vaccine, will gain some protection from hepatitis A vaccine or gammaglobulin given as soon as a family member develops jaundice. This must come from a reliable (i.e. developed country) source.

Infection with hepatitis usually gives life-long immunity to that form of hepatitis.

Please see further details in Appendix F, pages 209–12.

INTESTINAL WORMS

Worms, or helminths as they are known medically, are an occupational hazard of all but the most fastidious travellers, and perhaps the commonest cause of a scream from the loo. Here are the most widespread:

Pinworms (threadworms, Enterobius)

You don't have to leave the UK to catch pinworms, which are very common, especially among children. They are about one centimetre long, whitish, and look like threads. They usually reveal their presence by being passed in the stool or by the *symptom* of anal itching, especially at night. They are a nuisance, but not dangerous. *Prevention* depends on good personal hygiene. *Treatment* is with mebendazole 100 mg (Vermox) one, twice daily for three days (not in children under two, or in pregnancy) or piperazine (Pripsen). Piperazine can be used in children under two, but the dosages are quite complex and you will need medical advice or at the very least to read the instructions on the drug data sheet. Dosages are different for pinworms and roundworms.

Roundworms (Ascaris)

These are found throughout the tropics, especially affecting school-age children and those living among the local population. Roundworms look rather like earthworms; they are 20–30 cm long, smooth, round and non-segmented.

Symptoms include abdominal pain, a distended abdomen or occasionally loss of weight. Often there are no symptoms, and a junior member of the household discovers one or more, often with great astonishment, on passing a stool or, even worse, during a vomiting attack. Eggs are often *but not always* found on stool tests. *Prevention* depends on careful food and personal hygiene. *Treatment* is with mebendazole as described above or with piperazine.

Hookworms (Ankylostoma)

Hookworms occur quite commonly in expatriates, especially those who go barefoot or wear unprotected sandals or flip-flops. They are not noticed in the stool, but their eggs may show up on stool tests. Heavy infection with hookworm is harmful, especially in children because it leads to anaemia. Anyone who has *symptoms* of unexplained tiredness, shortness of breath or lack of energy should consider treating themselves for hookworm and having a haemoglobin test. *Prevention* depends on wearing shoes when walking outside the home. *Treatment* is with mebendazole, again as described above.

Another type of hookworm (Strongyloides) is spread in a similar way and can cause more severe symptoms. Eggs may show on stool tests, but an ELISA blood test is more likely to uncover it. Albendazole tablets, 400 mg daily for three days, with the same dose repeated after three weeks, usually cures it.

Tapeworms (Taenia)

You can become infected with tapeworm by eating undercooked beef (T. saginata) or pork (T. solium) or occasionally through poorly cooked food or salads contaminated with infected human faeces. Tapeworms are long, flat segmented worms, and sections may be noticed in the stool. Often they cause no obvious *symptoms* but their eggs, or worm segments, are found on stool tests.

Pork tapeworm occasionally leads to cysticercosis, a condition in which cysts can develop in other organs causing, for example, epileptic fits if one lodges in the brain. *Prevention* is through making sure that all meat, especially pork, is thoroughly cooked, meaning the centre of the meat should be brown or grey, not pink. Treatment is best done with praziquantel 20 mg/kg as a single dose after a light breakfast, or with niclosamide, but a doctor should confirm the diagnosis and supervise the treatment.

A *final suggestion*

For expatriate families or anyone living among the local population in a developing country, there is much to be said for a six-monthly 'worm-workout'. Dose yourself and any member of the family, unless under two or pregnant, with mebendazole 100 mg tablets, one twice daily for three days. Then do a final purge when you eventually get home. Mebendazole usually kills all the common worms except tapeworms.

LEISHMANIASIS

This disease comes in various forms. One is a serious illness affecting the whole body and known as visceral leishmaniasis (VL) or Kala Azar. This is rare in travellers but spreading in epidemic form in some areas of the world, such as Sudan and north India. More important for the traveller are the skin form, cutaneous leishmaniasis (CL) (more commonly known as oriental sore), and mucosal leishmaniasis (ML), which affects the mucous membranes of the mouth and nose.

All forms of leishmaniasis are caused by a one-celled parasite known as Leishmania, passed on by the bite of a sandfly that is active at dusk and dawn. CL is found around the Mediterranean, parts of Asia and the northern half of Africa and causes an ulcerating nodule following a sandfly bite on an exposed part of the body, especially the face, legs and arms. It may develop days, months or even years after the bite, and though not serious can leave a disfiguring scar.

ML is found in tropical America and gives a severe, ulcerating sore around the mouth and nose (Espundia), again leaving permanent scarring.

To *prevent* leishmaniasis, avoid sandfly bites in affected areas. Use insect repellents and permethrin-impregnated bed-nets, or sleep on the roof. Report to a doctor any bite that persists or ulcerates.

MENINGITIS

Meningitis is an infectious illness that causes inflammation of the brain lining. There are several forms, many caused by viruses spread by contaminated food and water. They commonly cause abdominal upsets and severe headache, which settle without treatment. Until recently, children between two months and five years were affected by Haemophilus meningitis, but Hib vaccine now makes this very rare in the UK and protects children when they travel abroad.

A much more serious form of meningitis is caused by an organism known as Meningococcus, or Neisseria, and the rest of this section refers to this form of the disease. It is spread by breathing in the germs from infected people or from healthy carriers. Meningococcal meningitis is found in many tropical countries, including the Sahel (countries bordering the southern Sahara, known as the 'Meningitis Belt'), though epidemics occur in countries to the south and the north of this area. There have been recent outbreaks in other parts of Africa, in Nepal and the UK.

The disease comes in various strains, and vaccines have been developed against forms A and C, which cause the most severe outbreaks, but not yet against form B. Meningitis tends to occur in the cool season when people crowd together – in the Sahel this coincides with our winter.

Symptoms include fever, severe headache, neck stiffness, nausea or vomiting, often preceded by a blotchy rash. In meningitis this rash does not go white when you press it. One easy way of testing this is to press a glass against the skin. If it does not blanch, assume this is meningitis and get immediate medical treatment (see below). Often meningitis is known to be present in the area. Children are at special risk.

The illness caused by forms A and C can be prevented by a single immunization (see Appendix F). Those visiting areas where the disease is known to occur, especially if working with children or in crowded communities, should be immunized, as should all children visiting affected areas. Anyone who has had their spleen removed should be immunized for any overseas travel. During epidemics try to avoid crowded conditions.

Treatment needs to be started immediately by a doctor as the disease can cause death within hours. In an emergency, health workers can give penicillin G two mega units, one injection intramuscularly into each buttock.

Please see further details in Appendix F (page 213).

MIGRAINE AND HEADACHES

Migraine and headaches in general often become worse when working overseas. Stress, dehydration and missing meals can contribute to this; so can monosodium glutamate (MSG), present in meals from many parts of the world, not just China. Sudden changes of altitude can also make headaches worse.

If you have a tendency to migraine, before you travel discuss in detail with your doctor how you will manage it. Take plenty of your preferred medication with you. A good first-line *treatment* is one tablet of metoclopramide 10 mg (Maxolon – prescription needed in UK), or domperidone (Motilium – not in pregnancy), followed ten minutes later by either soluble aspirin total 900 mg (usually three tablets) or soluble paracetamol total 1,000 mg (usually two tablets). Keep your fluid intake up, and consider a sweet snack between meals. Some find that giving up tea, cheese, coffee, chocolate or alcohol helps, though it may take you at least two weeks to become de-addicted to coffee, during which time headaches may be worse. Migraine can be worsened by the contraceptive pill.

It is worth knowing that there is a range of treatments available for migraine, both for prevention and cure, and if the medication you have been using is not working it is worth trying another. Sumatriptan (Imigran) is one example, but it is very expensive if you need to send back for more supplies when overseas as you will not be eligible for NHS prescriptions. Most GPs are experienced at dealing with migraine.

If headaches still seem to be getting worse, review your lifestyle and see if there are any changes you can make to reduce stress and overwork. Look at ways in which you can relax both on the job or at home, or how you might get away for a break or a holiday.

If headaches worsen for no obvious reason or they persist or start for the first time, this may be caused by a wide variety of infections and other conditions, including malaria. It would be sensible to consult a doctor.

MOUTH ULCERS

These can be a real nuisance among longer-term travellers. Often proguanil (Paludrine) contributes to mouth ulcers, but only change to another antimalarial if your mouth drives you crazy. Mouth ulcers can also develop if you are tired, run down or have repeated bowel problems. Sometimes they just occur for no reason.

They are best *treated* by making sure you eat a well-balanced diet, getting any bowel infection diagnosed and treated and making sure you have enough sleep and leisure. Some people find that taking vitamin B complex daily or folic acid 5 mg for a month seems to help. Try using an antiseptic mouth wash (e.g. chlorhexidine or povidone iodine) or carbenoxolone gel (Bioral) or hydrocortisone 2.5 mg lozenges (Corlan). If any single ulcer or mouth problems last longer than three weeks you should get checked out by a doctor.

PLAGUE

Plague, well known as the cause of the Black Death, still causes occasional outbreaks in parts of Asia, Africa and South America. Zaire, India, Madagascar and Mongolia have recently reported cases. Although the risk to travellers and expatriates is extremely remote, the fear of plague can cause much anxiety and it is therefore worth knowing about its prevention. There have been recent reports of resistance developing in some areas, meaning that plague may be harder to treat in future.

Plague is *caused* by a bacterium that affects rodents (especially rats) and occasionally other mammals, including humans. It is spread by fleas that come from an infected (often dying) animal and that are looking for another host. A bite from an infected flea causes *bubonic* plague, but a person so infected may pass on the germs (through coughing or breathing) to others, who then develop *pneumonic* plague.

Symptoms develop within a week, and in the case of bubonic plague include severe shivering, high temperature and pain, as well as swelling in the groin or armpit, caused by inflamed glands (bubos). Untreated cases have a 50/50 chance of survival.

Pneumonic plague starts and progresses rapidly, with fever, cough and severe shortness of breath, death usually occurring within forty-eight hours.

Prevention of plague consists of avoiding areas where outbreaks are known to be *currently* occurring. If this is not possible, take every effort to avoid flea bites by applying insect repellent and sleeping with permethrin-impregnated sheets or bed-nets. Both bed-nets and sheets must be well tucked in as fleas can otherwise jump from the floor to the bed. Bed legs should ideally be stood in jars of water. Kill off any potentially infected rodents, especially rats in or near the house. Regularly treat domestic pets with flea powder. Plague vaccines are not currently recommended, except for vets and zoologists working in affected areas.

Consider taking preventative antibiotics in the following three situations: definite contact with a case of plague; being in crowded areas where pneumonic cases are occurring; and the possibility of a flea bite from an infected animal.

Adults and children over the age of eight should take tetracycline or oxytetracycline 250 mg tablets four times daily for one week, if necessary repeating this if further contact occurs. Children between the ages of two and eight, if at high risk, can take ciprofloxacin 10 mg/kg daily in two divided doses for one week. (Ciprofloxacin is not otherwise used in children.) Children under the age of two, and pregnant women, should avoid areas where plague cases are occurring.

Treatment, if you develop any suspicious symptoms, must start immediately and be under medical supervision. The same antibiotics are used – twice the above dose of tetracycline or oxytetracycline, and 15 mg/kg of ciprofloxacin. Trimethoprim 200 mg twice daily has proved effective when resistance occurs, as in parts of Madagascar.

RABIES

Note: Even if you have had a course of three rabies injections before going abroad, you will still need further injections if you are bitten, licked or scratched by an animal that may have rabies (see below).

What is rabies?

Rabies is a virus infection of man and other mammals, spread by a bite, lick or scratch from an infected mammal. Certain mammals are well known as 'reservoirs' of infection. Examples are the dog almost worldwide, the fox in Europe and vampire bats in South America and the Caribbean. However, any mammal may be infected, and can in turn pass on the infection.

Rabies is found in over 150 countries, though the following are effectively free: the United Kingdom, Australia and New Zealand, Norway and Sweden, Japan, Papua New Guinea, most Pacific and many Caribbean Islands. Rabies is especially common in the Indian subcontinent, Afghanistan, Thailand including Bangkok, Vietnam and the Philippines, and parts of tropical Latin America and Africa. For more specific advice visit a travel clinic or ask your GP. Whether or not to be immunized is a matter of carefully weighing benefits and risks, including the cost (see Appendix F).

Risk to travellers

As a traveller or expatriate you have two risks, both of which need preventing: the small but important one of being infected with rabies, and the more common experience of anxiety following an encounter with a suspicious animal that you did nothing about. By being well informed and appropriately vaccinated you can be well protected against both these risks. Your maximum risk times are when travelling in rural areas, trekking or jogging, or when you or your children touch an apparently friendly but unknown dog, monkey, squirrel or cat.

The symptoms of rabies

These are well known. In animals there is often a change of behaviour, a dog becoming more aggressive or more docile than usual. There may be an aversion to water. Unprovoked attacks by dogs or by any animal that behaves aggressively should ring alarm bells, especially if rabies is common in the area. *Some infected (and infectious) animals behave quite normally.*

Humans can develop symptoms any time from four days to two years after being bitten (usually 30 to 60 days).

The symptoms progress rapidly from fever and headache to paralysis, bouts of terror and aggression to coma and death. There is no cure once symptoms have started.

Personal protection from rabies

This is through a series of three injections with Human Diploid Cell Vaccine (HDCV) or equivalent before travelling abroad. More details are given in Appendix F. HDCV is a simple and safe vaccine, given into the upper arm, with minimal side effects. All those spending six months or more in an area where rabies exists should have it, as should those on shorter journeys if travelling off the beaten path or in areas where rabies is known to be present. Remember, however, that these injections will *not* necessarily give you full protection.

When first taking up residence in a developing country, identify a safe source of HDCV (and HRIG – see below) by asking your embassy or another reliable source of information.

Keep anti-rabies injections up-to-date on domestic pets, especially dogs (see page 45).

Action after being bitten, licked or scratched by a suspicious animal

- Wash the wound carefully with soap and water, if possible under a running tap to remove infected saliva and dirt. Apply either tincture of iodine or alcohol (gin or whisky will do). It is better not to scrub. The wound should not generally be sutured.
- Consider as potentially rabid any animal that is *either* behaving strangely *or* is unknown *or* that disappears. Try to identify and observe the animal for ten days. Any animal alive after this time can be considered safe.
- Start rabies injections using one of the regimes below:
  – Either:
  The short regime – if you have definitely had a course of three primary injections in the past, with subsequent boosters every two to three years.

  Your should now have: one dose of 1 ml HDCV at the time of the bite and another 3–7 days later by the intramuscular route into the deltoid muscle (upper arm), or in a child into the upper outer part of the child's thigh.
  – Or:
  The full regime – if you have *not* had a full course of preventative injections with regular boosters as recommended above.

  You should now have: 1 ml of HDCV on days 0, 3, 7, 14 and 30 by the intramuscular route, the exact timing of the last one not being critical.

  In addition, if the incident happened within the last seven days, you will need to have an injection of either Human Rabies Immune Globulin (HRIG) 20 units per kg body weight *or* Equine Antirabies Serum (EARS) 40 units per kg body weight. HRIG and EARS should be given *after* HDCV (both may be hard to obtain). In either case half is infiltrated around the bite and half given by intramuscular injection. Because EARS may cause an allergic reaction, a doctor should be present with a supply of adrenalin (ideally a skin test should be done first).

  If the suspect animal is alive after ten days, rabies injections can be discontinued.
- In many developing countries post-mortem tests on the brain of an infected animal cannot be relied upon. However, where good facilities exist a brain fluorescent antibody test can be arranged.

- Ensure that your tetanus cover is up to date, and also that any infection is treated promptly with antibiotics.

Special situations

Delays

If *either* there is a delay in starting HDCV of more than forty-eight hours *or* if HRIG or EARS have been given *before* HDCV *or* the person at risk is either elderly, malnourished or with lowered immunity, the first HDCV should be trebled and given at three different sites of the body.

Even with longer delays of days or weeks it is still worth starting a course of HDCV injections if you come to recognize that you have had a suspicious encounter.

Rabies and children

Children and toddlers with their love for furry beasts have a higher risk of being exposed to rabies. Actively discourage them from touching unknown animals. Prophylactic (pre-exposure) injections are only currently recommended from one year upwards, but post-exposure treatment is given regardless of age.

Rabies and pregnancy

Pregnant women are not normally given prophylactic injections, but post-exposure treatment is essential and no serious reactions have been reported.

Note: If a local doctor suggests that a single injection or tablet alone are sufficient, *do not accept such advice*, rather follow the instructions above.

For further details on rabies immunization, see Appendix F.

RIVER BLINDNESS (Onchocerciasis)

This is found in scattered areas of tropical Africa and, less commonly, parts of Central America and the Yemen. It is spread by black flies (2–4 mm long), appropriately known as Simulium damnosum. They usually breed near fast-flowing rivers. Untreated, the disease can eventually lead to blindness, rare in travellers unless repeatedly reinfected. Those working in rural areas where it is known to occur are at risk.

Symptoms include an initial bite, often painful, which may be followed by skin nodules, especially over the lower trunk. Often itching or an itchy rash is the first symptom and this, along with swollen lymph nodes, may develop many months, or up to three years, after leaving the affected area. Eye symptoms are rare in travellers.

Prevention includes covering the skin and using insect repellents. Those working in high-risk areas can take prophylactic treatment under specialist advice. *Treatment* with ivermectin is effective but should be under medical supervision. Long-term follow-up is needed.

If you have been working in an area where the disease is known to occur, you should have a blood test on return, especially if you develop itching within weeks or months, with or without a rash. Usually the eosinophil count will be raised and a filaria serology test may be positive. A skin snip at a Tropical Disease Centre clinches the diagnosis. *Treatment* is quite simple – ivermectin under medical supervision.

SEXUALLY TRANSMITTED DISEASES (STDs)

These are theoretically the easiest diseases to *prevent*. You can forget about them if either you practise abstinence or have sex only in the context of a long-term stable relationship with a partner known to be unaffected. Pre- or extramarital sex always carries the risk of catching an STD, especially if you don't use a condom. Even in those committed to a risk-free lifestyle it is easy to slip up during a time of stress, loneliness – or celebration.

Those diseases always or most frequently transmitted sexually include: syphilis, gonorrhoea, chlamydia, lymphogranuloma, chancroid, trichomonas, genital herpes, pubic lice, hepatitis B and HIV infection.

There are two *symptoms* that should alert you to the probability of an STD: genital ulcers and a penile discharge. Vaginal discharge and pelvic pain have a greater variety of causes (see page 170). You should take these seriously because left untreated they can lead to pelvic infection and infertility.

If you suspect you may have an STD, try to see a reliable doctor as soon as possible. Only if this is not possible should you self-treat. Make sure your partner also gets checked out. If you have an STD confirmed, try and contact anyone else you have recently had sex with, and encourage them to get checked as well. Treatments usually effective for STDs include:

Tetracycline 500 mg four times daily *or* doxycycline 100 mg twice daily for seven days *or* ciprofloxacin 500 mg single dose *or* azithromycin one gram single dose. These drugs are not suitable in pregnancy – instead use erythromycin 500 mg four times daily for fifteen days.

If you've been at any risk, have a full medical check when you get home, ideally at an STD clinic (no appointment usually necessary), and consider having an HIV test, always done with counselling.

SKIN CONDITIONS

The combination of sun, heat, biting insects and lack of hygiene means that skin problems are common in developing countries. Aid workers, adventure travellers, children, and volunteers on low budgets need to take special care. The following are some of the common problems.

Blisters

These can develop very quickly, may be slow to heal and often become infected.

Prevent them by wearing well-fitting shoes, loose cotton socks and if trekking or walking any distance, by *wearing-in your shoes or boots for several days before*. Sandals, especially if worn without socks in dusty areas, quickly lead to blisters.

Treat blisters as follows: if the skin is broken, wash carefully, apply antiseptic cream and a non-adherent bandage, secured with an adhesive dressing. If unbroken leave intact if possible, otherwise pierce roof of blister with sterile needle, apply gauze covered with thin layer of Vaseline and secure with adhesive dressing. Avoid the offending footwear.

Boils and infected bites

These are very common in the tropics, often developing at times of overwork, stress or when due for home leave or a holiday. They often start as bites, which become infected through scratching.

Prevent boils by trying to develop a balanced lifestyle with adequate rest and relaxation; eat a well-balanced diet with fresh fruit and vegetables. Wash regularly with soap and water. Salt water is helpful either through bathing in the sea (where unpolluted) or, if you are prone to boils, by adding a handful of salt to bath water where possible. If living in an institution, make sure your sheets are properly cleaned and take care over your laundry.

Treat boils as follows: wash gently with soap and water and apply antiseptic cream. Do not squeeze, especially if on the head and neck, but allow the boil to come to a point and burst naturally, at which time you can apply absorbent gauze with Vaseline. Larger boils, especially in the armpit, may need lancing by a doctor or nurse using a sterile blade.

Those with a tendency for troublesome boils should take flucloxacillin capsules 500 mg every six hours for a week, or if allergic to penicillin, erythromycin 500 mg every six hours for one week, in each case starting when the boil first develops. Because the germs causing boils often live in the nostrils, also apply a cream containing both an antibiotic and an antiseptic (marketed in the UK as Naseptin) into both nostrils by using your cleaned little finger twice daily for a week. Ideally also use this in all household members – especially children. If you are troubled by boils, take a supply of one of these antibiotics and Naseptin with you.

Boils are occasionally caused by tumbu flies (see page 114).

Creeping eruption (Larva migrans, sandworm)

This is caused by a larva that penetrates the skin and causes a red, slowly moving itchy line. It is usually caught on tropical beaches, especially if there are a lot of dogs about.

The chief *symptom* is a red itchy line, usually either on the sole of the foot or the buttock. It can be *prevented* by lying on a towel rather than directly on the beach, and by walking barefoot only *below* the high tide mark. It can be *treated* either by allowing it to disappear naturally or by taking albendazole 400 mg tablets, two daily for five days.

Fungal infections (Tinea)

Fungi like warm, moist conditions, and are therefore very common in tropical climates. The main *symptom* is a red, rough itchy patch, often circular with a spreading edge.

Athlete's foot (Tinea pedis) causes itching between the toes; groin itch (Dhobie's itch, Tinea cruris) causes itching in the groin and between the legs. Other 'ringworm' infections occur in the scalp or anywhere on the body surface.

Thrush commonly causes a reddish line in the folds of the groin and the breast, especially in the overweight; thrush is also the commonest cause of itchy vaginal discharge (see page 170). You can help *prevent* fungal infections by bathing regularly, wearing loose-fitting cotton underpants (Dhobie's itch) and open-toed shoes or sandals with cotton socks changed daily (athlete's foot). Trainers or any shoe with an internal rubber sole are likely to make athlete's foot worse.

You can *treat* athlete's foot by applying an antifungal dusting powder, e.g. Mycota, between the toes and into the socks. Treat other fungus infections by applying clotrimazole cream (Canesten) three times daily until two weeks after symptoms have cleared. Fungal infections (except thrush) that fail to clear respond to griseofulvin tabs 500 mg twice daily until at least all signs of the infection have disappeared, or itraconazole 100 mg once daily for fifteen days (see Appendix A). Avoid both of these in pregnancy.

Travellers often notice a scaly rash with some paling of the skin, usually over the back and trunk. This is known as Pityriasis versicolor and is best treated by an antifungal cream such as terbinafine applied for two weeks. Patches that continue to look pale usually brown over once you are cautiously back in the sun.

Impetigo (infected skin)

This is a common bacterial infection of the skin that tends to occur when you are tired, hot or run-down. You recognize it by the *symptom* of a spreading, slightly itchy rash that weeps golden-coloured pus. It is very infectious.

Treat by gently removing crusts with povidone-iodine (or another antiseptic) or salty water, and applying a topical antibiotic cream or ointment such as fucidic acid or mupirocin. If it continues to spread, or you develop red, hot skin in patches or streaks, with or without swollen lymph nodes, start oral antibiotics such as flucloxacillin 500 mg four times a day, amoxycillin 500 mg three times a day or, if allergic to penicillin, erythromycin 500 mg four times daily, in each case for seven days. You should see a doctor.

Prickly heat

This is an itchy condition caused by the blocking up of sweat ducts. It is common in children and those not acclimatized. *Symptoms* consist of small reddish spots on a pinkish skin, which develop mainly on the upper trunk, armpits, waist and the backs of the knees and neck. It disturbs sleep and can be very irritating, especially for children.

You can *prevent* it by wearing light-fitting cotton clothing and by avoiding excessive soap. Dust talcum powder into clothes that rub against the skin.

It is best *treated* by applying calamine lotion and keeping as cool as possible. Air conditioning helps to reduce it, but most expatriates improve anyway after acclimatization.

Skin cancer

Those most at risk from skin cancer include long-term residents of the tropics, the fair-skinned and anyone exposed to prolonged or excessive sun in childhood. Make sure you take sensible precautions to avoid too much sun (see pages 106–8).

The two commonest cancers are:

Malignant melanomas: these usually arise in existing moles. If a mole starts to enlarge, darken, become less regular, or begins to itch, ooze or bleed, report it to a doctor.

Basal cell carcinomas (BCCs or rodent ulcers): these are locally malignant but do not spread to other parts of the body, meaning treatment is always successful. The face is the commonest site, and they usually occur in older people. If you notice any persistent nodule, lump or rough patch that ulcerates, oozes or bleeds, see a doctor. It could be a BCC or it could be another form of skin cancer that needs more urgent treatment.

In addition, older people or those exposed to years of sun often develop scaly, sometimes darkened patches on the face, neck, forearms or backs of the hands. If you have these, known as solar keratoses, show them to a doctor as occasionally they lead to skin cancer. Equally, if you have lived in a hot climate for a long time or are worried about your skin, have this looked at during your regular tropical check-up on return home.

See also page 21, which tells you how some pre-existing skin conditions are affected by hot climates.

SLEEPING SICKNESS (Trypanosomiasis)

Sleeping sickness is present in scattered rural areas across tropical Africa, and is becoming commoner in some areas. It is caused by the bite of an infected Tsetse fly (about 1 cm in length and like a large housefly), which flies during the day (see Figure 11). Expatriates visiting known areas, especially on wildlife safaris in east Africa or working on development programmes, are at slight risk of getting it.

Symptoms start with a boil-like, usually painful, swelling at the site of the bite. Fever may then develop within two to three weeks (east Africa), sometimes months later (west and central Africa), often with enlarged lymph nodes, especially in the neck. Headache and drowsiness gradually increase.

If you have suspicious symptoms, consult a doctor experienced in tropical diseases without delay. *Treatment* must be under medical supervision but *prevention* is quite straightforward: use insect repellents, cover exposed areas of your body and avoid wearing the colour blue (a favourite with many Tsetses) when in known areas.

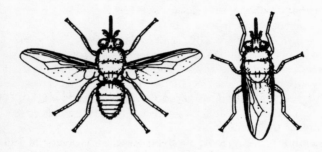

Figure 11 Tsetse fly (about 1 cm long)

TICK-BORNE RELAPSING FEVER (TBRF)

This disease is sometimes known as tick-bite fever, though this can also refer to tick typhus, caused by Rickettsia organisms (see page 193). TBRF is found mainly in east Africa, e.g. Tanzania, but cases also occur in west Africa and elsewhere in the tropics. It is caused by an organism known as Borrelia, which is spread by infected ticks that live in cracks and crevices and that bite during the night. Those sleeping in mud huts in known areas are at risk.

Symptoms depend on the area. Commonly TBRF mimics malaria, with high fever, head and muscle ache and vomiting, the symptoms usually lasting four to seven days. It commonly relapses after about seven further days, sometimes on repeated occasions, each attack gradually becoming less severe. It is dangerous in pregnancy.

Treatment is with tetracycline tablets 250 mg four times a day for one week. (An alternative should be used in pregnancy.) However, symptoms should first be treated as for malaria, unless this has been excluded on a blood slide.

Prevention is to avoid sleeping in mud huts in areas where the disease is known to occur, using insect repellents and mosquito nets, sleeping as high off the floor as possible and removing any ticks as soon as they are discovered (see page 114).

TONSILLITIS AND SORE THROATS

You will not necessarily escape such mundane problems as colds and sore throats by living in the tropics. If you have suffered from tonsillitis before going abroad, you may well find it recurs, especially at times of stress, overwork or exhaustion.

The *symptoms* of tonsillitis are fever, sore throat and swollen lymph nodes. Very occasionally throat infections may be caused by diphtheria (foul breath, greenish membrane on throat).

Prevention is to give priority to holidays, one or two days off in seven, and trying to achieve a balanced lifestyle. If you have a tendency to tonsillitis, consider starting antibiotic treatment *as soon as symptoms start*.

If you have had several severe attacks in the recent past, discuss with your doctor whether you should have a tonsillectomy before going abroad or when you get home.

Many sore throats and most attacks of tonsillitis are caused by a germ called Streptococcus (Strep throat), and any sore throat, especially if accompanied by swollen neck glands and a fever, is worth *treating* with antibiotics for ten days.

Use either penicillin V 250 mg four times daily or amoxycillin 500 mg three times daily. If you are allergic to penicillin, try erythromycin 500 mg four times daily. Some people find that gargling with aspirin can soothe the pain, but this should not be used in those under 12.

Remember, however, that many sore throats are caused by viruses, and although antibiotics will cause no harm, neither will they make any difference.

Glandular fever is a common cause of sore throat, especially in younger travellers (see page 162).

TOOTH PROBLEMS

Reasons for taking toothcare seriously

Severe toothache and dental abscesses are surprisingly common in those living overseas. It is worth giving your teeth a high degree of priority for the following reasons:

- Severe toothache can ruin a visit, an important programme or a holiday.
- Tooth abscesses often occur when you are tired or run-down, as for example during a tough assignment or at the end of a volunteer year.
- Dental care overseas is often unreliable, may be very expensive and carries a small but definite hepatitis B and HIV risk in some countries.
- The water used as a coolant or to rinse your mouth may be contaminated.

Recommendations for looking after your teeth

- Have a thorough dental check well before you leave. Have any fillings attended to, any ill-fitting dentures replaced and any pre-emptive treatment of impacted or painful wisdom teeth. Whenever you come on leave, have a further check.
- Choose any dentist overseas with care and on personal recommendation. Check as far as you are able that all needles and syringes are sealed, disposable and not reused; also that all instruments are steam-sterilized.
- Consider taking an emergency dental kit and a supply of antibiotics (see Appendix A).
- Clean your teeth regularly using boiled, filtered or bottled water unless tap water is known to be safe. Keep a supply in the bathroom or wherever you clean your teeth.

Common dental problems

- *Toothache*. This may be caused either by injury, the loosening of a filling or a dental abscess that is starting to form. If pain becomes severe or prolonged, try to find a reliable dentist and in the meantime start treatment with antibiotics, as detailed below. Oil of cloves can ease the pain, as can aspirin placed at the base of the tooth. In children, give paracetamol tablets or syrup by mouth, rather than aspirin.
- *Tooth abscess*. This is usually obvious because of severe pain on moving the tooth or pressing the root. Sometimes you may develop a swollen cheek or jaw (which may be painful or painless). *Treat* an abscess by taking antibiotics such as amoxycillin 500 mg three times a day for seven days (not if allergic to penicillin) or erythromycin 500 mg four times daily. See a dentist, who may either remove the tooth or recommend root canal treatment. If the latter, enquire *carefully* how many treatments are likely and the cost of each.
- *Lost dentures*. Consider taking a spare pair, and try to remove them before any attack of vomiting.
- *A broken front tooth*. If clean, soak in salty boiled water and replace within half an hour, pressing in firmly the right way round. Get to the dentist as soon as possible.
- Known heart problems such as past history of rheumatic fever, heart valve disease, or presence of prosthetic valves. Antibiotic cover will be needed for all dental work – discuss this with your dentist before going overseas. Widely used is amoxycillin 2 gm by mouth thirty minutes before and 1 gm six hours after any dental work, or if allergic to penicillin, erythromycin 1.5 gm before and 1 gm after.

Preventing tooth problems

This is through regular dental cleaning, at least twice a day. Dental floss is valuable. Avoid excessive sweets and too much oversweetened tea or soft drinks, unless there is nothing else safe to drink.

A small amount of fluoride helps prevent tooth decay; too much leads to tooth mottling and discolouration. Natural levels of fluoride in the water tend to be higher in tropical countries. Use fluoride tablets only if local levels are known to be very low or absent. Fluoride toothpaste can still be used, but make sure children don't eat it.

A *dental kit*

These are available and widely used by those living in remote conditions or where dental facilities are unreliable. They usually contain equipment for temporary replacements of crowns, bridges and caps, as well as material for temporary fillings. After using a kit, see a reliable dentist as soon as you can. If you take a kit, make sure you also have a supply of antibiotics.

TUBERCULOSIS

Expatriates occasionally develop TB, usually if they have been working with TB cases or living long term among the local population. With the spread of AIDS, TB is becoming commoner, meaning that those working in HIV-affected areas are at an increased risk.

Tuberculosis is most commonly a disease of the lungs, caused by germs spreading from an infectious case or from reactivation of a previous (often unknown) lesion. Only rarely is it spread in the tropics from infected milk. TB is spreading in many parts of the world, especially Africa, Asia, the former Soviet States and Eastern Europe.

Symptoms include loss of weight, fever and declining health, plus symptoms specific to the organs involved. Most commonly the lungs are affected, giving persistent cough with sputum (sometimes blood-stained), chest pain and evening fever. Children may simply lose weight or fail to gain it, only developing specific symptoms later.

TB is partly *prevented* by having a BCG vaccination. This is only given if a tuberculin test (Mantoux, Heaf or Tine test) carried out before is negative, showing that no natural immunity is present. Babies and young children who have not knowingly been exposed to TB can be given BCG without prior testing (see Appendix F).

Everyone going to live for any length of time in a developing country should make sure they have either had a BCG vaccination or a positive tuberculin test. As immunity may not be lifelong, adults at high risk should not depend on the BCG they had at school but should be retested and, if negative, given BCG unless a scar from a previous BCG is present. Similarly, those serving long term overseas in high-risk occupations should consider regular tuberculin testing. There are two reasons for this: the first is to make sure the test is not negative (if it is, a further BCG should be considered). The second is to make sure the test is not strongly positive (if it is, it could indicate early infection). It is worth noting that American guidelines on the use of BCG differ widely from British guidelines.

If you develop suspicious symptoms either abroad or after you come home, consult a doctor as soon as possible. You should have a special TB microscopy and culture of any sputum you cough up, as well as a chest X-ray and repeat tuberculin test. If TB is caught early it can be fully *treated* using multi-drug therapy under careful medical supervision.

TYPHUS

This is a group of diseases caused by an organism known as Rickettsia. There are various forms in different parts of the world, but two types are most commonly seen in travellers.

Scrub typhus is the most serious, found in rural Asia (especially South-East Asia) and some Pacific Islands. It is caused by small red mites called chiggers (not to be confused with jiggers), found in long grass and jungle areas (see page 115).

Tick typhus comes in several forms and is mainly found in Africa (especially southern Africa, e.g. Kruger Park area) and in the Middle East and southern Europe. Ticks become attached to your skin while walking in long grass or savannah.

Both forms of typhus give you the *symptoms* of a feverish illness, severe tiredness, aches and pains (sometimes severe), four to fourteen days after being infected. Often there is a dark, round skin patch with a reddish border at the place you were bitten (known as a tache-noire or eschar). This is often on the ankle, which may swell up. Lymph nodes may develop in the groin. Sometimes a rash develops.

Prevention is being aware of the risk and protecting your lower limbs by wearing trousers, strong shoes or boots, and tucking trousers into long socks. If you are on serious walking safaris or expeditions in affected areas, apply a DEET-based insect repellent to your skin and soak your socks in permethrin.

Treatment is to start on doxycycline 100 mg capsules, two together, then one daily for one week for tick typhus, and two daily for one week in scrub typhus, which remember is usually a more serious disease.

Your symptoms may baffle not only you but also your doctor, so it is worth being aware of this condition, which is being seen more commonly. A special blood test confirms the diagnosis.

URINARY TRACT INFECTION (UTI)

The *symptoms* of this are usually but not always obvious – an urge to pass urine, accompanied by pain or a burning sensation. Hot, bumpy journeys, dehydration and increased sexual activity on holidays can contribute. For expatriates living in hot climates, urinary infections are sometimes associated with a kidney or bladder stone.

Women tend to get urinary infections more commonly than men, and any infection in a man should always be investigated by a doctor, as should repeated infections in a woman. Children who start, or restart, wetting their bed for no obvious reason may have a urinary infection.

If you are unable to see a doctor or arrange a urine test, have plenty to drink and *self-treat* with either trimethoprim 100 mg, two tablets twice daily for five to seven days, or amoxycillin 250 mg three times daily for five to seven days. If there is a risk of having a sexually transmitted disease, see a doctor. Also see page 183.

It is sensible to have a urine test on return home, to make sure no infection persists.

YELLOW FEVER

Yellow fever is a virus infection found in the tropical belt of South America, and in Africa, especially west Africa (Figure 12). It is unknown in Asia. The risk to travellers is small, and becomes negligible in those immunized within the past ten years.

Yellow fever is spread by the bite of the Aedes mosquito. 'Jungle' yellow fever is found in forested areas and is spread by mosquitoes from infected monkeys. 'Urban' yellow fever is spread by the mosquito from an infected person. In practice, those at greatest risk are forest workers in Brazil and children in west Africa.

Symptoms are a sudden onset of fever, abdominal pain, backache, vomiting and headache, followed by signs of kidney and liver failure,

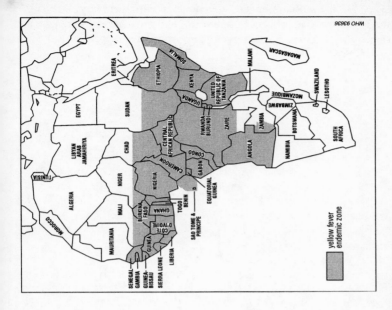

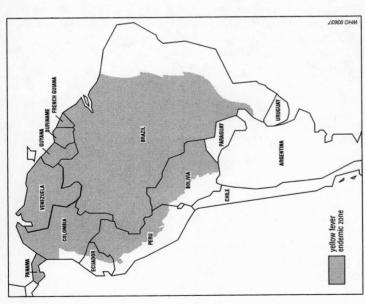

Figure 12 Areas where yellow fever is found (WHO 1999)

including jaundice. Symptoms always develop within six days of being infected. There is no specific *treatment*, but *prevention* is easy – a reliable, safe vaccine repeated every ten years (see Appendix F).

"It wasn't like this in Basildon."

APPENDIX A

Checklist of useful medicines

A supply of medicines or a medical kit is worth taking with you if you are working in a remote area or a place where you cannot easily obtain or trust essential medicines.

Pre-packed kits are available (see Appendix C for suppliers). Alternatively you can make up your own.

Please consult manufacturer's instructions and the text in this manual for further details, notes of side effects, interactions with other drugs, safety in pregnancy and when breastfeeding, and for exact dosages.

Dosages given are those commonly used for adults. They refer to the drugs listed in capitals, *not* to the alternatives.

Items marked # are available on prescription only. They can be obtained from your doctor, usually on a private rather than on an NHS prescription. Drugs not so marked are available over the counter.

Generic (scientific) names are given first; common brand names are in brackets.

P = avoid in pregnancy; B = avoid if breastfeeding.

Basic list

This is a suggested list of standard items for a tropical kit (some common alternatives are given).

Name	What used for	How used (normal adult dose)	P or B
AMOXYCILLIN # 250 mg caps (Amoxil)	General-purpose antibiotic Avoid if allergic to penicillin	One, three times daily for one week Double the dose in severe infections	
Alt. CO-AMOXICLAV # (Augmentin)			P
ANTACID tablets (various brand names)	Indigestion, heartburn	One or two as needed	
ANTISEPTIC CREAM (various brand names)	To prevent and treat skin infections	Rub in as needed. Start antibiotics by mouth if skin infection severe	
Alt. ANTIBIOTIC cream e.g. FUSIDIC ACID # (Fucidin) or MUPIROCIN # (Bactroban)			
CHLORPHENIRAMINE # 4 mg tabs (Piriton)	Allergy, hay fever, itching May cause drowsiness; take care driving	One, four-hourly as needed Double dose if severe allergic reaction	
CINNARIZINE 15 mg tabs (Stugeron)	Travel sickness May cause drowsiness	Two, two hours before flying, then one every eight hours if needed	
CIPROFLOXACIN # 250 mg tabs (Ciproxin)	To treat severe diarrhoea and dysentery. Avoid in children under 16 unless very ill	Two, twice daily for one day in severe diarrhoea; for three days in dysentery	P
CLOTRIMAZOLE cream (Canesten)	Fungal infections of the skin, vaginal thrush (pessaries also needed – see below)	Rub in as needed	
Alt. MICONAZOLE cream (Daktarin)			
ERYTHROMYCIN # 250 mg tabs	General-purpose antibiotic for those allergic to penicillin	One, four times daily for one week Double if infection severe	

Name	What used for	How used (normal adult dose)	P or B
GENTAMICIN # (Genticin) eye drops	Eye infections, especially conjunctivitis See a doctor if no rapid improvement	Use 1–2 drops every two hours, then gradually reduce. Continue 48 hours after infection cleared	
Alt. *CHLORAMPHENICOL* # *eye ointment or drops*			P
HYDROCORTISONE 1% cream	For bites, eczema, itchy skin conditions. Avoid if infected	Rub in twice daily for up to seven days	
INSECT REPELLENT containing DEET (various brand names)	To repel mosquitoes, sandflies and other biting insects	Rub in to exposed areas	
LOPERAMIDE 2 mg tabs (Imodium)	Emergency treatment of diarrhoea Avoid in children under four	Two, then one every four hours until diarrhoea controlled	P
MEBENDAZOLE # 100 mg tabs (Vermox)	Treatment of pin, round, whip and hookworm Not in children under two	One, twice daily for three days	
METOCLOPRAMIDE # 10 mg tabs (Maxolon)	Nausea, sickness	One, three times daily as needed	P
METRONIDAZOLE # 400 mg tabs (Flagyl, Zadstat)	Amoebiasis, giardiasis	Two, three times daily for five days	P
Alt. *TINIDAZOLE* # *(Fasigyn)*			P
ORAL REHYDRATION SALTS (Dioralyte, Rehidrat)	Diarrhoea, dehydration	One sachet with water, frequently	
PARACETAMOL 500 mg tabs (Panadol, Tylenol)	Pain, fever	Two, four- to six-hourly	
PARACETAMOL syrup (Calpol) is very useful in children			
SENOKOT tabs	For constipation, along with plenty to drink	2–4 tabs at bedtime as needed	

Additional list

You should also consider whether you need any of the following:

Name	What used for	How used	P or B
ANTIMALARIALS	See text	For prevention/treatment	P
ACETAZOLAMIDE # 250 mg tabs (Diamox)	To help prevent and treat acute mountain sickness	Two, 24 hours before ascending to 3,000 metres, continue two daily if climbing higher	P
CALAMINE lotion	Sore, inflamed, itchy skin	Apply as needed	
CLOTRIMAZOLE # pessaries (Canesten) *Alt. NYSTATIN pessaries*	Vaginal thrush	Insert one for six nights	P, B
FLUCLOXACILLIN # 250 mg caps (Floxapen)	To treat recurrent boils early if known tendency Avoid if allergic to penicillin	Two, four times daily for seven days	
ITRACONAZOLE # 100 mg tabs (Sporanox)	Avoid if taking antihistamines, erythromycin Avoid grapefruit and grapefruit juice	Vaginal thrush: two twice daily for one day Fungal skin infections: one daily for fifteen days	P, B
OIL OF CLOVES	Toothache	Apply to painful tooth and gum	
ORAL CONTRACEPTIVE PILL #	To prevent conception, delay periods, reduce menstrual flow	As instructed	P, B
TEMAZEPAM # 10 mg tabs (Normison) *Alt. ZOLPIDEM (Stilnoct)* #	Difficulty sleeping	One as needed, especially when crossing time zones	
TRIMETHOPRIM # 100 mg tabs	To treat urinary infections if known tendency	Two, twice daily for three to seven days	P

APPENDIX B

Checklist for first-aid kits

Please see pages 10–12 for further details of the types of kit recommended. A wide variety of kits is available from suppliers (see Appendix C) to cover the varying needs of travellers. Alternatively you can make up your own.

A simple first-aid kit could contain some or all of the following:

Crepe bandage
Plasters/band aids
Micropore tape
Triangular bandage
Cotton wool
Skin closure strips, e.g. Steristrips
Mediswabs
Non-adherent dressings, e.g. Melolin
Rubber gloves
Gauze swabs
Scissors
Safety pins
Tweezers
Savlon antiseptic
Clinical thermometer (preferably non-mercury)
Wound dressing
First-aid instructions
Documentation for customs
Contents list

You may also wish to take a needle and syringe kit for sterile supplies in an emergency. This could in addition include some or all of the following:

Needles – small, medium, large
Syringes – 2 ml and 5 ml
Malaria lancets
Skin suture with needle
Non-adherent dressings
Surgical tape, i.e. zinc oxide 1.25 cm wide
Butterfly needles for children

If in addition you plan to travel extensively in areas where HIV disease is common, you may wish to take an AIDS Protection Kit, which in addition to the above would include an intravenous giving set and fluid such as Hartmann's solution.

APPENDIX C

List of suppliers

ECHO International Health Services Ltd, 2 Ullswater Crescent, Coulsdon, Surrey CR3 2HR. Tel: 020–8660 2220; Fax: 020–8668 0751; e-mail: CS@echohealth.org.uk
Provides a wide range of bulk-supply medicines and equipment for overseas health projects.

InterHealth, 157 Waterloo Road, London SE1 8US. Tel: 020–7902 9000; fax: 020–7928 0927; e-mail: Interhealth@compuserve.com
InterHealth supplies a wide range of first-aid and medicine kits, mosquito nets, water filters, medicines and antimalarials. Also a catalogue describing items provided in detail, combined with health information. Available on request.

Mission Supplies Ltd, Dawson House, 128–130 Carshalton Road, Sutton, Surrey SM1 4TW. Tel: 020–8643 0205; fax: 020–8643 3937; e-mail: mission_supplies@compuserve.com
Provides a range of both small and large equipment needed by people and programmes overseas.

Nomad, 3–4 Wellington Terrace, Turnpike Lane, London N8 0PX. Tel: 020–8889 7014; fax: 020–8889 9529; e-mail: Nomad.travstore@virgin.net
Provides clothing, equipment, kits. Also runs a pharmacy and immunization clinic.

APPENDIX D

List of travel health facilities

1 Travel clinics and tropical medicine units

Travel clinics provide a full range of immunizations, health advice for those going abroad and usually a variety of useful equipment and books. There is a large network of **British Airways Travel Clinics** throughout much of the UK. Phone 01276 685040 to find out the address of the one nearest to you. Remember too that GPs can arrange most immunizations, many of them on the NHS.

Travel clinics in London include:

InterHealth, 157 Waterloo Road, London SE1 8US. Tel: 020–7902 9000; fax: 020–7928 0927; e-mail: Interhealth@compuserve.com InterHealth has discounted rates for all those involved in voluntary work overseas, including aid workers, missionaries and volunteers.

Nomad, 3–4 Wellington Terrace, Turnpike Lane, London N8 0PX. Tel: 020–8889 7014; fax: 020–8889 9529; e-mail: Nomad.travstore@virgin.net

Trailfinders Ltd, 194 Kensington High Street, London W8 7RG. Tel: 020–7938 3999; fax: 020–7938 3305.

Hospital for Tropical Diseases, Mortimer Market, Capper Street London WC1E 6AU (outpatients and travel clinic).

Travel clinics elsewhere include:

Birmingham
Department of Infection and Tropical Medicine, Birmingham Heartlands Hospital, Bordseley Green East, Bordseley Green, Birmingham B9 5SS. Tel: 0121–766 8752, ext. 4403/4535/4382.

Dublin
The Medical Centre, 34 Grafton Buildings, Grafton Street, Dublin 2. Tel: 00 3531 6719200.

Edinburgh
The Travel Clinic, Western General Hospital, Crewe Road South, Edinburgh EH4 2XU. Tel: 0131–537 2822.

Glasgow
The Brownlee Centre, Gartnavel Hospital, Glasgow G12 0YN. Tel: 0141–211 1074.

Liverpool
Liverpool School of Tropical Medicine, International Travel Health Clinic, Pembroke Place, Liverpool L3 5QA. Tel: 0151–708 9393; info. line: 0906–708 8807; fax: 0151–708 8733; e-mail: stwelby@liverpool.ac.uk

Your first point of contact should normally be your GP. Alternatively, you can attend the accident and emergency department at your nearest district general hospital if you have a serious or sudden health problem on return from overseas.

Travel clinics worldwide

International Association for Medical Assistance to Travellers (IAMAT). Provides details of English-speaking doctors abroad and foreign health information. 736 Centre Street, Lewiston, NY 14092, USA. Tel: 001 716 754 4883.

2 Health care for expatriates serving abroad

Care for Mission provides a range of services for members of Christian missions and aid agencies. Contact Dr Michael Jones, Care for Mission, Elphinstone Wing, Carberry, Musselburgh, Edinburgh EH21 8PW. Tel: 0131–653 6767; fax: 0131–653 3646; e-mail: 100633.2065@compuserve.com

InterHealth provides comprehensive health care including medicals, psychiatric support and counselling for any traveller, and specializes in aid workers, missionaries, volunteers and those working with NGOs. Phone, fax and e-mail on page 203.

3 Sources of specialist advice

AIDS

The national AIDS helpline is 0800 567123.

The UK NGO AIDS Consortium provides advice on funding and technical assistance for projects, and a book, *HIV/AIDS and Working Overseas: A Guide for Employees (1998)*. Contact UK NGO AIDS Consortium. Tel: 020–7401 8231; fax: 020–7401 2124; e-mail: ukaidscon@gn.atc.org

Alcohol

The National Alcohol Helpline is 0500 80102.

Back pain

The Back Pain Association can be contacted on 020–8977 5474.

Blood donation

The National Blood Transfusion Service will tell you how and where to give blood (and find out your blood group). Tel: 0345 711711.

Careers and job vacancies

Christian Vocations matches jobs with personnel available for the Christian sector. It publishes annually *The Short-Term Service Directory* and *Jobs Abroad Directory*. Contact Christian Vocations, Holloway Street West, Lower Gornall, Dudley, W. Midlands DY3 2DZ. Tel: 01902 882836; fax: 01902 881099; e-mail: Info@christianvocations.org

InterChange specializes in careers advice for those returning from overseas. Contact Joy Lankester on 01892 661421, or InterHealth on 020–7902 9000.

REACH has lists of vacancies in part-time charitable work for retired professionals. Tel: 020–7928 0452; fax: 020–7928 0798; e-mail: volwork@BTinternet.com

Counselling

The British Association for Counselling can be contacted on 01788 550899.

InterHealth can arrange counselling for anyone who has been working overseas with a charitable organization.

Diabetes

The British Diabetic Association has useful information on travel. Tel: 020–7323 1531; Careline: 020–7636 6112; fax: 020–7637 3644; e-mail: BDA@diabetes.org.uk

Disability

Two organizations provide helpful information:

The Disabled Living Foundation. Tel: 020–7289 6111.

RADAR. Tel: 020–7250 3222; fax: 020–7250 0212; e-mail: Radar@radar_org.uk

Dive Hotline

Tel: 020–7596 2723.

Expeditions

Expedition Advisory Service (Royal Geographical Society). Tel: 020–7591 3000; fax: 020–7591 3031; e-mail: eac@rgs.org

Foreign Office Advice Line

Worldwide details on safety for travellers. Tel: 020–7238 4503.

Health Line

The Hospital for Tropical Diseases has an automated recorded phone advisory service on 0839 337722 and 337733.

Insurance

The Banner Group in association with InterHealth specializes in travel and health insurance for those travelling with voluntary agencies. Tel: 01342 717917; fax: 01342 712534; e-mail: Info@bannergroup.dial.iql.co.uk; or contact InterHealth.

Malaria

There are pre-recorded messages on antimalarials and also advice in case of special difficulty on 0891 600350.

Maps

Stanfords. Maps and travel books. Tel: 020–7836 1321; fax: 020–7836 0189; e-mail: sales@stanfords.co

Marriage enrichment

Mission to Marriage runs courses countrywide from a Christian perspective. Tel: 01442 215414; fax: 01422 403062.

Relate (previously the Marriage Guidance Council) has trained counsellors throughout the United Kingdom. Contact them at local centres or through the national office. Tel: 01788 573241; fax: 01788 535007.

Medical Advisory Service for Travellers Abroad

MASTA provides detailed briefs on immunizations, recommended antimalarials and health hazards for each country of the world. Tel: 0891 224100.

Medic Alert

Provides bracelets, tags etc. for those with allergies or special conditions. Tel: 020–7833 3034; fax: 020–7278 0647.

Rape and personal safety

The Suzy Lamplugh Trust provides details on the awareness and avoidance of situations involving personal danger. It also publishes *Your Passport to Safe Travel*, M. Hodson, 1998, £6.99 + pp. Tel: 020–8392 1839; fax: 020–8392 1839;
Website: http://www.susielamplugh.org.

Safe blood

The Blood Care Foundation. Screened blood worldwide. Tel: 01293 425485; fax: 01293 425488; e-mail: Julian.bruce@virgin.net

Travel agents

Key Travel specializes in economic fares for members of charitable organizations: 92–96 Eversholt Street, London NW1 1BP. Tel: 020–7387 4933; fax: 020–7387 1090;
e-mail: reservations@keytravel.co.uk

Trailfinders arranges low-cost prices worldwide for any traveller. Tel (N. America and shorthaul): 020–7937 5400; (longhaul): 020–7938 3939; fax: 020–7938 3305.

APPENDIX E

Incubation periods of important illnesses

The incubation period is the time between being infected by an organism (e.g. from the bite of a mosquito, the swallowing of a diarrhoea-causing organism) until the first symptoms appear. This can be useful as it may help you work out what disease may be causing (or not causing) your symptoms.

Amoebiasis	At least 7 days, sometimes weeks or months.
Bilharzia (schistosomiasis)	4 weeks or more.
Brucellosis	3 weeks, sometimes much longer.
Chickenpox	2–3 weeks.
Cholera	A few hours to 5 days.
Dengue fever	5–8 days.
Diphtheria	1–5 days.
Filariasis	6 months or more.
Food poisoning (bacterial)	Variable: 1 hour to 12 days.
German measles (rubella)	2–3 weeks.
Giardiasis	Usually 2–6 weeks.
Gonorrhoea	2–7 days.
Hepatitis A	2–6 weeks.
Hepatitis B	6 weeks–6 months.
Herpes (genital)	2–12 days.
HIV infection	2 weeks to 10 years or more.
Jap. encephalitis	4–14 days.
Lassa fever	3–21 days.
Leprosy	Usually 2–4 years; occasionally shorter or much longer.
Malaria	Usually about 2 weeks. May be much longer; is never less than 7 days.
Measles	1–2 weeks.
Meningococcal meningitis	Usually 1–3 days. Always less than 1 week.
Mumps	2–3 weeks.
Onchocerciasis (River blindness)	1 year or more.
Plague	Usually less than 1 week.
Polio	10–15 days.
Rabies	2 weeks to more than 1 year.
Scabies	2–6 weeks.
Sleeping sickness	2 weeks–2 months
Syphilis	10 days to 10 weeks.
Tetanus	Usually about 2 weeks; may be much quicker or much longer.
Typhoid	Usually about 10 days. Can vary between 3 and 60.
Typhus	4–14 days.
Visceral leishmaniasis	3 months or more.
Yellow fever	3–6 days.

APPENDIX F

Notes on individual vaccines

BCG (for tuberculosis)

Type of vaccine: live, injected intradermally. BCG gives partial protection only.

A Tuberculin test (also known as a Mantoux, Heaf or Tine test) is often given before BCG to see whether immunity is present. Positive means there is immunity, and that BCG is not necessary.

Countries where TB is a risk: see page 192.

Risk to travellers: those with no immunity are at risk especially if working or living in close contact with the local population.

Number and spacing of doses: there are three categories for those travelling to at-risk situations:

- Babies and young children should be given BCG.
- Older children and adults who have never had BCG should be tested to see whether they have immunity. If they test negative they should be given BCG.
- Those who have previously had BCG. If a scar is present, no further BCG is needed. If no scar is present they should have a repeat Tuberculin test, and if negative should be given one further BCG.

BCG gives a significant degree of protection after two months. It is not known exactly how long this protection lasts.

Precautions: BCG should not be given to anyone seriously ill, with high fever, who is pregnant, taking steroids, has a positive tuberculin test or who is HIV positive.

How obtained: some GPs and most travel clinics can arrange testing and give BCG; others will refer you to a clinic where this can be done.

Reaction with other vaccines: can be given at the same time as other killed or live vaccines. If not given on the same day as other live vaccines, three or more weeks should be left between them. For those requiring gammaglobulin this should ideally be given at least three weeks after BCG (or three months before).

Certification: none necessary.

Recommendations: all those travelling to a developing country for more than one month should either have had a positive Tuberculin test or have received BCG.

Hepatitis A vaccine
(Adults: Havrix Monodose, Avaxim.
Children: Havrix Junior, Vaqta Paediatric)

Note: this highly effective vaccine has largely superseded the use of gammaglobulin for trips abroad longer than three months, and for frequent travellers.

Type of vaccine: killed, injectable.

Countries where hepatitis A occurs: see page 171.

Risk to travellers: adults and older children are at risk. Those under about ten years of age, when infected with hepatitis A, usually have a less severe or unrecognized illness and then develop lifelong immunity.

Number and spacing of doses: one 1 ml dose of Havrix Monodose provides coverage for up to one year, taking effect two weeks after immunization. A booster dose six to twelve months after the first gives persistent immunity for up to ten years. It is given by intramuscular injection into the deltoid muscle. Children under 16 should be given 0.5 ml or the Junior version, with a booster six to twelve months later.

Precautions: should not be given to anyone seriously ill, with high fever or known hypersensitivity to the vaccine. Side effects are usually mild, with slight soreness and redness at the injection site, and less often fever, headache and nausea. Pregnant women should receive gammaglobulin rather than hepatitis A vaccine.

Reactions with other vaccines: none. May be given at the same time but at a different site.

How obtained: is usually available on the NHS to those travelling to developing countries. Can also be given at travel clinics. Some doctors will want to check your hepatitis A antibodies before giving it, or use gammaglobulin for trips of three months or less.

Storage: should be kept between 2° and 8 °C and should be protected from light. Should not be frozen. Is thought to retain its potency if briefly warmed in transit for up to about seven days. Has a short shelf-life of two years.

Recommendations: hepatitis A vaccine is recommended for those aged 16 and over travelling to developing countries for three months or more or who are regular travellers. If travelling for more than 12 months an additional booster should be given (see above). Pregnant women are currently advised to have gammaglobulin, and unimmunized contacts of infectious cases either hepatitis A vaccine or gammaglobulin. Those immunized less than two weeks before travel can be given hepatitis A vaccine and gammaglobulin at the same time but at different sites. Anyone born before 1945, brought up in a developing country or with a history of jaundice may have immunity and can be tested for antibodies to see if immunization is necessary.

Children between one and fifteen should receive the Junior form, though children under five are only immunized in high-risk areas.

Gammaglobulin – against hepatitis A

Type of vaccine: a protein (immunoglobulin) derived from human serum. It gives passive, short-lived but valuable protection. Supplies manufactured in a developing country should not be used.

Number and spacing of doses: a dose according to manufacturer's instructions, ideally within one to two weeks of departure. Gives protection immediately.

Precautions: can be safely given to anyone unless a known hypersensitivity exists. Side effects amount to no more than sore buttocks for twenty-four hours. Serious reactions are rare. Can be given in pregnancy.

How obtained: usually free on the NHS for those travelling to developing countries.

Reactions with other vaccines: none with any killed vaccines or with yellow fever vaccine, which can be given at the same time though at a different site. Gammaglobulin may reduce the effectiveness of the following live vaccines: oral polio, mumps, measles, rubella and BCG, oral typhoid, oral cholera. It should ideally be given at least three weeks after (or three months before) these vaccines, though there is no danger from the injection if these intervals are not followed.

Recommendations: see under hepatitis A vaccine.

Hepatitis B vaccine

Note: because hepatitis B is a serious illness and can lead to liver cancer later in life, the World Health Organisation has drawn up plans to introduce universal immunization.

Type of vaccine: killed, injectable.

Countries where hepatitis B is a risk: worldwide, but most common in Africa, South and South-East Asia, China, the Pacific Islands and parts of South America, Eastern Europe and the former Soviet States.

Risk to travellers: generally (though not exclusively) spread in a similar way to AIDS, therefore blood transfusions, dirty needles and sexual intercourse with carriers are the main methods of spread. Health workers have an increased risk, as do very young children who can catch it through close contact with a carrier.

Number and spacing of doses: there are two methods:
- *Regular course*: three injections, leaving at least one month between the first and second, five months between the second and third (0, 1, 6), given by intramuscular route.
- *Quick course* if insufficient time for regular course: three injections at intervals of at least one month followed by a booster one year after the first (0, 1, 2, 12).

Whichever course you have followed, boosters can be given every five years. Where full cover is important, e.g. among health workers, a blood test can be done to see whether a booster is necessary, or it can be carried out two to four weeks after completing a course or having a booster to ensure a sufficient level of antibody has developed (100 iu/ml or more).

The vaccine gives protection immediately after the third dose, or after any booster. It can be given at any age.

Precautions: hepatitis B vaccine should not be given to anyone with fever or known hypersensitivity either to the vaccine or to yeast. It should be avoided in pregnancy (unless risk very high). Side effects include local soreness, occasionally with nodule formation, and fever, nausea and headache.

How obtained: the vaccine is available from travel clinics and on the NHS for accredited health workers and those in training.

Storage: if you need to take doses abroad with you the vaccine should be kept between 2° and 8 °C. It is thought to remain effective if temporarily heated up to 25 °C for between four and six days, provided it is then re-refrigerated. It should not be frozen.

Reaction with other vaccines: none. May be given at the same time but at a different site.

Recommendations: all health workers, those working with drug abusers, the mentally handicapped, street children or in institutions, including orphanages, should be protected, regardless of their length of stay. Others, particularly children, living or working in developing countries for more than three months, should be immunized. Further advice can be obtained from your travel health adviser.

A combined hepatitis A and hepatitis B vaccine is available under the name Twinrix, both in adult and paediatric forms. This does not work out more economical, but will mean fewer injections if you need protection against both hepatitis A and hepatitis B. Twinrix is useful for those previously unimmunized against both hepatitis A and B who need both immunizations, because of frequent travel or a prolonged trip abroad.

Japanese encephalitis vaccine

Type of vaccine: killed, injectable.

Countries where the disease occurs: South-East Asia, parts of India (especially Nepal border area and the south), Nepal, China, Japan, the Philippines, Malaysia, Indonesia, south-eastern areas of the Russian Federation, Korea, Pakistan (especially Sind).

JE is spread by Culex mosquitoes and can cause a dangerous illness with severe headache, sometimes leading to death or long-term disability. It is, however, rare in travellers.

Risk to travellers: low except in known high-risk districts during and shortly after the rainy season, where those residing in rural rice-growing areas, especially where pigs are kept, are at some risk.

Number and spacing of doses: the normal schedule is three doses, on days 0, 7–14 and 28, with a booster every three years. Protection starts ten to fourteen days after completing the course and immediately after any booster. Children aged one to three should receive half the dose; those under twelve months should not be given the vaccine.

Precautions: the vaccine should not be given to anyone who has had a serious reaction to a previous dose, nor to anyone with a fever, cancer or with any serious illness, especially of the heart, liver or lung. It should not be given in pregnancy. Side effects include local soreness, occasionally fever and headache. More serious reactions have occasionally been reported after second or subsequent doses, sometimes hours or days after the injection. Those vaccinated should wait in the clinic for 30 minutes, and the course should ideally be completed ten days before leaving.

How obtained: expensive and not available on the NHS. It is available from travel clinics, and some GPs will order it and give it privately.

Reaction with other vaccines: none. Can be given at the same time but at a different site.

Recommendations: only recommended for travellers spending one month or more during the time of year when, and at a location where the disease is known to occur. Consult your travel health adviser if in doubt.

Meningitis vaccine

Note: this vaccine protects only against meningococcal meningitis strains A and C, two of the most serious forms of meningitis.

Type of vaccine: killed, injectable.

Countries where these strains of meningitis occur: see page 176.

Risk to travellers: an appreciable risk occurs during outbreaks or when visiting the meningitis belt during the dry season. Children or those working with children are at greater risk.

Number and spacing of doses: a single dose of 0.5 ml at least three weeks before departure, with boosters every three years. Form 'AC Vax' can be given from two months of age; form 'Mengivac' from 18 months. Gives protection after 15 days, and probably sooner.

Precautions: should not be given to anyone with fever or severe illness, known hypersensitivity nor during pregnancy unless risk very high. Side effects include local soreness as well as occasional chills and fever in the first 24 hours.

How obtained: not normally free under the NHS, though many GPs will obtain it or write a prescription for you to collect. Otherwise it is available in travel clinics.

Reactions with other vaccines: none. Can be given at the same time but at a different site.

Recommendations: as described above. Also needed (with certificate) for all going on Haj pilgrimage to Saudi. Those who have had their spleen removed must have this vaccine, regardless of country of travel. The distribution of meningitis changes frequently. Consult your travel health adviser a few weeks before departure.

Polio vaccine (oral)

Type of vaccine: live, oral. In some countries, killed, injectable polio vaccine is used instead.

Countries where polio occurs: polio is rapidly disappearing after a worldwide immunization programme. At the time of writing there are still cases occurring in parts of Africa and Asia, especially India.

Risk to travellers: extremely low. Although polio is disappearing, the World Health Organisation recommends everyone to keep their immunizations up to date.

Number and spacing of doses: most children and those born after 1956 (when the vaccine was introduced) should have received a primary course of three injections. For such people boosters are needed every ten years to guarantee immunity.

Those who have not had a primary course of three in the past, or who are unsure, should do so before going abroad, with three injections at intervals of one month or more.

Precautions: should not be given to anyone with fever, serious illness, diarrhoea and vomiting, or those with low immunity. It should not be given in pregnancy. There are usually no side effects.

How obtained: polio vaccine is generally free on the NHS, though adults requiring a primary course may be charged.

Reactions with other vaccines: may be given on the same day as any other vaccine, live or killed. In the case of other live vaccines, if not given on the same day should be given at an interval of three weeks or more. Those needing gammaglobulin should ideally receive this three weeks or more after (or three months before) polio vaccine.

Recommendations: all travellers should be in date for polio. Expatriate children brought up overseas must be fully immunized.

Rabies vaccine (HDCV)

Note: contrary to some fears, modern rabies vaccine is both simple and safe. It *does not*, *however*, give full protection, and after any encounter with a potentially rabid animal further doses are needed.

Type of vaccine: killed, injectable 'Human Diploid Cell Vaccine' or HDCV.

Countries affected by rabies: see page 179.

Risk to travellers: the risk to most careful travellers is relatively low, but intrepid travellers, rural workers, vets, zoologists and children are at higher risk. Many travellers and expatriates worry that their last encounter with a suspicious dog might have sealed their fate.

Number and spacing of doses: three injections are needed with seven to fourteen days between the first and second, about 21 between the second and third (0, 7–14, 28). Boosters are needed every two to three years, or every year for those working with animals. If longer than three years has elapsed since your last booster, the full course must be repeated. An alternative regime of two intradermal injections 28 days apart gives almost as good protection and is sometimes used.

Gives protection after second or third dose, *but* two further injections are still needed after a bite or lick from a suspect animal, the first ideally immediately after the bite and the second between the third and seventh day (0, 3–7). If preventative rabies injections have not been completed or have lapsed, five post-exposure injections are needed, along with Human Rabies Immunoglobulin (HRIG). See page 181.

Rabies injections should usually be given by the intramuscular (IM) route (into the upper arm, not the buttock). Health workers very experienced with the technique can give the injection intradermally using only one tenth of the IM dose. Injections given to those who are currently taking chloroquine should generally include the full dose via the IM route, as chloroquine may reduce the effect of the intradermal injection.

The vaccine is thought to retain its potency for a cumulative total of 14 days if unrefrigerated. It should, however, be kept as cool as possible, ideally in a vacuum flask. It must not be transported in the aircraft hold, where freezing may destroy it.

Rabies injections in children under the age of 12 months may not be fully effective (though they are sometimes used from six months onwards). For this reason you should take enough rabies vaccine with you so that children can be immunized from the age of one upwards.

Rabies vaccines are increasingly becoming available in developing countries. Purified Chick Embryo Culture Vaccine (PCEC) is considered to be safe and effective, provided it has been kept reliably refrigerated since manufacture (hard to verify). It is used in the same way as HDCV. Purified Vero Rabies Vaccine (PVRV) and Purified Duck Embryo Vaccine (PDEV) are also acceptable.

Precautions: rabies vaccine should be avoided in anyone with a high fever or who is seriously ill. Pregnant women should only receive it if their risk is very high, though after any possible exposure it is essential. Side effects are few, and include local swelling and redness and occasionally fever and headache.

How obtained: not usually available on the NHS. It is available from travel clinics and privately from many GPs.

Reactions with other vaccines: none. Can be given at the same time but at a different site.

Advantages of having rabies injections before going abroad:

- It reduces from five to two the number of further HDCV or equivalent injections you need after an encounter with a suspicious animal.
- It means you will not need a special immunoglobulin (HRIG or EARS) injection as well.
- It limits the risk of delays in obtaining vaccine when in remote areas, allowing you 48 before having post-exposure injections.

Recommendations: those going to affected areas whose occupation, style of travel or remoteness puts them at risk, or who may be more than 24 hours from a reliable source of vaccine, should be immunized, regardless of their length of stay; so also should all those, including children over 12 months, spending six months or more in a country where rabies is known to occur.

Tetanus toxoid vaccine (TT) or Tetanus with low-dose diphtheria (Td, Diftavax)

Type of vaccine: killed, injectable. Tetanus with low-dose diphtheria (Td) is used for those aged 10 and above.

Countries where tetanus occurs: worldwide, but much commoner in the tropics; rare at high altitudes. *Diphtheria* occurs in many developing countries, the former Soviet States, the Russian Federation and in parts of Eastern Europe.

Risk to travellers: in the absence of completed immunization, any wound, even a trivial one, may cause tetanus. So also may delivery, surgery, middle-ear infections, bites and boils.

Number and spacing of doses: those born after 1961 will normally have received a course of DPT in childhood, and those who have served in the armed forces a course of TT. Others should make sure they have completed a primary course of three injections before travelling abroad. The best spacing is six to eight weeks between the first and second, four to six months between the second and third, but three injections at monthly intervals will confer full immunity. Td boosters are needed every ten years. If, however, you have had a tetanus booster alone in the past ten years, you can receive a single low-dose Diphtheria injection instead.

Protection takes effect immediately after the third dose or any booster.

Precautions: should not be given to anyone with high fever or who is seriously ill, or has known hypersensitivity. May cause fever and pain at the injection site, especially if less than five years have elapsed since last booster. It is safe in pregnancy.

How obtained: Tetanus Toxoid, DPT and Td are usually available on the NHS.

Reactions with other vaccines: none. Can be given at the same time but at a different site.

Recommendations: all those travelling overseas should have completed a primary course of three Td, TT or DPT injections at some time in their lives, and have had a booster within the past ten years. It is now best practice to use Td vaccine rather than TT (when available).

Tick-borne encephalitis

Type of vaccine: non-live, injectable.

Countries where TBE occurs: in scattered areas of Scandinavia, Central and Eastern Europe, including the former Yugoslavia, and in a band across the temperate parts of Russia and the former Soviet States. TBE can cause a dangerous illness with severe headache, and occasionally death and disability. It is very local, being found mainly in forests, forest margins and clearings. Most common in late spring and summer when the ticks that cause it are active.

Risk to travellers: low unless camping, trekking or working in forested areas in summer where the disease is known to occur. Take precautions to avoid tick bites (see page 113).

Number and spacing of doses: two doses four to twelve weeks apart protect for one year. A booster can be given after one year and then every three years.

Precautions: should not be given to anyone allergic to egg protein or to thiomersal (the preservative). Headache, local soreness and mild symptoms may occur for 24 hours, and occasionally a mild rash.

How obtained: from travel clinics. It is not available on the NHS.

Recommendations: see above. Obtain specialist advice from a travel clinic. Whether you need it or not will depend on exactly where and when you will be travelling, and what you will be doing.

Typhoid vaccine
(Typhim Vi, Typherix)

Type of vaccine: killed, injectable.

Countries where typhoid occurs: the Indian subcontinent, Indonesia and other parts of Asia, tropical South America and Africa.

Risk to travellers: there is an appreciable risk.

Number and spacing of doses: a single injection gives substantial protection for three years. Boosters are needed every three years. Protection takes effect 14 to 21 days after the injection.

Precautions: should not be given to anyone with a fever or who is seriously ill, nor to those under 18 months old. It should only be given in pregnancy if the risk is high. Side effects include minor pain, swelling and redness at the injection site for two to three days, with occasional mild fever or headache. Side effects are less marked than with the previously used vaccine.

How obtained: usually available on the NHS and from travel clinics.

Certification: not normally required.

Reactions with other vaccines: none. May be given at the same time but at a different site.

Recommendations: travellers to developing countries, Eastern Europe, Russia and the former Soviet states from age five upwards should be immunized. Children between 18 months and five years, and pregnant women, should only be covered if the risk of catching the disease is high. Precautions with food and water are essential.

Live oral typhoid vaccine (Vivotif) is used in some centres as an alternative to Typhim Vi. Three doses are necessary, taken on alternate days with a cool drink on an empty stomach. Doses must be kept in the refrigerator. A full three-dose course has to be taken every year to maintain protection. It should not be used in children under six, nor in pregnant women.

Yellow fever vaccine

Type of vaccine: live, injectable.

Countries where yellow fever occurs: tropical Africa between approximately 16° north and 16° south; tropical South America between 10° north and 20° south (see pages 194–5).

Some countries within this belt are reportedly free.

Risk to travellers: there is an appreciable risk in several countries in the YF zone, especially to rural travellers.

Number and spacing of doses: a single injection to all those over nine months of age, with a booster every ten years.

Precautions: should not be given to anyone with fever, who is seriously ill, has depressed immunity, is allergic to neomycin, polymixin or hens' eggs. YF vaccine should not be given to children under nine months, nor to pregnant women unless travelling in a high-risk area. Side effects, which affect about one person in ten, include local pain, headache and fever, five to ten days after the injection.

How obtained: from Yellow Fever Vaccination Centres, including some GP surgeries. Your travel health adviser or GP will advise you where the nearest one is. It is not available on the NHS.

Reactions with other vaccines: can be given at the same time as any other vaccine but at a different site. Being a live vaccine, if not given on the same day as other live vaccines it should be given at an interval of three weeks or more. There is no interaction with gammaglobulin, which can be given at the same time or any time before or after YF.

Certification: an international certificate should be filled in and carried when travelling abroad. It is valid for ten years, taking effect ten days after the first vaccination and immediately after any further dose. Some countries outside the YF zone will demand to see a valid certificate if you have travelled from or passed through a country within the zone in the last six days. An exemption certificate should be carried by anyone who for any reason cannot be vaccinated.

Recommendations: anyone nine months or over travelling through or residing in a country in the YF zone should keep their injection and certificate up to date.

FURTHER READING

Except where otherwise indicated, the following may be obtained from bookshops.

On health care while abroad

Traveller's Health, Dr Richard Dawood, Oxford University Press (475 pages), third edition, 1992. Regular new editions. A standard and very detailed reference book for the serious traveller.

Where There is No Doctor, D. Werner MacMillan, 1993, and special Africa edition. A really valuable book for anyone living in areas with absent or unreliable health services. Translated into many languages. Available from bookshops, InterHealth etc.

Health Advice for Travellers, Department of Health, 1999 and updated annually. Basic information directed at tourists and concentrating on Europe. Free from Post Offices or tel: 0800 555777.

Travel in Health, G. Fry, V. Kenny, third edition, 1999, International Safari Health, Dublin. An easy-to-read book for tourists and travellers.

International Travel and Health – vaccination requirements and health advice. WHO, Geneva, 1999 and updated annually. Available from WHO Distribution and Sales, 1211 Geneva, along with details of wide range of books on health. Designed for those giving health advice.

Healthy Travel: Bugs, Bites and Bowels, J. W. Howarth, Cadogan, 1995. An enjoyable and informative read. Second edition due 1999.

Stay Healthy Abroad, R. Ryan, Health Education Authority, 1995. A humorous and informative approach to travellers' health.

Practical First Aid, British Red Cross, Dorling Kindersley, 1998. An excellent, easy-to-follow manual, recommended and designed for the general traveller.

For expeditions and adventure travel

Expedition Medicine, ed D. Warrell, S. Anderson, Royal Geographical Society, Profile Books, 1998. An excellent guide for those travelling to inhospitable areas or planning adventure travel.

The High-Altitude Medicine Handbook, A. Pollard, D. Murdoch, Radcliffe Medical Press, Oxford, 1997. Everything you need to know about high-altitude trekking and expeditions. Also available as MicroEdition weighing less than 60 gm.

For the disabled and elderly

Guide for the Disabled Traveller, Automobile Association, 1991. Available from the AA.

Nothing Ventured: Disabled People Travel the World, A. Walsh (ed.), Rough Guide Series (Penguin), 1992. An inspiring read for anyone.

For those with children

Your Child's Health Abroad: A Manual for Travelling Parents, J. Wilson-Howarth, M. Ellis, Bradt Publications, 1998. The kids' and parents' survival kit we've all been waiting for, giving practical and comprehensive information for parents and families.

For those in stressful situations

Honourably Wounded, M. Foyle, Marc Europe, 1987. Very useful insights and suggestions, written specifically for those involved in Christian work overseas, all of whom should consider obtaining a copy before leaving. Translated into many languages. New edition targetted for 2002.

INDEX